Dishes for Special Occasions

Recent Titles in
Foodservice Menu Planning Series

Volume Feeding Menu Selector by Alta B. Atkinson
Eulalia C. Blair, Editor

Luncheon and Supper Dishes
Eulalia C. Blair

Salads and Salad Dressings
Eulalia C. Blair

Breakfast and Brunch Dishes
Eulalia C. Blair

Dishes for Special Occasions

FOR
FOODSERVICE
MENU
PLANNING

Selected

by

EULALIA C. BLAIR

Jule Wilkinson, Editor

CAHNERS BOOKS

A Division of Cahners Publishing Company, Inc.
89 Franklin St., Boston, Massachusetts 02110
Publishers of Institutions/VF Magazine

Library of Congress Cataloging in Publication Data
Main entry under title:

Dishes for special occasions.

 (Foodservice menu planning series)
 Recipes selected from Volume feeding management
magazine.
 1. Cookery for institutions, etc. I. Blair,
Eulalia C.
TX820.D57   641.5'7   75-4684
ISBN 0-8436-2058-7

ISBN 0-8436-2058-7

Cover Picture, American Spice Trade Association

Printed in the United States of America

CONTENTS

ACKNOWLEDGEMENTS

THE RECIPES THAT make up this book reflect the creative thinking of many minds. Because this is so, there are many people to thank for these recipes, for their down-to-earth practical qualities and for the imaginative new ideas that set them far apart.

I should like to express my most sincere "Thank You" to the talented technicians who have worked in the various test kitchens to develop and perfect these recipes. Thanks should also go to my business and professional associates allied with food processors, manufacturers, public relations firms, advertising agencies, associations and institutions who supplied the recipe material that appeared in Volume Feeding Management Magazine *during the years it was a separate publication. I should like to thank them as well for furnishing the photographs that illustrate this book.*

I also want to voice my appreciation to the foodservice operators across the nation who, time and time again, shared treasured recipes from their kitchens.

In addition, I want to thank Book Editor, Jule Wilkinson for her capable help in designing, editing and handling the many details concerned with publishing this book.

Eulalia C. Blair

Steak, Special Occasion Style

Cling Peach Advisory Board

INTRODUCTION

THIS RECIPE BOOK is planned to lend a hand to the men and women in the foodservice field who are called upon to create menus for special group functions—luncheons, dinners, receptions and various other social occasions at which invariably "refreshments will be served."

The recipes were selected from the large collection from which, over the years, material was chosen for inclusion in the Recipe File section in past issues of Volume Feeding Management Magazine.

Included are an extensive variety of hot and cold hors d' oeuvres, tea breads, sandwich fillings, small cakes, cookies, punch bowls and other festive beverages.

The recipes for luncheon and dinner items take in a broad selection of appetizers, hot and chilled soups, entrees, vegetables and desserts. In addition, there are a number of recipes for dishes especially suited for service on a buffet.

Although salads are easily identified as an important part of luncheon and dinner menus, salad recipes, by intent, were omitted from this book since the subject is quite thoroughly covered in another of the cookbooks in the series for foodservice menu planners. It is entitled Salads and Salad Dressings, *and was published by Cahners Books in 1974.*

While Dishes for Special Occasions *is designed to be a recipe book rather than a menu book, it does include a sampling of luncheon and dinner menus that feature recipes from the book. Hopefully, these will prove of help as they are presented and will also suggest other pleasing combinations that will assure your catering efforts continued success.*

Show Stoppers for Cocktail Receptions

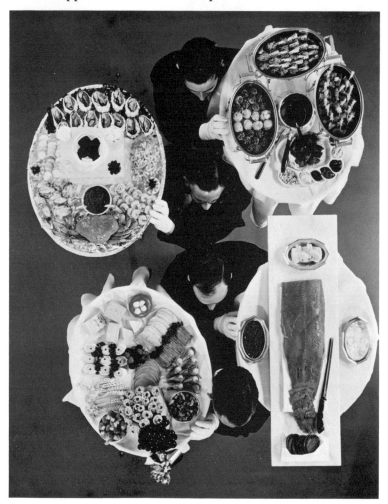

COCKTAIL RECEPTION FARE

Appetizers and Hors D'Oeuvres

WHETHER IT IS a small intimate cocktail party or a large reception, the hors d'oeuvres that you serve can make the difference between just one more affair and a gala occasion. Attractive before-the-meal food helps get conversation going, puts people at ease. It sparks pleased comments, establishes the climate for a festive mood.

Hors d'oeuvres can be as simple or as elaborate as you choose. The scope is broad. It includes appetizing morsels that are served hot, others served cold. In addition, there are canapes, dainty sandwiches, dips and spreads as well as olives, salted nuts, crisp vegetable strips and other nibbles or tidbits. A wide variety of crackers, pretzels and other items of the kind comes ready to serve.

The hors d' oeuvres that star as beverage accompaniments are small, tastefully seasoned, and easy to eat. At most, they are not more than two or three bites. Moreover, they are not too filling since they are intended to coax the appetite rather than satisfy it completely.

Chicken wings, pastry turnovers, chafing dish specialties and bacon-wrapped savories are among the hot hors d'oeuvres that have a strong appeal. Barbecued riblets, stuffed mushroom caps and small wedges of a warm quiche are among other items that go over well.

The first joint of a chicken wing, resembling a miniature drumstick, is a natural to hold in the fingers and dip in a flavorful sauce. Tiny meatballs, cocktail sausages and squares of fried fish are designed to spear with a pick and dip in a sauce. Remember that any food meant to be speared should be firm enough to stay on the pick. Always be sure to have plenty of napkins at hand when sauces or dips are involved.

Hot or cold, hors d'oeuvres that feature fillings get hearty applause. Take deviled eggs, miniken puff shells with a savory filling and crisp celery ribs stuffed with cheese as three of the examples that prove the rule.

Stuffed items look impressive yet they actually take little time when you line them up on a tray and work with pastry bag and tube. Cheese spreads, guacamole, and other flavorful soft fillings manage well for this procedure. Cherry tomatoes, cucumber cups (scooped-out chunks), artichoke bottoms, and cornucopias made with thin slices of salami or other round luncheon meat indicate the variety that you can achieve in a short time.

Sandwiches, cut small and delicately thin, are popular before-the-meal pick-ups. Well-seasoned little sandwiches filled with cheese mixtures, ham, tongue or rare roast beef never go begging. The rolled soup tea sandwiches (see chart on page 44) are as delightful with cocktails as with tea, and they offer an added advantage since they can be made ahead, frozen and held until they are needed.

There is probably nothing more showy than a well-arranged tray of dainty canapes, fashioned in various shapes and tastefully decorated. This type of hors d'oeuvres includes the small, savory tidbits, hot or cold, which are prepared on a bread, cracker or pastry base. Caviar, smoked salmon, sardines, lobster, shrimp, anchovies, liver pate, pimiento, olives, *eggs and cream cheese are among the toppings that you can use to get eye-catching effects.*

These handsome creations do take hand work and a measure of skill. If or when this poses a problem, attractive assortments of this type of hors d' oeuvres come frozen, ready to thaw or to bake.

Hot and Cold Hors d'Oeuvres

Left to right above: Seafood Filled Turnovers; Fried Chicken Wings; Bacon-Water Chestnut Hors d'oeuvres (recipe, page 30); Spicy Cocktail Franks in Chafing Dish (recipe, page 27); Small Puff Shells (recipe, page 22); Filled Cherry Tomatoes; Sausages Wrapped in Pastry. Below in picture: Raw Vegetables and Two Cheese Dip (recipe, page 8).

Breads

SEEDED BREAD STICKS

Yield: 24 portions (3 sticks per portion)

Ingredients

ENRICHED BREAD, sliced	24 slices
BUTTER or MARGARINE, melted	1/2 cup (1/4 pound)
CARAWAY or POPPY SEEDS	1/4 cup

Procedure

1. Trim crusts from bread slices; arrange on an ungreased bun pan 18-inch by 26-inch by 1-inch.

2. Brush melted butter over top of each slice. Sprinkle seeds evenly over tops.

3. Toast in oven at 350°F. for 12 minutes or until crisp and golden brown.

4. Cut each slice into 3 equal-sized strips. Serve hot or cold.

PARMESAN RYE TOASTIES

Yield: 48 portions (3 slices each)

Ingredients

BUTTER or MARGARINE	1/2 pound
PARMESAN CHEESE, finely grated	1 cup
PARTY RYE BREAD, thin-sliced	4 loaves
	(7-1/2 to 8 ounces each)

Procedure

1. Combine butter and cheese in a 1-quart mixing bowl.

2. Arrange 72 slices (2 loaves) of small-loaf rye bread on each of 2 bun pans 18-inch by 26-inch by 1-inch. Spread 1/2 teaspoon Parmesan butter on each slice.

3. Toast in oven at 400°F. for 10 minutes. Serve hot or cold as a cocktail tidbit or with dips.

GARLIC RYE TOASTIES

Yield: 48 portions (3 slices each)

Ingredients

GARLIC	6 cloves
BUTTER or MARGARINE, melted	11 ounces
PARTY RYE BREAD, thin-sliced	4 loaves
	(7-1/2 to 8 ounces each)

Procedure

1. Cut garlic cloves in quarters; add to melted butter. Let stand for 1 hour to allow flavor to permeate butter; remove garlic pieces.

2. Arrange 72 slices (2 loaves) of small-loaf rye bread on each of 2 bun pans 18-inch by 26-inch by 1-inch.

3. Brush with garlic butter allowing about 1/2 teaspoon for each slice.

4. Toast in oven at 400°F. for 10 minutes. Serve hot or cold as a cocktail tidbit or with dips.

SWISS TWISTS

Yield: approximately 7 dozen

Ingredients

SWISS CHEESE, grated	1/2 pound
PIE CRUST (dry mix)	1-1/4 pounds
EGG WHITE, slightly beaten	2 ounces
SALT	as needed
CAYENNE	as needed

Procedure

1. Add grated cheese to pie crust mix; add wetting and mix as pie crust dough.

2. Roll dough 1/4-inch thick. Brush with egg white; sprinkle with salt and cayenne.

3. Cut in 1/2-inch strips, 5 inches long. Twist by holding both ends and turning in opposite directions. Press ends of twists down on ungreased baking sheet.

4. Bake in oven at 425°F. for 10 minutes, or until crisp and golden brown.

SAVORY PRETZELS

Yield: 2 quarts

Ingredients

THIN PRETZEL STICKS	1 7-1/2 ounce package
THIN TWIST PRETZELS	1 8-ounce package
BUTTER or MARGARINE	4 ounces
GARLIC POWDER	1 tablespoon
PARMESAN CHEESE, grated	6 ounces

Procedure

1. Place pretzels in a baking pan.
2. Cut butter into pieces; place on top of pretzels. Sprinkle with garlic powder and cheese.
3. Bake in oven at 325°F. for 10 to 15 minutes, shaking the pan occasionally to coat all the pretzels.
4. Remove from oven. Cool. Store in airtight container.

Dips

TWO CHEESE DIP
(See picture, page 5)

Yield: 2 pounds, 6 ounces

Ingredients

BLUE CHEESE	6 ounces
COTTAGE CHEESE, SMALL CURD	2 pounds
CHIVES, chopped	2 tablespoons
SOUR CREAM	as needed

Procedure

1. Break up blue cheese, mashing thoroughly. Add cottage cheese; mix until blended. Add chives.
2. Add sour cream to moisten to desired consistency.

GUACAMOLE DIP

Yield: 1-1/4 quarts

Ingredients

AVOCADO, pitted, peeled	2 pounds, 8 ounces
ONION, chopped (reconstituted instant)	1-1/4 ounces
GARLIC, minced	2-1/2 cloves
CHILI POWDER	1-1/4 teaspoons
SALT	1/2 teaspoon
PEPPER	1/4 teaspoon
LEMON JUICE	5 teaspoons
MAYONNAISE	1 cup
TOMATOES, cut in 1/2-inch wedges	as needed
CORN CHIPS	as needed

Procedure

1. Mash avocado. Add onion, garlic, chili powder, salt, pepper and lemon juice.

2. Turn mixture into a narrow container. Spread mayonnaise on top, covering completely to edges. Store in refrigerator until just before serving.

3. At serving time, fold mayonnaise into dip. Place in an attractive bowl. Place bowl on platter or tray. Remove seeds from tomato wedges. Arrange tomatoes on one half of platter, corn chips on other half.

Note

Prepare dip on day it is to be served. Do not store overnight.

CHEESE SPREAD OR DIP

Yield: approximately 1-3/4 quarts

Ingredients

CREAM CHEESE, softened	1 pound
CAMEMBERT CHEESE	1/2 pound
COTTAGE CHEESE, SMALL CURD	2 pounds
PARMESAN CHEESE, grated	2/3 cup
SEASONED SALT	1-1/2 to 2 teaspoons

Procedure

1. Place cream cheese and Camembert (including skin) in mixer bowl. Using paddle at low speed, beat until smooth.

2. Add cottage cheese and Parmesan; blend. Add seasoned salt to taste.

3. If desired, garnish with toasted sesame seeds. Or, sprinkle thinly sliced radishes over top. Serve with slices of small-loaf rye bread, plain or toasted.

HUNGARIAN DIP

Yield: 2 quarts

Ingredients

ONION SOUP MIX	1 6-ounce can
SOUR CREAM	2 quarts
CARAWAY SEEDS	1 tablespoon
CAPERS, chopped	1/2 cup
PAPRIKA	3 tablespoons
PIMIENTO, chopped	1 cup

Procedure

1. Thoroughly blend soup mix into sour cream. Fold in caraway, capers, paprika and pimiento.

2. Cover; refrigerate 1 hour before using.

3. Garnish top with additional pimiento, if desired. Serve with green pepper, raw turnip strips, celery, cucumber or carrot sticks, and assorted crackers.

HAMBURGER STROGANOFF DIP

Yield: 4-1/2 cups

Ingredients

MUSHROOMS, FRESH, finely chopped	1/4 pound
ONION, chopped	1/2 cup
GARLIC, minced	1 clove
BUTTER or MARGARINE	2 ounces
PAPRIKA	1/2 teaspoon
BLACK PEPPER, GROUND	1/4 teaspoon
MONOSODIUM GLUTAMATE	1/4 teaspoon
CHOPPED BEEF	3/4 pound
CREAM OF CHICKEN SOUP, CONDENSED	1-1/4 cups
CORNSTARCH	2 tablespoons
RED BURGUNDY	1/2 cup
SOUR CREAM	3/4 cup
PARSLEY, snipped (for garnish)	as needed
ASSORTED SNACK CRACKERS	as needed

Procedure

1. Saute mushrooms, onion and garlic in butter 5 to 7 minutes, stirring occasionally.

2. Stir in seasonings and meat; cook until meat loses pinkness (4 to 5 minutes).

3. Add soup.

4. Blend cornstarch with burgundy. Add to meat mixture. Cook and stir over medium heat until mixture thickens and begins to bubble.

5. Stir in sour cream.

6. Garnish with parsley. Serve with snack crackers.

Spreads

CURRIED TURKEY MOUSSE

Yield: 24 portions

Ingredients

GELATINE, UNFLAVORED	1/4 cup
CHICKEN STOCK, cold	1 quart
SALT	1 tablespoon
PEPPER, WHITE	1/2 teaspoon
LEMON JUICE	1/4 cup
APPLESAUCE, CANNED	2 cups
TURKEY, cooked, finely chopped	1-1/4 quarts
CREAM, WHIPPING	2 cups
CURRY POWDER	1-1/2 tablespoons

Procedure

1. Soften gelatine in chicken stock. Place over low heat; stir until gelatine is dissolved.

2. Add salt, pepper, lemon juice and applesauce. Chill until slightly thickened; add turkey.

3. Combine cream and curry powder; whip until stiff. Gently fold into gelatine mixture.

4. Pour into two 2-quart molds. Chill until firm.

5. Unmold. Coat with chaud-froid. Decorate and glaze as desired.

OLIVE-CHICKEN LIVER PATE

Yield: 2 quarts

Ingredients

CHICKEN LIVERS	4 pounds
INSTANT CHOPPED ONION	1 cup
INSTANT CELERY STALK and	
LEAF GRANULES	1/2 cup
BAY LEAVES	4
SALT	2 teaspoons
THYME, crushed	1 teaspoon
INSTANT MINCED PARSLEY	1 teaspoon
WATER	1-1/2 quarts
BUTTER or MARGARINE, softened	1/2 pound
INSTANT MINCED GREEN ONION	1 tablespoon
MUSTARD, PREPARED	2 tablespoons
OLIVES, GREEN, PIMIENTO-STUFFED,	
chopped	2 cups
CHABLIS WINE or CHICKEN STOCK	2/3 to 1 cup
GELATINE, UNFLAVORED	2 ounces
STOCK FROM CHICKEN LIVERS	1 cup
MAYONNAISE	1/2 cup
OLIVES, GREEN, PIMIENTO-STUFFED,	
sliced	as needed

Procedure

1. Combine chicken livers, onion, celery, bay leaves, salt, thyme, parsley and water. Bring to a boil; cover and simmer 20 minutes. Cool; strain, reserving stock.

2. Put cooked livers through food grinder using fine plate. Blend in butter, green onion, mustard, chopped olives and Chablis wine. Chill thoroughly.

3. Shape mixture into a pyramid or other desired form. Chill again.

4. Soften gelatine in stock from chicken livers. Dissolve over low heat, stirring constantly. Gradually stir in mayonnaise; chill until slightly thickened.

5. Spoon gelatine mixture over pate. Decorate with sliced olives. Chill.

6. Serve with toast or crisp crackers.

Cheese Stuffed Celery (Recipe, page 20)

Florida Celery Committee

OLIVE-CHEESE ROLL

Yield: 6 dozen appetizers

Ingredients

RIPE OLIVES, PITTED	2 cups
CREAM CHEESE	1 pound
BLUE CHEESE	1 pound
BUTTER	4 ounces
LEMON JUICE	2 tablespoons
GREEN ONIONS, finely chopped	1/4 cup
PARSLEY, chopped	as needed

Procedure

1. Cut olives into chunks.

2. Combine cheeses and butter; blend until smooth. Add olives, lemon juice and onions.

3. Shape into 2 long rolls, about 1-1/2 inches in diameter. Roll in chopped parsley to coat.

4. Wrap in foil or plastic wrap. Chill at least 3 hours.

5. Slice; serve on crackers or toast rounds.

Cold Hors d'Oeuvres

PICKLED SHRIMP

Yield: 1 quart

Ingredients

VINEGAR, WHITE	3/4 cup
WATER	2 cups
SALAD OIL	1/4 cup
SEAFOOD SEASONING	2 tablespoons
SUGAR	1/4 cup
SHRIMP, SMALL, CANNED, drained	1 quart

Procedure

1. Combine vinegar, water, oil, seafood seasoning and sugar; bring to boiling.

2. Pour over shrimp. Cover; chill several hours or overnight.

HEN HOUSE HOMARDS ━━━━▶

Yield: 32 hors d'oeuvres

Ingredients

LOBSTER MEAT, FRESH or FROZEN, cooked	1 pound
MAYONNAISE or SALAD DRESSING	2/3 cup
CHILI SAUCE	1 tablespoon
GREEN PEPPER, chopped	1 teaspoon
ONION, grated	1 teaspoon
PIMIENTO, chopped	1 teaspoon
EGGS, HARD-COOKED	16
PARSLEY	as needed

SEAFOOD FILLED LEMON CUPS

Yield: 30 portions

Ingredients

OLIVE OIL	1-1/2 cups
LEMON RIND, grated	1 teaspoon
LEMON JUICE, FRESH	2/3 cup
SUGAR	1/2 cup
SALT	2 teaspoons
PAPRIKA	1-1/2 teaspoons
INSTANT MINCED ONION	1 teaspoon
HADDOCK,* cooked, flaked	2 quarts
SHRIMP, cooked, chopped	1 quart
CELERY, finely chopped	2 cups
LEMON CUPS	30
ANCHOVY FILLETS, ROLLED	30

Procedure

1. Combine oil, lemon rind, lemon juice, sugar, salt, paprika and onion. Beat well with wire whip. Chill.

2. Combine fish, shrimp and celery. Add chilled dressing; toss lightly. Chill for at least one hour.

3. Pile salad mixture into lemon cups. Garnish each with a rolled anchovy.

*Or other white fish.

Procedure

1. Thaw frozen lobster meat; drain. Remove any remaining shell or cartilage. Cut meat into small pieces.

2. Combine mayonnaise, chili sauce, green pepper, onion and pimiento. Add to lobster; toss lightly to mix.

3. Cut eggs in half lengthwise; remove yolks.* Fill each white with 1 tablespoon of lobster mixture.

4. Garnish with chopped parsley or parsley sprigs.

*Reserve to use in other recipes.

NIPPY CHEESE BALLS

Yield: 24 portions (3 balls each)

Ingredients

CHEDDAR CHEESE, NATURAL, grated	1 pound
EGGS, HARD-COOKED, chopped	4
MAYONNAISE	1/2 cup
GREEN PEPPER, very finely chopped	1/2 cup
DILL PICKLES, finely chopped	1/2 cup
PIMIENTO, chopped	1/2 cup
ONION, very finely chopped	1/4 cup
PARSLEY, snipped (optional)	as needed
NUTS, chopped (optional)	as needed
CRACKERS, BACON FLAVOR	72

Procedure

1. Combine cheese, eggs, mayonnaise, green pepper, dill pickles, pimiento and onion. Mix until well blended.

2. Refrigerate at least 6 hours or overnight.

3. Shape into 1-inch balls.

4. If desired, mix parsley and nuts; roll balls in mixture.

5. Chill cheese balls; place on crackers to serve.

CRISPY CHEESE BALLS

Yield: 20 full-size portions or 200 appetizer balls

Ingredients

CHEESE, NATURAL CHEDDAR, grated	3 pounds
FLOUR, ALL-PURPOSE	3/4 cup
SALT	1-1/2 teaspoons
CAYENNE	few grains
EGG WHITES	12 (1-1/2 cups)
EGGS, WHOLE	3
MILK	1 cup
CORN FLAKE CRUMBS	2 cups

Procedure

1. Combine cheese, flour, salt and cayenne.

2. Beat egg whites until stiff but not dry. Carefully fold into cheese mixture. Chill thoroughly.

3. Combine eggs and milk; beat thoroughly.

4. Portion cheese mixture with a No. 30 scoop. (For appetizer balls, portion mixture by rounded teaspoons). Shape into balls.

5. Coat balls first with egg mixture, then with cereal crumbs.

6. Fry in deep fat at 350°F. 2 to 3 minutes.

7. Serve regular size portions with hot sauteed pineapple ring, if desired.

CURRIED CASHEW NUTS

Yield: 1-1/2 quarts

Ingredients

BUTTER or MARGARINE	6 ounces
CASHEW NUTS, unsalted	1-3/4 pounds
CURRY POWDER	2 tablespoons
SALT	as needed

Procedure

1. Melt butter in a skillet. Add nuts and curry powder; saute until lightly browned.

2. Drain on paper towels. Sprinkle with salt to taste. Cool and serve.

DEVILED EGGS

Yield: 48 halves

Ingredients

EGGS, HARD-COOKED	24
INSTANT MINCED ONION	2 tablespoons
LEMON JUICE	3 tablespoons
PARSLEY, finely chopped	2/3 cup
SALT	1 teaspoon
PEPPER	1/8 teaspoon
MAYONNAISE	2/3 cup
LIQUID HOT PEPPER SEASONING	1/8 teaspoon
CURRY POWDER	1/4 teaspoon
RIPE OLIVES, chopped	9 ounces

Procedure

1. Peel eggs; cut in half. Remove yolks; press through a ricer or mash.

2. Combine onion and lemon juice. Add remaining ingredients. Combine with egg yolks, mixing well.

3. Fill egg whites with mixture using a pastry bag with large star tube. Refrigerate until used.

CRISP STUFFED RIPE OLIVES

Yield: 50 olives

Ingredients

WATER CHESTNUTS, LARGE, CANNED	9
ITALIAN DRESSING, BOTTLED	2/3 cup
RIPE OLIVES, EXTRA LARGE PITTED	50

Procedure

1. Drain water chestnuts; cut each into 5 or 6 wedges about the size of olive pits.

2. Cover with Italian dressing; chill overnight.

3. Stuff each olive with a drained wedge of water chestnut.

CHEESE STUFFED CELERY
(See picture, page 14)

Yield: 48 portions

Ingredients

CELERY	3 stalks
CREAM CHEESE, softened	2 pounds
ROQUEFORT CHEESE, crumbled	1 cup
MILK	1/2 cup
RED PEPPER, GROUND	1/4 teaspoon
RED CAVIAR	as needed
BLACK CAVIAR	as needed
NOVA SCOTIA SMOKED SALMON, thinly sliced	1/2 pound
GREEN PEPPER, cut in 1/2-inch strips	as needed
PAPRIKA	as needed

Procedure

1. Remove celery ribs from stalks; trim both ends. Cut ribs into 4-inch and 2-inch lengths depending on width.
2. Combine cheeses, milk and pepper; beat well.
3. Turn mixture into pastry bag; fill each celery rib.
4. Garnish with caviar, rolled salmon, green pepper and paprika as desired. Refrigerate until ready to serve.

OLD SOUTH STUFFED CELERY

Yield: 50 portions, 2 pieces each

Ingredients

CELERY, washed, trimmed	3 stalks (30 ribs)
CREAM CHEESE, softened	1-1/2 pounds
PECANS, chopped	1/2 cup
MAYONNAISE	1/3 cup

Procedure

1. Cut celery ribs into 2-inch lengths.
2. Combine cheese, pecans and mayonnaise. Chill 30 minutes.
3. Fill celery with cheese mixture.

SAGE CHEESE CELERY STUFFING

Yield: 24 portions

Ingredients

COTTAGE CHEESE (CREAMED STYLE)	2 pounds
CREAM CHEESE	12 ounces
SOUR CREAM	1/2 cup
ONION, finely chopped	1/4 cup
SAGE, rubbed	2 teaspoons
SALT	2 teaspoons
GARLIC, finely chopped	1/4 teaspoon
BLACK PEPPER, GROUND	1/2 teaspoon
CELERY RIBS	36
PAPRIKA	as needed

Procedure

1. Place cheeses, sour cream, onion, sage and pepper in a mixing bowl. Rub salt and garlic together. Add to ingredients in bowl; mix well. Place mixture in a pastry bag.

2. Cut celery in pieces about 3 inches long; fill with cheese mixture. Dust with paprika. Chill.

CELERY, ROQUEFORT STYLE

Yield: 2 cups filling

Ingredients

CHEESE, ROQUEFORT, crumbled	2 cups
CHEESE, CREAM, softened	6 ounces
RAISINS, SEEDLESS, finely chopped	1/4 cup
CELERY RIBS, chilled	as needed

Procedure

1. Combine cheeses; beat until smooth. Add raisins; mix.

2. Fill celery ribs. Chill. Cut across into serving size pieces.

PUFF SHELLS
(Small, for Hors d'Oeuvres)
(See picture, page 5)

Yield: 150

Ingredients

SHORTENING	1 pound
WATER, boiling	1 quart
FLOUR, ALL-PURPOSE, sifted	1 pound
SALT	1 teaspoon
EGGS (at room temperature)	16

Procedure

1. Put shortening and water in a saucepan over high heat.

2. When fat is melted and mixture is *actively* boiling, add flour all at once. Mixture should not stop boiling. Stir and cook until it comes from side of pan. Do not overcook.

3. Put into small mixer bowl with paddle attachment. Break eggs into a quart measure; add, one at a time to mixture with beater at high speed. Mix after each addition until egg is completely incorporated. After adding last egg, mix until smooth.

4. Drop on lightly greased and floured baking sheet using No. 60 scoop. Bake in oven at 400°F. for 8 minutes until puffed and set. Reduce heat to 300°F. and bake 25 minutes more or until pastry puffs are golden and dry.

Filled Fare for Punch Parties

Concord Grape Association

TUNA EUROPEAN
(Puff Shell Filling)

Yield: 3 quarts

Ingredients

TUNA, drained	3 pounds
OLIVES, PIMIENTO-STUFFED, chopped	3 cups
SOUR CREAM	2 cups
ONION, minced	3/4 cup
FILBERT GRANULES, toasted	3 ounces
LEMON JUICE	1/3 cup
HORSERADISH	1 tablespoon
SALT	as needed

Procedure

1. Flake tuna with fork; combine with olives.

2. Combine sour cream with remaining ingredients; add to tuna mixture; toss lightly to mix. Chill.

3. Serve in small puff shells as an appetizer.

JAVA LAMB
(Puff Shell Filling)

Yield: 3 quarts

Ingredients

LAMB, cooked, diced	3 pounds
CRUSHED PINEAPPLE, drained	3 cups
COCONUT, SHREDDED	3/4 cup
MAYONNAISE or SALAD DRESSING	3/4 cup
GINGER, GROUND	1-1/2 teaspoons
CURRY POWDER	1-1/2 teaspoons

Procedure

1. Combine lamb, pineapple and coconut.

2. Blend mayonnaise with spices. Add to lamb mixture; toss lightly to mix. Chill.

3. Serve in small puff shells as an appetizer.

SHRIMP ITALIANA
(Puff Shell Filling)

Yield: 3 quarts

Ingredients

SHRIMP, cooked, diced	2-1/2 pounds
CELERY or GREEN PEPPER, diced	3 cups
TOMATO SAUCE	2 cups
WORCESTERSHIRE SAUCE	2 tablespoons
HORSERADISH	1 tablespoon
LEMON RIND, grated	1 tablespoon
LIQUID HOT PEPPER SEASONING	generous dash
PARMESAN CHEESE, grated	3/4 cup

Procedure

1. Combine shrimp and celery.

2. Combine tomato sauce, Worcestershire, horseradish, lemon rind and pepper seasoning. Add to shrimp mixture; toss lightly to mix. Chill.

3. Spoon filling into small puff shells; sprinkle with cheese. Replace tops on shells. Serve as an appetizer.

ACAPULCO FILLING
(for Puff Shells)

Yield: approximately 3 quarts

Ingredients

CRABMEAT	2-1/4 pounds
AVOCADOS. medium size, *fully ripe*	8
CREAM CHEESE, softened	6 ounces
MAYONNAISE or SALAD DRESSING	1 cup
ONION JUICE	1-1/2 tablespoons
GARLIC SALT	3/4 teaspoon

Procedure

1. Flake crabmeat.

2. Mash avocado; add cream cheese, mayonnaise, onion juice and garlic salt. Mix well.

3. Add avocado mixture to crabmeat; toss lightly to mix. Chill.

4. Serve in small puff shells as an appetizer.

GARDEN RELISH
(Puff Shell Filling)

Yield: 3 quarts

Ingredients

COTTAGE CHEESE (CREAMED), LARGE CURD, drained	3 pounds
SOUR CREAM	3 cups
DILL PICKLES, chopped	1 cup
GREEN PEPPER, chopped	1 cup
GREEN ONIONS, chopped	1 cup
PIMIENTO, chopped	1/2 cup
SALT	1 teaspoon
PEPPER	1/2 teaspoon

Procedure

1. Combine ingredients. Chill thoroughly.
2. Serve in small puff shells as an appetizer.

Roquefort Stuffed Mushrooms (Recipe, pages 32-33)

American Mushroom Institute

Hot Hors d'Oeuvres

SPICY COCKTAIL FRANKS

(See picture, page 5)

Yield: 24 to 32 portions

Ingredients

RED CURRANT JELLY	1-1/2 pounds
MUSTARD, PREPARED	12 ounces
FRANKFURTERS, cut into bite-size pieces	2-1/4 pounds

Procedure

1. Melt jelly over low heat. Blend in mustard.
2. Add frankfurter pieces; heat through, stirring to coat all sides.
3. Serve hot from chafing dish, providing picks for spearing.

SWISS CHEESE QUICHE ⟶

Yield: 1 (9-inch)

Ingredients

BACON SLICES	12
CHEESE, NATURAL SWISS, grated	4 ounces (1 cup)
UNBAKED PIE SHELL, chilled	1 9-inch
EGGS	4
CREAM, HEAVY	2 cups
SALT	3/4 teaspoon
NUTMEG	dash
SUGAR	dash
CAYENNE	dash
PEPPER, WHITE	1/8 teaspoon
BUTTER	1 tablespoon

BARBECUED PORK NUGGETS

Yield: 24 portions (3 pieces)

Ingredients

PORK SHOULDER, BONELESS	4 pounds
ONION, chopped	14 ounces
BARBECUE SAUCE	2 cups
SALT	4 teaspoons
ROSEMARY LEAVES, crushed	2 teaspoons
BLACK PEPPER, GROUND	1/2 teaspoon
CRACKERS, ASSORTED SHAPES	as needed

Procedure

1. Trim excess fat from pork. Cut into 1-1/2-inch cubes to make 72 pieces.

2. Combine meat with onion, barbecue sauce and seasonings. Marinate overnight.

3. Place into shallow baking pan; bake in oven at 400°F. for 1 to 1-1/4 hours, or until done, turning occasionally.

4. Place a pick in each piece of pork. Serve with crackers.

Procedure

1. Cook bacon until crisp; crumble into small pieces. Sprinkle bacon and cheese in the pie shell.

2. Combine eggs, cream and seasonings; beat until blended; pour into pie shell. Cut butter in small pieces; distribute over top.

3. Bake in oven at 425°F. for 15 minutes. Reduce oven heat to 300°F.; continue to bake about 40 minutes or until set.

Variations

Quiche Lorraine: Omit cheese.

Quiche Louisiane: Omit bacon. Add 1 cup split, cooked cleaned shrimp, tossed with 2 tablespoons chili sauce and a dash of hot pepper sauce.

Quiche Americanne: Omit bacon. Add 1 cup finely cut cooked ham or tongue or 2 tablespoons cut-up anchovy fillets.

BAKED CHEESE AND OLIVE OMELET

Yield: 50 portions

Ingredients

EGGS, beaten	7-3/4 pounds (3-7/8 quarts)
EVAPORATED MILK	3 cups
WATER	3 cups
SALT	1/4 cup
CHEESE, PROCESS AMERICAN, ground	1-1/2 pounds
STUFFED OLIVES, chopped	3 cups

Procedure

1. Combine eggs, milk, water and salt. Mix thoroughly.

2. Add cheese and olives, combining well.

3. Pour mixture into well-greased baking pans, to a depth of 1 to 1-1/2 inches.

4. Bake in oven at 325°F. for 35 to 45 minutes or until omelet is set.

Note

Mixture can be prepared on a well-greased griddle. Allow 1/2 cup mixture per omelet. Cook at moderate heat until bottom is golden brown.

BACON-WATER CHESTNUT HORS D'OEUVRES
(See picture, page 5)

Yield: approximately 32 pieces

Ingredients

WATER CHESTNUTS, drained	2 5-ounce cans
SOY SAUCE	1/2 cup
SUGAR	as needed
BACON, long narrow strips	16

Procedure

1. Marinate water chestnuts in soy sauce for 30 minutes.
2. Drain chestnuts; roll lightly in sugar.
3. Cut bacon strips in half crosswise. Wrap each chestnut in a piece of bacon; secure with a pick or bamboo skewer.
4. Place on rack in a baking pan. Bake in oven at 400°F. until bacon is lightly browned and crisp. Drain on absorbent paper.
5. Serve hot as an hors d'oeuvre.

FRIED PRAWNS

Yield: 30 portions

Ingredients

FLOUR	1 cup
CORNSTARCH	1/2 cup
BAKING POWDER	1/4 teaspoon
SALT	2 teaspoons
WATER	3/4 cup
EGG, beaten	1
PRAWNS, large (15 or under)	2 pounds

Procedure

1. Sift flour, cornstarch, baking powder and salt together.
2. Combine water and beaten egg. Add to dry ingredients, stirring to make a smooth batter.
3. Clean prawns; split in half. Dip into batter. Fry in deep fat at 350°F. until golden brown.

ORANGE BARBECUED CHICKEN WINGS

Yield: 60 wings, 5 quarts sauce

Ingredients

CHICKEN WINGS, LARGE	60
SALT	as needed
SHORTENING or COOKING OIL	as needed
ORANGES, peeled	16 medium
ORANGE JUICE, FRESH	2 quarts
TOMATO SAUCE	2 quarts
SUGAR, BROWN	1/2 cup
WORCESTERSHIRE SAUCE	1/2 cup
INSTANT MINCED ONION	3 tablespoons
MUSTARD, DRY	1 tablespoon
LIQUID HOT PEPPER SEASONING	1/4 teaspoon

Procedure

1. Sprinkle chicken wings with salt. Brown in shortening. Arrange in 5 baking pans, one layer deep.

2. Cut peeled oranges into bite-size pieces. Combine with remaining ingredients; mix well.

3. Pour 1 quart sauce over each pan of wings. Bake in oven at 375°F. for 40 to 45 minutes.

BATTER FOR SHRIMP TEMPURA

Yield: for 2 pounds butterfly shrimp

Ingredients

EGGS, beaten	2
BUTTER, melted	2 tablespoons
FLOUR	1 cup
SALT	1/2 teaspoon
BEER, FLAT	1 cup
EGG WHITES	2

Procedure

1. Combine eggs and melted butter.

2. Combine flour and salt. Add egg mixture. Mix in beer, stirring only until smooth. Let stand until light and foamy (1 to 2 hours).

3. Beat egg whites until stiff but not dry. Fold into batter.

4. Use for dipping raw butterfly shrimp to fry in deep fat.

ROQUEFORT STUFFED MUSHROOMS ⟶
(See picture, page 26)

Yield: 144 mushrooms

Ingredients

MUSHROOMS, FRESH, SMALL SIZE	4 pounds
BUTTER or MARGARINE, melted	2 cups
ROQUEFORT CHEESE, crumbled	1 pound
CREAM CHEESE, softened	12 ounces
INSTANT ONION POWDER	1 teaspoon

BARBECUED LAMB RIBLETS

Yield: 25 portions

Ingredients

LAMB RIBLETS	12-1/2 pounds
SALAD OIL	as needed
SALT	2-1/2 tablespoons
PEPPER	1/2 teaspoon
PAPRIKA	1 tablespoon
MONOSODIUM GLUTAMATE	1/2 teaspoon
WATER	1-1/2 cups
VINEGAR	2-1/2 cups
BUTTER or MARGARINE	1/2 pound
CHILI SAUCE	1-1/2 cups
HORSERADISH, grated	1/4 cup
WORCESTERSHIRE SAUCE	1-1/2 tablespoons
SALT	3 tablespoons
SUGAR	2 tablespoons
ONION, finely chopped	1/2 cup
CHILI POWDER (optional)	1 tablespoon

Procedure

1. Cut riblets in serving size portions. Place in a baking pan, brush with oil. Season with a mixture of salt, pepper, paprika and monosodium glutamate.

2. Bake in oven at 325°F. for 1/2 to 3/4 hour.

3. Combine remaining ingredients; simmer for 10 minutes.

4. Cover the riblets with the sauce; continue baking and basting with sauce until riblets are glazed and fork-tender, approximately 1 to 1-1/2 hours. Serve any remaining sauce over meat.

Procedure

1. Rinse mushrooms, pat dry. Remove stems.
2. Brush mushroom caps with butter. Place on baking sheets; bake in oven at 450°F. for 5 minutes.
3. Blend Roquefort and cream cheese with onion powder. Fill hot mushroom caps using pastry bag fitted with star tip.
4. Serve warm as an hors d'oeuvre. Or, serve in snail dishes as an appetizer.

LAMB RIBLETS WITH TIGER TWISTER SAUCE

Yield: 24 portions

Ingredients

LAMB RIBLETS	12 pounds
TOMATO PUREE	1-1/2 pounds
CHILI SAUCE	2 cups
VINEGAR	2 cups
GINGER ALE	2 cups
ONION, chopped	2 cups
SUGAR	1/2 cup
SALT	2 tablespoons
ALLSPICE	2 tablespoons
SEASONED PEPPER	1 tablespoon
BLACK PEPPER, CRACKED	2 teaspoons
MACE	2 teaspoons
LIQUID HOT PEPPER SEASONING	1/2 teaspoon

Procedure

1. Brown riblets in oven at 325°F. Drain off excess fat.
2. Combine remaining ingredients; simmer 10 minutes.
3. Spoon sauce over riblets. Cover; bake 1-1/2 hours or until tender, basting 2 or 3 times
4. Serve riblets with sauce (for dipping).

SPICED HAM BALLS

Yield: 9 pounds, 12 ounces, 50 portions

Ingredients

*LUNCHEON MEAT, CANNED	6 pounds
ROLLED OATS, uncooked	1 pound (1-1/2 quarts)
EGGS	6
MILK	1 quart
WORCESTERSHIRE SAUCE	2 tablespoons
PREPARED MUSTARD	1/3 cup

Procedure

1. Grind luncheon meat.

2. Place ingredients in mixing bowl in order given. Combine thoroughly; if using mixer, beat at low speed about 1 minute.

3. Chill mixture; shape into 100 small balls, using a No. 32 scoop. Place in shallow baking pan. Bake in oven at 325°F. for 45 minutes.

4. Pour Sweet-Sour Sauce (recipe below) over the balls and continue baking for 15 minutes.

*Or, use 2-1/2 pounds ground lean ham and 3-1/2 pounds ground lean pork.

SWEET-SOUR SAUCE

Yield: approximately 8-1/2 cups, 50 portions

Ingredients

CORNSTARCH	1/2 cup
BROWN SUGAR	2 cups
VINEGAR	2/3 cup
DARK CORN SYRUP	2 cups
APPLE JUICE	1-1/4 quarts

Procedure

1. Combine cornstarch and brown sugar; add vinegar and blend.

2. Add remaining ingredients; cook until sauce is thickened and clear.

EAST-WEST PINEAPPLE BEEF BALLS

Yield: 24 entree portions or 48 portions hors d'oeuvres

Ingredients
MEAT BALLS

BEEF, LEAN, GROUND	6 pounds
ONION, finely chopped	3/4 cup
BREAD CRUMBS, fine dry	3 cups
PARSLEY, chopped	1/3 cup
GARLIC SALT	2 tablespoons
PEPPER	3/4 teaspoon
EGGS, slightly beaten	6
MILK	1 quart
PINEAPPLE TIDBITS (IN LIGHT SYRUP)	1 No. 10 can
BUTTER or MARGARINE	1/3 cup
OIL, COOKING	3/4 cup
CURRY POWDER	3/4 teaspoon

SAUCE

PINEAPPLE SYRUP AND WATER	3 cups
VINEGAR	2 cups
SOY SAUCE	1/3 cup
SUGAR	1-1/2 cups
CORNSTARCH	1/3 cup
SALT	3/4 teaspoon

Procedure

1. Combine beef, onion, crumbs, parsley, garlic salt, pepper, eggs and milk. Let stand, covered, about 1 hour.

2. Scoop or shape into 96 small balls.

3. Drain pineapple, reserving syrup for sauce. Press a pineapple tidbit into center of each meat ball.

4. Heat butter, oil and curry powder together. Brown meat balls on all sides; drain off fat.

5. Add water to pineapple syrup, if necessary to make required amount. Add vinegar and soy sauce. Heat.

6. Mix sugar, cornstarch and salt. Add to liquid; cook and stir until thickened and clear. Pour over meat balls.

7. Add remaining pineapple tidbits; heat 5 minutes.

GOLDEN CHICKEN NUGGETS PARMESAN ➤

Yield: 24 portions

Ingredients

BROILER-FRYER HALF-BREASTS, boned, skinned (5 to 6 ounces each)	24
BREAD CRUMBS, fine, dry	2 cups
CHEESE, PARMESAN, grated	1 cup
MONOSODIUM GLUTAMATE	1 tablespoon
SALT	1 tablespoon
THYME	1 tablespoon
BASIL	1 tablespoon
BUTTER or MARGARINE, melted	1/2 pound

BARBECUED SPARERIBS

Yield: 32 portions

Ingredients

PORK SPARERIBS	18 pounds
WATER, hot	3-1/4 quarts
ONION, CHOPPED (reconstituted instant)	8 ounces
GREEN PEPPER, chopped	3 ounces
TOMATO PUREE	1-1/4 quarts
CATSUP	1-1/4 quarts
VINEGAR	1-1/4 cups
SUGAR	10 ounces
WORCESTERSHIRE SAUCE	1/3 cup
SALT	2 ounces
PEPPER	2 teaspoons
CHILI POWDER	1/2 ounce
PAPRIKA	1 tablespoon
CAYENNE PEPPER	few grains

Procedure

1. Cook spareribs in strips as purchased. Arrange on trays. Brown in oven at 500°F. Drain; discard all fat. Transfer ribs to braising pan.

2. Combine water with remaining ingredients; pour over ribs. Bake in oven at 350°F. until meat is done, about 2 hours. Skim sauce thoroughly.

3. To prepare for service, cut strips into 3 rib sections; arrange in pan. Pour a small amount of sauce over ribs. Serve with additional sauce.

Procedure

1. Defrost half-breasts, if necessary. Dry with crumpled paper towels. Cut each breast half into 6 chunks or nuggets about 1-inch to 1-1/2-inch square.

2. Combine crumbs, cheese, monosodium glutamate, salt, thyme and basil.

3. Pour melted butter over chicken pieces in pans; coat well.

4. Roll chicken pieces in crumb mixture to coat thoroughly.

5. Place nuggets in single layer on foil-lined or well-greased baking pans.

6. Bake in oven at 400°F. for 10 to 15 minutes.

DELICE

Yield: 30 portions (3 croquettes each)

Ingredients

BUTTER	1/2 pound
FLOUR	1 pound
MILK	1-1/2 quarts
SWITZERLAND SWISS CHEESE	1 pound
GRUYERE CHEESE (BULK)	1 pound
EGG YOLKS	12
SALT	as needed
PEPPER	as needed
EGG WASH	as needed
BREAD CRUMBS, fine dry	as needed

Procedure

1. Melt butter; blend in flour. Cook and stir until golden.

2. Add milk; cook over low heat until thickened and smooth.

3. Remove from heat; blend in cheeses. Add egg yolks; mix well. Season with salt and pepper.

4. Turn into a flat pan. Chill overnight.

5. Shape into croquettes. Dip in egg wash; roll in crumbs. Saute in hot fat.

Festive Refreshment Service *(Choco-Cherry Bars, recipe, page 45;*
Miniature Cherry Filbert Meringues, recipe, page 65)

National Cherry Growers & Industries Foundation

REFRESHMENTS

"REFRESHMENTS" CAN follow a variety of patterns. The menu and service can take a very simple route, providing little more than coffee or a cup of punch. Again, it can become as elaborate and formal as the occasion demands.

A beverage with a pleasing accompaniment—dainty sandwiches, cookies or fancy small cakes—can provide a festive refreshment at most times of day. The drink can be coffee or tea (either hot or iced), steaming hot chocolate or a tangy punch. Be sure to keep in mind the merits of spiced cocoa or tea and some of the dressed-up coffee treats.

A well-appointed tea table has perennial charm. Custom dictates a pretty tablecover, candles and flowers and a choice of beverages, one available to guests at each end of the table. Trays arranged with an inviting assortment of tea sandwiches and/or other appropriate food complete the table and its decorative effect.

Variety in sandwiches can come with the use of several shapes as well as from the use of different breads and kinds of filling. Triangles, rectangles, fingers and squares give a fair sampling of the conventional styles. Adding some of the more elaborate rolled sandwiches, ribbon sandwiches and the garnished open-face creations can give a well-rounded assortment a fancy touch.

Thinly-sliced white, raisin or cracked wheat bread are among the choices for making tea sandwiches as are slices cut from the loaves of nut or fruit breads (made from a recipe or a mix). The nut or fruit breads work out best when simply spread with butter or whipped cream cheese.

An attractive array of sweets is easy to achieve. Cookies come both dark and light and offer an almost bewildering choice of flavor, texture and shape. As a "small cake," chocolate brownies are a temptation that few people resist.

A more elaborate display can include items such as petits fours and tiny lemon-filled tarts, flat chocolate-covered mints and assorted nuts.

Miscellaneous

TOASTED HONEY-SESAME STICKS

Yield: 16 dozen sticks

Ingredients

BREAD	48 slices
BUTTER or MARGARINE, melted	6 ounces
HONEY, STRAINED	12 ounces
SESAME SEEDS, toasted	3/4 cup (3-3/4 ounces)

Procedure

1. Trim crusts from bread slices.
2. Combine butter and honey; brush over bread.
3. Sprinkle toasted sesame seeds over butter mixture.
4. Cut each bread slice into 4 finger-length sticks; place on bun pans. Cover with foil or plastic film; refrigerate until needed.
5. At serving time, remove covering; toast in oven at 400°F. about 9 minutes or until crisp and browned.

RAISIN TOAST PICADORS

Yield: approximately 20 portions

Ingredients

BUTTER or MARGARINE	1 pound
LEMON RIND, grated	2 teaspoons
LEMON JUICE	1/4 cup
PIMIENTO	8 ounces
RAISIN BREAD	4 1-pound loaves

Procedure

1. Blend butter, lemon peel, lemon juice and pimiento in blender.
2. Quarter slices of raisin bread.
3. Spread both sides with seasoned butter; thread on skewer.
4. Toast in oven at 370°F. for about 15 minutes, until browned. Serve hot.

ANGELIC HONEY FINGERS

Yield: 48

Ingredients

COCONUT, SHREDDED (firmly packed)	2 cups (5-1/2 ounces)
HONEY, strained	1 cup
ANGEL FOOD LOAF CAKE, 1-inch slices	16

Procedure

1. Combine coconut and honey.
2. Cut each slice of cake into three equal-sized "fingers."
3. Spread 1 teaspoon coconut mixture on each strip of cake.
4. Place on a bun pan; toast under medium broiler heat until brown, about 3 minutes.

LEMON CURD

Yield: 3 quarts filling

Ingredients

BUTTER or MARGARINE	1 pound
GRATED LEMON RIND from	4 lemons
LEMON JUICE	2 cups
SALT	1 teaspoon
SUGAR, GRANULATED	1-1/2 quarts
EGGS, WHOLE	12 (2-1/2 cups)
EGG YOLKS	12 (1 cup)

Procedure

1. Melt butter, add lemon rind and juice, salt and sugar.
2. Beat whole eggs and yolks together; combine with lemon and sugar mixture.
3. Cook over boiling water, stirring constantly, until thick and smooth.

Note

Filling will keep, covered, in the refrigerator for several weeks. Use as a filling for cake, for small tea sandwiches, or small cream puffs as well as for tarts.

ANGEL PECAN CAKE FINGERS

Yield: 48

Ingredients

ANGEL FOOD LOAF CAKE, 1/2-inch slices	16
BUTTER or MARGARINE, melted	1/4 pound
ORANGE JUICE	1/2 cup
CONFECTIONERS' SUGAR	3 cups
PECANS, finely chopped	1-1/2 cups
GRAHAM CRACKER CRUMBS	1 cup

Procedure

1. Cut each slice of cake into 3 equal-sized "fingers."
2. Combine melted butter, orange juice and confectioners' sugar.
3. Combine pecans and graham cracker crumbs.
4. Dip each strip of cake into orange icing; roll in nut mixture.
5. Place on bun pan. Refrigerate at least 1 hour before serving.

Note

This will not freeze satisfactorily. It can be prepared a day in advance of serving.

MINTED WALNUTS

Yield: 2-1/2 pounds

Ingredients

CORN SYRUP, LIGHT	1/2 cup
SUGAR, GRANULATED	2 cups
WATER	1 cup
ESSENCE OF PEPPERMINT	2 teaspoons
MARSHMALLOWS	20
WALNUT HALVES	6 cups (1-1/4 pounds)

Procedure

1. Combine syrup, sugar and water in saucepan. Cook over medium heat, stirring constantly, until mixture boils.
2. Continue cooking to soft ball stage (238°F.) or until a small amount of mixture forms a soft ball when tested in very cold water.
3. Remove from heat; quickly add peppermint and marshmallows. Stir until marshmallows are melted.
4. Add walnut halves; stir until well-coated. Pour onto waxed paper. Separate nuts while still warm.

SOUP-FILLED TEA SANDWICHES

Yield: 30 sandwiches (using 30 slices of enriched bread)

Sandwich Name	Condensed Soup Variety (10-1/2 to 11-1/2 ounce can)	Outside Coating (1 cup)
Chicken Almond Dainties	Cream of Chicken	Coarsely Chopped Almonds
Mushroom Rollups	Cream of Mushroom	Shredded or Flaked Coconut
Zesty Turn-A-Rounds	Bean (add 5 tablespoons of hot water)	Finely Chopped Onion
Shrimp Rolls	Cream of Shrimp	Shredded Carrots
Irish Fancies	Cream of Asparagus	Chopped Parsley
Soup 'n Sesame Twists	Green Pea (add 5 tablespoons of hot water)	Sesame Seeds
Potato-Corned Beef Pixies	Cream of Potato	Shredded Corned Beef
Clam Chowder Treats	Clam Chowder	Chopped Ripe Olives
Tomato-Parmesan Rollups	Tomato Bisque	Grated Parmesan Cheese
Cheese 'n Bacon Curls	Cheddar Cheese	Chopped Cooked Bacon

Procedure

1. Trim crusts from 30 slices of fresh enriched or wheat bread.

2. Spread 2 teaspoons soup on each slice of bread. Roll each slice up as for jelly roll; fasten edge with a toothpick.

3. Spread the outside of each sandwich with 1/2 teaspoon soft (not melted) butter and roll in specified outside coating.

4. Place sandwiches on a baking sheet; toast in oven at 400°F. until browned, or about 5 minutes.

5. Remove toothpicks. Serve piping hot with beverages, salads, fruit cups, fruit juices or cocktails.

Note

For advance preparation, make up sandwiches, omitting the butter and outside coating. Freeze until ready to use. At serving time, brush melted or soft butter over outside of frozen sandwiches and immediately dip or sprinkle coating over each sandwich. Toast in oven at 400°F. until browned, or about 10 minutes.

Cookies

CHOCO-CHERRY BARS
(See picture, page 38)

Yield: 200 bars

Ingredients

SUGAR	2-1/4 cups (1 pound)
SALT	1-1/2 teaspoons
EGGS	5
VANILLA	3/4 teaspoon
BUTTER or MARGARINE, soft	6 ounces
CHOCOLATE, UNSWEETENED, melted	6 ounces
FLOUR, ALL-PURPOSE, sifted	1-1/2 cups (6 ounces)
MARASCHINO CHERRIES, drained, chopped	1-1/2 cups (8 ounces)
COCONUT, flaked	2-1/4 cups (8 ounces)

Procedure

1. Combine sugar, salt, eggs and vanilla; beat until thick and lemon-colored.
2. Add soft butter and melted chocolate; blend.
3. Add flour; mix until blended.
4. Add cherries and coconut.
5. Spread in a greased 18-inch by 26-inch baking pan. Bake in oven at 350°F. for 30 to 40 minutes or until done.
6. Cool. Spread with white frosting.*
7. Cut into 2-inch by 1-inch bars. Garnish with pieces of red and green maraschino cherries, as desired.

*WHITE FROSTING

Yield: spreads 1 pan 18-inch by 26-inch

Ingredients

BUTTER or MARGARINE, soft	4 ounces
CONFECTIONERS' SUGAR	1-1/4 pounds
VANILLA	1 teaspoon
MILK	3 to 4 tablespoons

Procedure

Combine ingredients; beat, adding enough milk to make frosting smooth and creamy.

Stained Glass Cookies, (recipe, page 66); Cherry Tea Bars, (recipe on facing page); Cherry Roll-Up Cookies, and Cherry Bird's Nest Cookies, (recipe, page 63)–popular accompaniments for coffee, tea or punch.

National Cherry Growers & Industries Foundation

CHERRY TEA BARS
(See picture, facing page)

Yield: 8 dozen

Ingredients

BUTTER or MARGARINE	1 pound
SUGAR	2 cups
VANILLA	1-1/2 tablespoons
EGGS	8
FLOUR	1-1/2 pounds
BAKING POWDER	4 teaspoons
SALT	1 teaspoon
NUTMEG	2 teaspoons
GLACE CHERRIES, chopped	2 cups
CITRON or CANDIED PINEAPPLE, chopped	1 cup
RAISINS	1 cup
CONFECTIONERS' SUGAR	1 pound
LEMON JUICE	2 tablespoons
WATER	3 to 4 tablespoons

Procedure

1. Cream butter and sugar until light. Beat in vanilla and eggs.
2. Sift flour, baking powder, salt and nutmeg.
3. Add sifted dry ingredients and fruit to egg mixture; mix well.
4. Pour into paper-lined 18-inch by 26-inch by 1-inch sheet pan. Bake in oven at 350°F. for 25 to 30 minutes or until done.
5. Turn out onto a rack; peel off paper. Turn right side up.
6. Combine confectioners' sugar and lemon juice; add water gradually, beating until mixture will spread easily.
7. Spread top with glaze; cut into bars.

BUTTERSCOTCH BROWNIES ➡

Yield: 3 pans (180 brownies, approximately 2-1/2 inches square)

Ingredients

EGGS	36 (3-3/4 pounds)
SUGAR, BROWN	11-1/4 pounds
BUTTER, melted	4-1/2 pounds
FLOUR	6 pounds
BAKING POWDER	4 ounces
SALT	2 tablespoons
VANILLA	2 tablespoons
PECANS, medium pieces	4-1/2 quarts

CHEWY PEANUT BUTTER BARS

Yield: 10 dozen bars 1-inch by 3-inch

Ingredients

FLOUR	1 pound
BAKING POWDER	4 teaspoons
SHORTENING	10 ounces
PEANUT BUTTER	1 pound, 2 ounces
SUGAR, BROWN	6 ounces
SUGAR, GRANULATED	1-3/4 pounds
SALT	1 teaspoon
EGGS	13 ounces (8 eggs)
VANILLA	1-1/2 tablespoons
COCONUT	10 ounces

Procedure

1. Sift flour and baking powder together.

2. Combine shortening, peanut butter, brown and granulated sugar, salt, eggs and vanilla in mixer bowl. Mix at low speed until well blended.

3. Add dry ingredients; mix only until blended. Mix in coconut.

4. Spread mixture in greased baking sheets to a depth of 1/2 inch. Bake in oven at 350°F. for 20 to 25 minutes, or until done. When cool, cut into bars about 1-inch by 3-inches.

Procedure

1. Beat eggs until thick and frothy. Add sugar.
2. Add melted butter; mix well.
3. Sift flour, baking powder and salt together. Add to sugar mixture; mix.
4. Add vanilla and pecans.
5. Spread in greased 24-inch by 16-1/2-inch by 1-inch pans.
6. Bake in oven at 350°F. for 20 minutes or until done.   Cool; cut pans 6 x 10 or as desired.

CHEWY SQUARES

Yield: 1 pan, 18-inch by 26-inch

Ingredients

SUGAR, GRANULATED	2 pounds
BISCUIT MIX	1 pound (1 quart)
SHORTENING	7 ounces (1 cup)
EGGS	8
NUTS, chopped	3 cups
DATES, chopped	1-1/4 quarts
MARASCHINO CHERRIES, drained, cut in fourths	2 cups
SUGAR, CONFECTIONERS'	as needed

Procedure

1. Combine granulated sugar, biscuit mix, shortening and eggs. Mix at low speed for about 1 minute.
2. Fold in nuts, dates and cherries.
3. Spread in a well-greased 18-inch by 26-inch sheet pan. Bake in oven at 350°F. for 35 minutes or until done.
4. Cool slightly; cut into squares. Roll in confectioners' sugar.

FIRST PRIZE FUDGE BROWNIES ⟶

Yield: 48

Ingredients

CHOCOLATE, UNSWEETENED, melted	4 ounces
BUTTER or MARGARINE, melted	8 ounces
EGGS	4
SUGAR	2 cups
FLOUR, ALL-PURPOSE	8 ounces
BAKING POWDER	1 teaspoon
SALT	1/2 teaspoon
APPLESAUCE, CANNED	2 cups
WALNUTS, chopped	2 cups
RAISINS	1 cup
VANILLA	2 teaspoons

CHOCOLATE NUT DROP COOKIES

Yield: 6 dozen (2-inch)

Ingredients

BUTTER or MARGARINE	1/2 pound
SUGAR, LIGHT BROWN	12 ounces
EGGS, beaten	1/2 cup
FLOUR, CAKE	10-1/2 ounces
SALT	1 teaspoon
BAKING SODA	1 teaspoon
MILK	1 cup
CHOCOLATE, UNSWEETENED, melted	4 ounces
WALNUTS or PECANS, chopped	1/2 pound
VANILLA	2 teaspoons

Procedure

1. Cream butter; add brown sugar gradually, continuing to beat until light and fluffy.

2. Add eggs; mix well.

3. Combine flour, salt and soda; sift.

4. Add flour mixture to egg mixture alternately with milk, mixing until smooth.

5. Add chocolate, nuts and vanilla; blend well.

6. Drop by teaspoonfuls onto greased baking sheet.

7. Bake in oven at 375°F. for 12 to 15 minutes or until done.

Procedure
1. Combine chocolate and butter.
2. Beat eggs until light and lemon colored. Gradually add sugar, continuing to beat.
3. Blend in chocolate mixture. Beat 1 minute.
4. Sift flour, baking powder and salt. Add to chocolate mixture; beat only until mixed.
5. Add applesauce, nuts, raisins and vanilla.
6. Spread in a greased 12-inch by 18-inch by 2-inch pan. Bake in oven at 350°F. for 30 minutes or until just done.

HOLIDAY DROP COOKIES

Yield: 16 dozen

Ingredients

FLOUR, ALL-PURPOSE	2 pounds
BAKING SODA	2 teaspoons
SALT	2 teaspoons
SHORTENING	14 ounces
SUGAR, LIGHT BROWN	1-1/2 pounds
EGGS, beaten	4
BUTTERMILK	1-1/3 cups
PECANS, chopped	2 cups
CANDIED CHERRIES, cut in quarters	2 cups
DATES, cut	1 quart
CANDIED FRUITS AND PEELS	1 pound

Procedure
1. Combine flour, soda and salt; sift.
2. Cream shortening. Add sugar and eggs; beat until light and fluffy.
3. Add buttermilk alternately with flour mixture.
4. Fold in pecans and fruits.
5. Chill dough thoroughly.
6. Drop by teaspoonfuls on lightly greased baking sheet.
7. Bake in oven at 375°F. for 8 to 10 minutes or until done.

GLAZED MINT BROWNIES ⟶

Yield: 16 dozen 3-inch by 3/4-inch

Ingredients

CHOCOLATE MINT BROWNIES*	1 24-inch by 18-inch pan
BUTTER or MARGARINE	6 ounces
CONFECTIONERS' SUGAR	1-3/4 pounds
CREAM, LIGHT	3/4 cup
PEPPERMINT FLAVORING	1 tablespoon
CHOCOLATE, UNSWEETENED	6 ounces
BUTTER or MARGARINE	2 ounces

*CHOCOLATE MINT BROWNIES

Yield: 7 pounds, 16 dozen 3-inch by 3/4-inch

Ingredients

CHOCOLATE, UNSWEETENED	12 ounces
BUTTER, MARGARINE or SHORTENING	1 pound
FLOUR	1 pound
BAKING POWDER	4 teaspoons
SALT	1-1/2 teaspoons
EGGS	1-1/4 pounds (2-1/2 cups)
SUGAR	2-3/4 pounds
PEPPERMINT FLAVORING	1 tablespoon
PECANS or WALNUTS, chopped**	12 ounces

Procedure

1. Melt chocolate and shortening over hot water. Cool slightly.

2. Mix flour, baking powder and salt together thoroughly.

3. Beat eggs in mixer bowl. Add sugar and flavoring, beat well.

4. Add chocolate mixture; blend. Add flour mixture and nuts; beat only until well-mixed.

5. Spread batter in one 24-inch by 18-inch pan or in six 9-inch by 9-inch by 2-inch pans (about 1-1/4 pounds batter per pan).

6. Bake in oven at 350°F. for 20 to 25 minutes or until edges begin to shrink slightly from sides of pan. Cool. Finish with glaze, if desired.

**Or, use 12 ounces lightly toasted chopped almonds.

Procedure

1. Let brownies cool in pan.
2. Cream butter; add sugar alternately with cream, blending until of spreading consistency.
3. Add peppermint flavoring. Spread on brownies. Let stand until frosting sets.
4. Melt chocolate and butter together; blend. Drizzle or spread evenly over frosting.
5. Let stand a few minutes before cutting. Cut into strips 3-inches by 3/4-inch.

CHOCOLATE CHIP PEANUT COOKIES

Yield: 24 dozen

Ingredients

FLOUR, ALL-PURPOSE	3-3/4 pounds
BAKING POWDER	1-1/2 tablespoons
SALT	1-1/2 tablespoons
BAKING SODA	2-1/2 tablespoons
BUTTER or OTHER SHORTENING	2 pounds, 3 ounces
SUGAR, BROWN	3-3/4 pounds
EGGS, unbeaten	10 (1 pound)
VANILLA	2-1/2 tablespoons
MILK	3-1/3 cups
SALTED PEANUTS, chopped	1 pound, 14 ounces
SEMI-SWEET CHOCOLATE CHIPS	3-3/4 pounds

Procedure

1. Sift together flour, baking powder, salt and soda.
2. Cream butter; add sugar gradually, creaming thoroughly.
3. Add eggs, a few at a time, beating well after each addition.
4. Combine vanilla and milk.
5. Add flour mixture to creamed mixture alternately with milk, a small amount at a time, blending after each addition. Mix until smooth.
6. Add peanuts and chocolate chips.
7. Drop from No. 30 scoop onto greased baking sheets.
8. Bake in oven at 375°F. for 10 to 12 minutes or until done.

CREAM CHEESE BROWNIES

Yield: 8 dozen

Ingredients

CHOCOLATE, UNSWEETENED	12 ounces
BUTTER or MARGARINE	1 pound
FLOUR, ALL-PURPOSE	1-1/4 pounds
BAKING POWDER	4 teaspoons
SALT	1-1/2 teaspoons
CREAM CHEESE	2 pounds
MILK	1/2 cup
EGGS	1-1/4 pounds (2-1/2 cups)
SUGAR	2-3/4 pounds
VANILLA	2 tablespoons
WALNUTS, chopped	12 ounces

Procedure

1. Melt chocolate and butter over hot water; cool slightly.

2. Mix flour, baking powder and salt together thoroughly.

3. Blend cheese with milk.

4. Beat eggs. Add sugar and vanilla; beat well. Blend in chocolate mixture.

5. Add flour and nuts; beat just to blend.

6. Spread half the batter in a well-greased 24-inch by 18-inch pan. Cover with cream cheese mixture. Spread with remaining batter.

7. Bake in oven at 350°F. for about 30 minutes or until edges shrink slightly from sides of pan.

8. Cool thoroughly. Cut into squares.

Variation

For Marbled Cream Cheese Brownies, spread batter in pan. Spoon cream cheese mixture on top; swirl mixtures together with a spatula just to marble. Bake in oven at 350°F. for about 30 minutes or until edges shrink slightly from edges of pan.

GLAZED CINNAMON CREAM CHEESE COOKIES

Yield: 8 dozen 2-inch cookies

Ingredients

BUTTER, softened	8 ounces
CREAM CHEESE, softened	3 ounces
CINNAMON, GROUND	3/4 teaspoon
VANILLA EXTRACT	1 teaspoon
SUGAR	1 cup
EGG	1
MILK	1 tablespoon
FLOUR	10 ounces
BAKING POWDER	1 teaspoon
SALT	1/2 teaspoon
CHOCOLATE GLAZE*	2 cups
CHOCOLATE SPRINKLES or CHOPPED NUTS	as needed

Procedure

1. Cream together butter, cream cheese, cinnamon and vanilla. Blend in sugar.

2. Add egg and milk; beat.

3. Sift flour, baking powder and salt; add to sugar mixture; mix well.

4. Using pastry bag with narrow ribbon tube, shape 2-inch cookies onto cold cookie sheet.

5. Bake in oven at 375°F. for 8 to 10 minutes or until edges are a golden brown. Cool on racks.

6. Dip ends of cookies in chocolate glaze, then in chocolate sprinkles or chopped nuts.

*CHOCOLATE GLAZE

Yield: approximately 2 cups

Ingredients

SEMI-SWEET CHOCOLATE PIECES	12 ounces (2 cups)
MILK	1/2 cup

Procedure

1. Melt chocolate pieces over hot water.

2. Add milk; beat until smooth.

PEACH DAISIES

Yield: approximately 24 dozen

Ingredients
COOKIE DOUGH

SUGAR	1-1/2 pounds
BUTTER	1-1/2 pounds
SHORTENING	1-1/2 pounds
VANILLA	1/4 cup
SALT	1 tablespoon
EGGS	4-1/2 ounces
FLOUR, PASTRY	4-1/2 pounds
CLING PEACH JAM	
CLING PEACHES, PIE PACK	1 No. 10 can
SUGAR, GRANULATED	5 pounds
SALT	1 tablespoon
CORNSTARCH	3 ounces
WATER	5 ounces

Procedure

(Cookies)

1. Mix first amount of sugar, butter, shortening, vanilla and salt together at 1st speed. Do not cream.

2. Blend in eggs.

3. Add pastry flour; mix only until incorporated.

4. Divide into 1-pound pieces. Shape into long slender rolls. Cut into 1/2-ounce pieces. Place on pans, cut side up.

5. Make indentations in center. Fill with peach jam.

6. Bake in oven at 360°F. for 10 to 12 minutes.

7. To make jam: chop peaches fine. Add remaining ingredients; bring to boil.

8. Blend cornstarch with water. Add to peach mixture; simmer 15 minutes. Add egg coloring, if desired. Cool.

FILBERT CRESCENTS

Yield: 16 dozen

Ingredients

SUGAR, CONFECTIONERS'	10 ounces
SALT	1 teaspoon
BUTTER or MARGARINE	2 pounds
EGG YOLKS	3 ounces
VANILLA	1 tablespoon
FLOUR, ALL-PURPOSE	2-1/2 pounds
FILBERTS, coarsely ground, toasted*	1 pound
SUGAR, CONFECTIONERS'	as needed

Procedure

1. Sift first amount of confectioners' sugar and salt.
2. Cream butter; blend in sugar mixture, egg yolks and vanilla.
3. Gradually mix in flour and filberts until thoroughly blended. Chill dough until firm.
4. Divide dough in fourths. Roll one portion at a time, keeping remainder chilled. Roll on lightly floured or canvas-covered board to 1/4-inch thickness. Cut into narrow strips 2-1/2-inch to 3-inches long and form in small crescents; place on sheet pans.
5. Bake in oven at 375°F. for 10 minutes or until lightly browned. Cool slightly; roll in confectioners' sugar.

Note

To store, place in container with tight fitting cover.

*To toast filberts, spread on sheet pan. Place in oven at 400°F. for 10 to 15 minutes. Shake pan occasionally to brown evenly avoid burning.

MANY WAY BUTTER COOKIES ⟶

Yield: approximately 3-1/4 pounds dough

Ingredients

BUTTER	1 pound
SUGAR, CONFECTIONERS'	10 ounces
EGGS	4 ounces
VANILLA	2 teaspoons
FLOUR, ALL-PURPOSE	1-1/2 pounds
SODA	2 teaspoons
CREAM OF TARTAR	2 teaspoons
SALT	1/2 teaspoon

Procedure

1. Cream butter on medium speed of mixer. Gradually add sugar; continue to beat 3 minutes.
2. Add eggs and vanilla; beat thoroughly.
3. Sift together flour, soda, cream of tartar and salt.
4. Turn mixer to low speed, add flour mixture.
5. Shape dough according to desired variations.

Variations

Rolled Butter Crispies 1. Chill dough.

2. Roll out on lightly floured surface to 1/8-inch thickness.
3. Cut into desired shapes. Using broad spatula, transfer to baking sheet. Sprinkle with granulated sugar.
4. Bake in oven at 400°F. for 6 to 8 minutes.
5. Remove at once onto rack to cool. Decorate before or after baking, as desired. Yield: approximately 6 dozen.

Jewel Drops 1. Add 1 cup chopped mixed candied fruit to basic dough.

2. Drop by rounded teaspoons onto baking sheet.
3. Bake in oven at 400°F. for 8 to 10 minutes.
4. Remove at once onto rack to cool. Yield: 5 to 6 dozen.

Butter Thins 1. Chill dough.

2. Shape into rolls 2 inches in diameter.
3. Wrap rolls in waxed paper; chill several hours or overnight.
4. Cut into 1/8-inch slices; place on baking sheet. Sprinkle with chopped nuts.
5. Bake in oven at 400°F. for 6 to 8 minutes. Remove at once onto rack to cool. Yield: 5 to 6 dozen.

Snowballs 1. Add 1 cup finely chopped walnuts to basic dough.

2. Chill dough.

3. Shape into balls about 3/4-inch in diameter. Place on baking sheet.

4. Bake in oven at 400°F. for 8 to 10 minutes.

5. Remove at once; roll in confectioners' sugar. Cool on rack.

6. When cool, sprinkle with additional sugar. Yield: 9 to 10 dozen.

Snicker-Doodles 1. Chill dough.

2. Shape into balls about 1-inch in diameter; roll in a mixture of 1/4 cup sugar and 1 teaspoon cinnamon.

3. Place on baking sheet.

4. Bake in oven at 400°F. for 10 to 12 minutes. Remove at once onto rack to cool. Yield: 6 to 7 dozen.

Chocolate Refrigerator Cookies 1. Add 2 ounces unsweetened chocolate, melted and cooled, to basic dough.

2. Chill dough.

3. Shape into rolls 2 inches in diameter.

4. Wrap rolls in waxed paper; chill several hours or overnight.

5. Cut into 1/8-inch slices; place on baking sheet. Sprinkle with chopped nuts, if desired.

6. Bake in oven at 400°F. for 6 to 8 minutes. Remove at once onto rack to cool. Yield: 5 to 6 dozen.

Many Way Butter Cookies (Recipe on these pages)

United Dairy Industry Association

SPICED REFRIGERATOR COOKIES ⟶

Yield: 10 dozen cookies

Ingredients

SHORTENING	2 cups
SUGAR, GRANULATED	1 cup
SUGAR, BROWN	1 cup
EGGS	2
FLOUR, sifted	4-1/2 cups
	(1 pound, 2 ounces)
SODA	1 teaspoon
SALT	1 teaspoon
CINNAMON	4 teaspoons
NUTMEG	1 teaspoon
CLOVES	1 teaspoon
WALNUTS or PECANS, chopped	1 cup

TOP-OF-THE-STOVE COOKIES

Yield: 8 dozen

Ingredients

SUGAR	1 quart
MILK	1 cup
BUTTER or MARGARINE	1/2 pound
VANILLA	2 teaspoons
OATMEAL, QUICK COOKING, RAW	1-1/2 quarts
COCOA	6 tablespoons
NUT MEATS, chopped	1 cup
COCONUT, SHREDDED	1 cup

Procedure

1. Mix sugar, milk, butter and vanilla in a sauce pan; bring to a rolling boil; boil for one minute.

2. Mix oatmeal, cocoa, nuts and coconut. Add boiled mixture. Drop from a teaspoon onto waxed paper.

3. Let stand 15 minutes until firm.

Procedure

1. Cream together the shortening and sugars. Add eggs; beat well.

2. Sift together the dry ingredients; add to the creamed mixture. Add nuts; blend.

3. Shape into rolls about 2-1/2 inches in diameter; wrap in wax paper. Chill thoroughly.

4. Slice very thin. Bake on a greased baking sheet in oven at 350°F. for 5 to 7 minutes or until delicately browned. Remove at once to cooling rack.

LEMON-ICED TEA COOKIES

Yield: 15 dozen

Ingredients

BUTTER or MARGARINE	1 pound
SUGAR, GRANULATED	1-1/2 cups
LEMON FLAVORED ICED TEA MIX	3/4 cup (6 ounces)
EGGS	3
FLOUR, ALL-PURPOSE	1 pound, 14 ounces
COCONUT, FLAKED	1-1/2 cups
NUTS, finely chopped	1-1/2 cups

Procedure

1. Combine butter, sugar and iced tea mix. Beat until creamy, using medium speed of mixer. Add eggs; beat until light and fluffy.

2. Blend in flour, coconut and nuts. Chill dough.

3. Shape into rolls about 2-1/2 inches in diameter. Wrap in waxed paper; chill at least 2 hours.

4. Cut dough into 1/4-inch slices. Place on ungreased baking sheets.

5. Bake in oven at 375°F. for 8 to 10 minutes or until edges are light brown. Cool on racks.

PARTY COCONUT KISSES

Yield: 5 dozen

Ingredients

EGG WHITES	4
SALT	1/4 teaspoon
INSTANT COFFEE	2 tablespoons
SUGAR	1 cup
COCONUT	2 cups
VANILLA	1/2 teaspoon

Procedure

1. Beat egg whites and salt until foamy. Combine coffee powder and sugar; add to egg whites gradually, continuing to beat until mixture stands in peaks.

2. Fold in coconut and vanilla.

3. Drop from teaspoon onto well-greased baking sheet. Bake in oven at 250°F. for 30 minutes or until done.

SHORTBREAD

Yield: 1 pan (18-inch by 26-inch)

Ingredients

BUTTER (use only butter)	2 pounds
SUGAR	1 pound, 4 ounces
EGGS	4
FLOUR, PASTRY	3 pounds, 12 ounces

Procedure

1. Mix butter and sugar together.

2. Add eggs, one at a time, continuing to mix.

3. Add flour; mix.

4. Turn out on a board; knead lightly (just until dough holds together).

5. Place on a shallow 18-inch by 26-inch pan; roll out to 3/4-inch thickness. Prick top with a fork about 1 inch apart.

6. Bake in oven at 400°F. for 35 to 40 minutes or until done. Check after 25 or 30 minutes; cover with brown paper, if necessary, to prevent browning.

7. Cut into squares while warm.

CHERRY BIRD'S NEST COOKIES

(See picture, page 46)

Yield: 16 dozen 2-inch cookies

Ingredients

BUTTER or MARGARINE	1-1/2 pounds
SUGAR, BROWN	12 ounces
EGG YOLKS	6
FLOUR	1-1/2 pounds
EGG WHITES	6
PECANS, chopped	1-1/2 pounds
GLACE CHERRIES, WHOLE	16 dozen

Procedure

1. Cream butter and sugar. Beat in egg yolks. Mix in flour.
2. Form dough into 1-inch balls.
3. Beat egg whites slightly. Dip balls in egg white, then in chopped pecans. Place on baking sheets; flatten slightly.
4. Bake in oven at 350°F. for 8 minutes. Remove from oven; press small depression in the center. Bake 10 minutes longer. (In an electric oven, bake with the top unit on high and bottom unit on low, or bake cookies in a double pan.)
5. Loosen cookies from pans while still warm.
6. Place a whole glace cherry in center of each.

LEMON DATE MERINGUES (COOKIES) ⟶

Yield: approximately 6 dozen

Ingredients

DATES, FRESH, PITTED	3 cups (1 pound)
EGG WHITES	1 cup
SALT	1/2 teaspoon
GINGER, POWDERED	1 teaspoon
SUGAR	3 cups
LEMON RIND, grated	1 teaspoon
LEMON JUICE	1/4 cup

CHOCOLATE MERINGUE COOKIES

Yield: 5 pounds dough or 13-1/2 dozen cookies

Ingredients

CHOCOLATE, UNSWEETENED	15 ounces
EGG WHITES	1 pound (2 cups)
SUGAR, CONFECTIONERS'	2-1/2 pounds (2-1/2 quarts)
FLOUR	1/3 cup
SALT	1-1/4 teaspoons
VANILLA	1-1/2 tablespoons
COCONUT, FLAKED	10 ounces (1 quart)

Procedure

1. Melt chocolate. Cool slightly.
2. Beat egg whites to stiff peaks.
3. Sift together sugar, flour and salt.
4. Gradually add sugar mixture to beaten whites, beating just until blended.
5. Fold in vanilla, coconut and cooled chocolate, by hand, stirring just enough to distribute evenly.
6. Drop on greased baking sheets, using a scant No. 40 scoop or 1/2 ounce per cookie. Bake in oven at 375°F. for about 10 minutes or until done.
7. Cool about 1 minute before removing from sheets. Store in a loosely-covered container.

Procedure

1. Chop dates.
2. Beat egg whites with salt to soft peaks.
3. Combine ginger and sugar. Add to egg whites gradually, continuing to beat until stiff peaks form.
4. Fold in lemon rind and juice. Carefully fold in dates.
5. Line a baking sheet with well-greased brown paper. Using a No. 40 scoop or teaspoon, drop mixture onto paper.
6. Bake in oven at 325°F. for 20 to 30 minutes, or until slightly browned.
7. Remove from paper at once; cool on rack. Store in airtight container.

MINIATURE CHERRY FILBERT MERINGUES

(See picture, page 38)

Yield: approximately 14 dozen

Ingredients

MARASCHINO CHERRY HALVES (RED)	2 cups
EGG WHITES	4 ounces (1/2 cup)
SALT	1/2 teaspoon
SUGAR	1 pound
SYRUP FROM CHERRIES	4 teaspoons
FILBERTS (GRANULES or finely ground)	6 ounces (1-1/2 cups)

Procedure

1. Drain cherries, reserving required amount of syrup.
2. Combine egg whites and salt; beat until soft peaks form. Gradually add sugar, continuing to beat until meringue is stiff but not dry.
3. Fold in reserved cherry syrup and filbert granules.
4. Drop by teaspoonfuls onto baking pans covered with unglazed wrapping paper.
5. Top each meringue with a cherry half.
6. Bake in oven at 350°F. for 10 to 12 minutes, or until done.
7. Cool on paper 2 to 3 minutes. Remove to wire racks to cool thoroughly.

Note

For a chewy cookie, store in containers with tight-fitting covers.

Poppy Seed Tea Bread (Recipe, facing page)

American Spice Trade Association

STAINED GLASS COOKIES
(See picture, page 46)

Yield: approximately 8 dozen

Ingredients

BUTTER or MARGARINE	1/2 pound
CONFECTIONERS' SUGAR	2 cups
VANILLA	2 teaspoons
LEMON JUICE	2 tablespoons
EGG YOLKS, hard-cooked	8
FLOUR, sifted	3 cups (12 ounces)
NUTMEG	1/2 teaspoon
GLACE CHERRIES, diced	2 cups

Procedure

1. Cream butter; gradually beat in sugar. Add vanilla, lemon juice and egg yolks. Beat until well blended.

2. Add flour, nutmeg and cherries; mix until blended.

3. Pack firmly into greased 6- or 8-ounce cans or form into rolls, about 3 inches in diameter. Freeze or chill thoroughly.

4. Slice very thin; place on ungreased baking sheets. Bake in oven at 300°F. about 15 to 18 minutes.

Breads (Tea Loaves)

POPPY SEED TEA BREAD WITH LEMON FROSTING
(See picture, facing page)

Yield: 5 1-pound loaves

Ingredients

POUND CAKE or TEA CAKE MIX	5 pounds
MILK	2-1/2 cups
EGGS	10
MILK	1-1/4 cups
POPPY SEED	3 cups
FROSTING MIX, VANILLA FLAVOR	3 cups
LEMON JUICE	1/4 cup
LEMON RIND, grated	3 tablespoons
POPPY SEED	3/4 cup

Procedure

1. Place cake mix in mixer bowl. Add first amount of milk; blend at low speed for one minute.

2. Add eggs, one at a time, blending well after each addition.

3. Add remaining milk and first amount of poppy seed. Blend until smooth. Scrape bowl occasionally during mixing.

4. Pour batter into 5 greased and lightly floured 9-inch by 5-inch by 3-inch loaf pans.

5. Bake in oven at 325°F. for 1 hour, 10 minutes or until done.

6. Cool in pans 20 minutes. Turn out on wire racks. Cool completely.

7. Prepare frosting mix according to package directions, replacing part of the liquid with the lemon juice.

8. Add lemon rind. Spread frosting on tops of cooled loaves. Sprinkle with remaining poppy seed.

PRUNE ORANGE NUT BREAD

Yield: 4 3-pound loaves, 30 to 32 slices per loaf

Ingredients

ORANGES, 2-1/2 INCH DIAMETER	4
or ORANGE JUICE	1-1/2 cups
PRUNES, plumped, pitted	1 quart
APPLESAUCE, CANNED	1 quart
FLOUR, ALL-PURPOSE, sifted	4 pounds
BAKING POWDER, DOUBLE-ACTING	6 tablespoons
BAKING SODA	2 tablespoons
SUGAR, GRANULATED	2 pounds
SALT	2 tablespoons
NUT MEATS, broken or chopped	1 pound
EGGS, slightly beaten	8
MARGARINE or SHORTENING, melted	1 cup

Procedure

1. Cut oranges in half. Put through grinder with prunes.
2. Combine orange (or juice) and prune mixture with applesauce.
3. Sift dry ingredients together; add nuts.
4. Combine eggs, margarine and fruit mixture.
5. Add moist ingredients to dry ingredients, mixing only until blended.
6. Scale three pounds into each of 4 oiled loaf pans. Bake in oven at 350°F. for one hour, or until done.
7. Turn on rack to cool. Place in plastic or tin container; cover tightly.
8. Chill in refrigerator overnight before slicing.

BANANA DATE BREAD

Yield: 3 loaves

Ingredients

FLOUR, ALL-PURPOSE	2 pounds
SALT	1-1/2 teaspoons
BAKING POWDER	2 tablespoons
BAKING SODA	3/4 teaspoon
GINGER, GROUND	1-1/2 teaspoons
MACE, GROUND	3/4 teaspoon
SUGAR, LIGHT BROWN	14 ounces
WALNUTS or PECANS, chopped	1-1/2 cups
EGGS, slightly beaten	6 (10 ounces)
BUTTERMILK	3/4 cup
BUTTER or MARGARINE, melted	1 pound, 2 ounces
DATES, chopped	1-1/2 pounds
BANANAS, ripe, mashed	3 cups

Procedure

1. Combine flour, salt, baking powder, soda and spices; sift. Add sugar and nuts.
2. Combine eggs, buttermilk, melted butter, dates and bananas. Add to dry ingredients; mix until moistened.
3. Turn into 3 greased 9-inch by 5-inch loaf pans.
4. Bake in oven at 375°F. for 1 to 1-1/4 hours or until done.
5. Cool in pan 10 minutes. Turn out on rack; finish cooling.
6. Wrap in foil. Store overnight before slicing.

FRUITED QUICK BREAD

Yield: 3 9-inch by 5-inch loaves

Ingredients

FLOUR, ALL-PURPOSE	2 pounds
SALT	1-1/2 teaspoons
BAKING POWDER	2 tablespoons
CARDAMOM, GROUND	1 teaspoon
or MACE, GROUND	1-1/2 teaspoons
SUGAR	3 cups
BUTTER or MARGARINE	3/4 pound
GLACE RED CHERRIES (READY TO USE),	
cut in half	3 8-ounce jars
LEMON PEEL (READY TO USE), diced	3 4-ounce jars
DATES, chopped	8 ounces
EGGS, beaten	9 (15 ounces)
MILK	1-1/2 cups

Procedure

1. Combine flour, salt, baking powder and spice; sift. Add sugar.

2. Cut in butter until mixture resembles coarse meal.

3. Add cherries, lemon peel and dates. Mix well.

4. Combine eggs and milk. Add, all at once, to dry ingredients. Mix until just moistened.

5. Turn into 3 greased 9-inch by 5-inch loaf pans. Bake in oven at 375°F. for 1-1/4 hours or until done. Cool in pan 10 minutes. Remove to rack to finish cooling.

6. Wrap in foil or waxed paper. Store overnight before slicing.

BRAN CREAM CHEESE BREAD

Yield: 2 9-inch by 5-inch loaves

Ingredients

WHOLE BRAN	1 quart
BUTTERMILK	1 cup
MOLASSES	1/2 cup
EGGS, beaten	4
BUTTER or MARGARINE, melted	1/2 pound
CREAM CHEESE, softened	1 pound
SUGAR, LIGHT BROWN	9 ounces
FLOUR, ALL-PURPOSE	12 ounces
SALT	1 teaspoon
BAKING POWDER	4 teaspoons
SODA	1/2 teaspoon
CINNAMON, GROUND	1-1/2 teaspoons
NUTMEG, GROUND	1/2 teaspoon
WALNUTS, chopped	1-3/4 cups
WALNUTS, chopped	1/4 cup

Procedure

1. Combine bran, buttermilk, molasses, eggs and melted butter; allow to stand 5 minutes.

2. Blend cream cheese and sugar.

3. Combine flour, salt, baking powder, soda and spices; sift. Add first amount of the chopped walnuts.

4. Add dry ingredients to cream cheese mixture alternately with bran mixture, beginning and ending with dry ingredients.

5. Turn batter into 2 greased 9-inch by 5-inch loaf pans. Sprinkle 2 tablespoons chopped walnuts over each loaf.

6. Bake in oven at 350°F. for 1-1/4 hours or until done. Cool in pan 10 minutes. Turn out on rack to finish cooling.

7. Wrap in foil or waxed paper. Store overnight before slicing.

Sandwich Fillings

CHERRY-CHEESE SANDWICH FILLING

Yield: 1 quart

Ingredients

CREAM CHEESE, softened	1-1/2 pounds
MARASCHINO CHERRY SYRUP	1/4 cup
MARASCHINO CHERRIES, well drained, chopped	2 cups
ALMONDS, SLIVERED, toasted or	
PECANS, chopped, toasted	1 cup

Procedure

1. Combine cream cheese and cherry syrup; beat until well blended.
2. Mix in cherries and nuts.
3. Spread on white, raisin or Boston brown bread.

CURRIED CHICKEN-EGG SANDWICH FILLING

Yield: 1-1/2 quarts

Ingredients

CANDIED GINGER, finely chopped	1 tablespoon
SALT	1-1/2 teaspoons
MUSTARD, DRY	1 tablespoon
CURRY POWDER	3/4 teaspoon
LEMON JUICE	1 tablespoon
MAYONNAISE or SALAD DRESSING	1-1/2 cups
CHICKEN, cooked, chopped	3 cups
EGGS, hard-cooked, chopped	3 cups

Procedure

1. Combine ginger, salt, mustard, curry powder, lemon juice and mayonnaise.
2. Add chicken and eggs; toss together lightly.

Note

Also good as a hot grilled sandwich.

VOLUME FEEDING
RAISIN SPREAD

Yield: about 1 quart, filling for 24 sandwiches (bread slice size)

Ingredients

RAISINS, LIGHT or DARK	2 cups
AMERICAN CHEESE, grated	1 pound
SALAD DRESSING	1 cup

Procedure

1. Rinse and drain raisins. Chop coarsely. Blend with remaining ingredients.

CHILI CHEESE FILLING

Yield: 1 gallon, 96 sandwiches* (No. 24 scoop)

Ingredients

CHEESE, PROCESS AMERICAN, grated	6 pounds
CHILI SAUCE	3 cups
RIPE OLIVES, chopped	3 4-1/2-ounce cans
GREEN PEPPER, chopped	2 cups

Procedure

1. Combine ingredients; mix well.
*Bread slice size.

HAM AND ALMOND SANDWICH FILLING

Yield: 7 pounds, 75 sandwiches* (1-1/2 ounces each)

Ingredients

HAM, ground	3 pounds
EGGS, hard-cooked, chopped	12
ALMONDS, DICED ROASTED	1 pound
MAYONNAISE	1 quart
HORSERADISH	3 ounces

Procedure

1. Combine ingredients; chill.
*Bread slice size.

CHICKEN-PIMIENTO FILLING

Yield: 2 quarts, 48 sandwiches* (No. 48 scoop)

Ingredients

CHICKEN, cooked, ground	1-3/4 pounds
CELERY, finely chopped	3 cups
PIMIENTO, chopped	1/2 cup
SALT	1 teaspoon
MAYONNAISE or SALAD DRESSING	2-1/2 cups

Procedure
1. Combine ingredients; mix well.
*Bread slice size.

SWISS MISS SANDWICH

Yield: 24 sandwiches (bread slice size)

Ingredients

SWISS CHEESE, grated	1-1/2 pounds
OLIVES, RIPE, chopped	3/4 cup
MUSTARD, DRY	1 tablespoon
MAYONNAISE or SALAD DRESSING	3/4 cup
BREAD, WHOLE WHEAT	48 slices

Procedure
1. Combine cheese, olives, mustard and mayonnaise.
2. Make 24 sandwiches, using No. 24 scoop of filling and 2 slices bread per sandwich. Cut as desired.

ALMOND COTTAGE SANDWICH FILLING

Yield: 1/2 gallon

Ingredients

ALMONDS, DICED ROASTED	3 cups
COTTAGE CHEESE	3 pounds
GREEN ONIONS, sliced	1/3 cup
MAYONNAISE	1-1/2 cups

Procedure
1. Combine ingredients, mixing well.
2. Keep refrigerated.

Rolled Sandwiches—Good Beverage Companions

American Mushroom Institute; American Spice Trade Association

LEMON-TUNA-NUT SANDWICH FILLING

Yield: 1 quart

Ingredients

BUTTER or MARGARINE, soft	1/2 pound
TUNA, drained, flaked	3-1/2 cups (1 pound)
LEMON JUICE	1/4 cup
LEMON RIND, grated	2 tablespoons
SALT	1 teaspoon
PEPPER	1/2 teaspoon
ALMONDS, SLICED, toasted	1-1/2 cups

Procedure

1. Whip butter until light and fluffy. Blend in tuna, lemon juice and rind, salt and pepper.
2. Stir in almonds.

CHEESE AND DEVILED EGG SANDWICHES

Yield: 24 sandwiches (bread slice size)

Ingredients

COTTAGE CHEESE, CREAMED	2-1/2 pounds
EGGS, hard-cooked, finely chopped	8
SALT	2 teaspoons
DRY MUSTARD	1-1/2 teaspoons
SOUR CREAM (COMMERCIAL)	1 cup
ENRICHED WHITE BREAD, buttered	24 slices
WHOLE WHEAT BREAD, buttered	24 slices

Procedure

1. Combine cottage cheese and eggs.

2. Mix salt and mustard; add to sour cream; blend. Add to cheese mixture; mix thoroughly.

3. Make sandwiches using a No. 20 scoop of filling between one slice of white bread, one of whole wheat. Cut as desired.

FESTIVE SANDWICH FILLING

Yield: 2-1/4 quarts

Ingredients

RIPE OLIVES, pitted, drained	3 cups
ONION, finely chopped	1/4 cup
SALT	1 teaspoon
LEMON JUICE	2 tablespoons
MAYONNAISE	1-1/2 cups
EGGS, hard-cooked, chopped	1-1/2 quarts
CRABMEAT, cooked, flaked	1 pound

Procedure

1. Chop olives.
2. Combine onion, salt, lemon juice and mayonnaise; mix well. Fold in olives, eggs and crabmeat, mixing well.
3. Keep refrigerated for use.

OLIVE-NUT FILLING

Yield: 55 sandwiches (bread slice size) (1/4 cup each)

Ingredients

RIPE OLIVES, pitted, chopped	1-1/4 quarts
CELERY, finely chopped	3 cups
WALNUTS, chopped	1 quart
EGGS, hard-cooked, finely chopped	1-1/2 dozen
SALT	2 teaspoons
SALAD DRESSING	2 cups

Procedure

1. Combine ingredients; mix well. Chill.

Punch with Spicy Character

American Spice Trade Association

THE PUNCH BOWL

A FESTIVE WELL-FILLED punch bowl radiates hospitality on an impressive scale. Yet it is an easy way to provide refreshment for a large—or lingering—crowd.

A successful punch is a drink with character. It is either definitely hot or thoroughly chilled, has a pleasing tang and is never too sweet. It delights the eye as well as the taste and maintains its strength to the very last cup.

Wines and all types of spirits can combine with fruit juices and sugar for brisk, taste-teasing punches to quench the thirst. Or a well planned selection of juices makes delightful mild-mannered drinks without any spirits at all. A fragrant brew of tea can provide a pleasing base, and a carbonated beverage introduce a tingle of bubbles.

Hot punches add warmth and cheer at holiday time and at other times of year when there's a nippy wind and a flurry of snow. Eggnog is another drink with a long tradition closely associated with the holiday season.

In summer, when people assemble for refreshments and talk, there's nothing more sociable than a flavorfully concocted punch bowl that is sparkling cool.

Cold punches benefit from being mixed ahead and allowed to blend. For optimum chilling and strength, chill ingredients thoroughly before placing them in the bowl with ice to avoid too rapid melting and a diluted punch. When sparkling wines or carbonated beverages are used, chill separately and add just before serving time.

A large single block of ice will not melt as quickly as small cubes. Ice molds are a decorative addition to the punch bowl. They are especially attractive when the water for making them is colored and/or when a pattern of berries or pieces of fruit is frozen into them. Small scoops of sherbet or water ice can take the place of ice and at the same time provide a decorative effect. When using sherbet or ice, be sure to take into account the sweetness they give.

For added charm, surround your punch bowl with ivy, fern or other forms of greenery. Garnish the punch with thin slices of lemon, orange or lime. Or, use sliced fresh strawberries, melon balls or small fresh pineapple fans. As an added fillip, try sprinkling a little grated fresh coconut on cups of fruit punch.

Trays of dainty sandwiches, small cakes and an assortment of cookies make gracious companions for hot or cold punch and add to the attractiveness of the refreshment table.

Hot Punches

HOLIDAY HOT TEA PUNCH

Yield: approximately 6-1/2 quarts

Ingredients

WATER, boiling	5 quarts
TEA, LOOSE	1/3 cup
WHOLE CLOVES	3 tablespoons
CINNAMON STICKS	12 2-inch sticks
ORANGE JUICE	3 cups
LEMON JUICE	1-1/2 cups
HONEY	2 cups

Procedure

1. Bring water to a full rolling boil. Immediately pour over tea and spices. Cover; steep 5 minutes. Strain.

2. Add fruit juices and honey. Stir until blended. Keep hot.

3. Serve in cups or mugs garnished with lemon slices and whole cloves, if desired.

THE BISHOP

Yield: 4-1/2 quarts

Ingredients

LEMON JUICE from	8 lemons
LEMON RIND from	4 lemons
WHOLE CLOVES	24
WATER	1 quart
SUGAR	1 cup
CALIFORNIA PORT, TOKAY or MUSCATEL WINE	4 4/5-quart bottles
LEMON SLICES	for garnish

Procedure

1. Combine lemon juice, lemon rind, whole cloves, water and sugar. Simmer gently for 15 minutes. Strain.

2. Add spiced liquid to wine. Heat, but do not allow to boil.

3. Serve piping hot, garnished with lemon slices.

HOT MULLED APPLE JUICE

Yield: 1 gallon

Ingredients

APPLE JUICE	1 gallon
CINNAMON STICKS	4 2-inch sticks
WHOLE CLOVES	16
SUGAR	1 cup

Procedure

1. Combine apple juice, cinnamon (broken in small pieces), cloves and sugar.

2. Bring to boiling point; simmer 10 minutes.

3. Strain. Serve hot.

WASSAIL (Non-Alcoholic)

Yield: 50 portions

Ingredients

WHOLE CLOVES	2 tablespoons
WHOLE ALLSPICE	4 teaspoons
CINNAMON STICKS	4
APPLE CIDER	2 quarts
PINEAPPLE JUICE	1 quart
APRICOT NECTAR	1 quart
ORANGE JUICE	1-1/2 quarts
LEMON JUICE	2 cups
GRAPEFRUIT JUICE	2 cups
SUGAR	1 cup

Procedure

1. Tie cloves and allspice in a cheesecloth bag. Combine with remaining ingredients; simmer 15 minutes.

2. Remove spice bag. Pour hot mixture into a heat-proof punch bowl. Garnish with thin slices of oranges and lemons stuck with whole cloves, if desired. Serve hot.

GLOGG

Yield: approximately 1 gallon

Ingredients

CLARET WINE	2 bottles
PORT WINE	2 bottles
ORANGE PEEL, grated	2 tablespoons
CARDAMOM SEEDS	20
CINNAMON STICKS	6
WHOLE CLOVES	25
ALMONDS, WHOLE, blanched	1 pound
RAISINS	1 pound
COGNAC	1 bottle
LUMP SUGAR	1 pound

Procedure

1. Combine wines in a large kettle, suitable for serving. Add orange rind and spices tied in a cheesecloth bag. Heat slowly; simmer 15 minutes.

2. Add almonds and raisins; simmer 10 minutes longer. Remove from heat; discard spice bag.

3. Add cognac, reserving 1 cup.

4. Place a narrow wire grill over the kettle. Spread lump sugar on the grill. Gradually pour reserved cognac over sugar. Ignite.

5. Ladle glogg over sugar while it melts and drips down to sweeten glogg. When sugar is melted, remove grill. Put out flame by covering the kettle.

6. Ladle hot glogg into demitasse cups. Make sure there are a few almonds and raisins in each cup. Serve with a small spoon to be used in eating raisins and nuts in the bottom of cup.

Cold Punches

NEW YEAR CHEER PUNCH

Yield: 20 1/2-cup portions

Ingredients

SUGAR	1 cup
CRANBERRY JUICE COCKTAIL	1 quart
ORANGE JUICE	2 cups
PINEAPPLE JUICE	1 cup
LEMON JUICE	3/4 cup
GINGERALE	2 cups
LEMON, LIME or PINEAPPLE SHERBET	3/4 to 1 quart

Procedure

1. Add sugar to cranberry cocktail; stir until dissolved.

2. Combine with fruit juices; pour into punch bowl over ice. Add gingerale. Float small scoops of sherbet over top.

TROPICAL FRUIT PUNCH

Yield: 3 gallons

Ingredients

PINEAPPLE, FRESH, diced	3 quarts
ORANGE JUICE, FRESH	2 quarts
LEMON JUICE, FRESH	2 quarts
GRAPEFRUIT JUICE, FRESH	2 quarts
SUGAR	3 pounds
WATER	2 quarts
GINGERALE	2 quarts

Procedure

1. Put the pineapple into an electric blender for about 5 minutes, or until finely minced. (If blender is not available, use fine knife of grinder.)

2. Combine pineapple and fruit juices.

3. Combine sugar and water; bring to a boil, stirring until sugar is dissolved. Cool. Combine with fruit juices.

4. Add gingerale. Serve garnished with ice mold.

HOLIDAY FRUIT PUNCH

Yield: approximately 2 gallons

Ingredients

WATER, boiling	2 quarts
TEA, LOOSE	1/4 cup
LEMON JUICE	2 cups
ORANGE JUICE	1 quart
SUGAR	2 cups
CRANBERRY JUICE	1-1/2 quarts
WATER	2 quarts
GINGERALE	1 quart
LEMON, sliced	1 lemon
LIMES, sliced	2 limes
MARASCHINO CHERRIES	as needed

Procedure

1. Bring 2 quarts of water to a full rolling boil. Immediately pour over tea. Brew 5 minutes. Stir; strain. Cool at room temperature.

2. Combine cold tea, fruit juices and water. Chill.

3. At serving time, pour over a large piece of ice, an ice ring or ice cubes. Add gingerale. Garnish with fruit.

CRANBERRY FRUIT PUNCH

Yield: 3-3/4 quarts

Ingredients

CRANBERRY JUICE COCKTAIL	1-1/2 quarts
ORANGE JUICE	3 cups
LEMON JUICE	1-1/4 cups
PINEAPPLE JUICE	1-1/2 cups
SUGAR	1-1/2 cups
WATER	3 cups

Procedure

1. Combine cranberry juice cocktail and fruit juices.

2. Dissolve sugar in water; add to punch mixture; mix well. Chill.

3. Serve over crushed ice or ice cubes.

STRAWBERRY-RHUBARB PUNCH

Yield: 3 gallons

Ingredients

PINK RHUBARB, FRESH	10 pounds
SUGAR	5 pounds
WATER	1-1/2 gallons
STRAWBERRIES, FRESH, hulled	4 quarts
ORANGE RIND, grated	1/4 cup
LEMON RIND, grated	1/4 cup
ORANGE JUICE, FRESH	1 quart
LEMON JUICE, FRESH	2 cups
ICE	16 pounds

Procedure

1. Cut rhubarb in 1-inch pieces. Wash thoroughly; combine with sugar and water. Bring to a boil, stirring occasionally. Cook until tender. Remove from heat. Reserve 2 cups of rhubarb for garnish.

2. Puree remaining rhubarb through a fine strainer. Add 3 quarts of crushed or sliced berries, grated rinds and fruit juices.

3. Add the ice. Chill well. Serve garnished with reserved rhubarb and the remaining quart of whole strawberries.

CUCUMBER LEMONADE

Yield: 3 gallons

Ingredients

SUGAR	3 pounds
WATER	1 gallon
LEMON JUICE, FRESH	3 quarts
WATER, cold	1 gallon
CUCUMBERS	8
GRENADINE (optional)	1 cup
ICE CUBES	12 pounds

Procedure

1. Combine sugar and water. Cook 5 minutes, stirring until dissolved. Cool.

2. Add fresh lemon juice and cold water. Score cucumbers with the tines of a fork. Slice; add to punch. Add grenadine, if desired. Serve over ice cubes.

APPLE "CHAMPAGNE" PUNCH

Yield: 3 quarts

Ingredients

STRAWBERRIES, FRESH, unhulled	1 pint
GRAPES, SEEDLESS	1 cup
WATER	as needed
APPLE JUICE, chilled	1-1/2 quarts
GINGERALE, chilled	1-1/2 quarts

Procedure

1. Wash unhulled berries and grapes. Freeze in water in a 1-1/2 quart ring mold.

2. At serving time, unmold ice ring. Place in chilled punch bowl. Pour apple juice and gingerale over frozen mold.

TRADITIONAL AMERICAN EGGNOG

Yield: 20 portions

Ingredients

EGG YOLKS	12 (1 cup)
SUGAR	8 ounces
MILK	1 quart
RUM, GOLD	1 bottle (1/5 gallon)
CREAM, WHIPPING	1 quart
NUTMEG	as needed

Procedure

1. Beat egg yolks until light. Add sugar gradually, continuing to beat until mixture is thick.

2. Add milk and rum. Chill 3 hours.

3. Pour into chilled punch bowl.

4. Whip cream until thick and shiny. Fold into eggnog mixture. Chill 1 hour. Dust with nutmeg.

Note

To make with dairy eggnog, add 1 cup rum to 1 quart of eggnog. Fold in 1 cup heavy cream, whipped. Chill; add nutmeg.

FRUIT FRESHER

Yield: approximately 1 gallon

Ingredients

APPLE JUICE, chilled	2 quarts
PINEAPPLE JUICE, chilled	1 quart
LIME JUICE, FRESH	1/2 cup
GINGERALE, chilled	1 quart

Procedure

1. Combine apple juice, pineapple juice and lime juice. Add gingerale.
2. Pour over ice cubes in tall glasses.

SPICED FRUIT PUNCH

Yield: 3 gallons

Ingredients

SUGAR	3 pounds
WATER	1 gallon
GRAPEFRUIT JUICE, FRESH	1 quart
LEMON JUICE, FRESH	1 quart
ORANGE JUICE, FRESH	3 quarts
PINEAPPLE, FRESH, finely minced	2 quarts
LEMON RIND, grated	1/4 cup
ORANGE RIND, grated	1/4 cup
WHOLE CLOVES	2 tablespoons
CINNAMON, STICK	12 2-inch pieces
WHOLE ALLSPICE	2 tablespoons
TEA, strong	2 cups
CRACKED ICE	10 pounds

Procedure

1. Combine sugar and water; cook 5 minutes, stirring occasionally. Cool. Combine with fruit juices and pineapple which has been put through a blender.

2. Add rinds. Steep spices in tea for 15 minutes; strain into the fruit juices. Chill. Serve over cracked ice.

SCOTTISH EGGNOG

Yield: 5-3/8 quarts

Ingredients

DAIRY EGGNOG	4 quarts
SHERRY, SPANISH, DRY	1 quart
BRANDY	1 cup
RUM, BACARDI	1/2 cup

Procedure

1. Combine ingredients. Refrigerate, covered, for 2 to 4 hours to mellow.

2. Serve in punch cups. Sprinkle tops with mixture of 1 part nutmeg to 3 of cinnamon.

Note

This is a mild flavored eggnog, not over-rich.

APPLE MINT REFRESHER

Yield: 6-1/2 quarts, 35 6-ounce portions

Ingredients

APPLE JUICE	6 quarts
LEMON JUICE	1 cup
MINT EXTRACT	1 teaspoon
SUGAR, GRANULATED	1 cup
WATER	1 cup

Procedure

1. Combine apple juice, lemon juice and mint extract; set aside to blend.

2. Combine sugar and water; bring to a boil. Add to juice mixture. Chill.

3. Garnish each glass with a sprig of fresh mint or a thin slice of lemon.

Special Service for Cafe Diable *(Recipe, page 94)*

Concord Grape Association

SPECIAL BEVERAGES

SPICED TEA

Yield: 1 gallon

Ingredients

CINNAMON, STICK	1 ounce (10 3-inch sticks)
CLOVES, WHOLE	2 tablespoons
SUGAR	1-1/2 cups
WATER, boiling	1 gallon
TEA	1 ounce (1 iced tea bag)
LEMON JUICE	1/2 cup

Procedure

1. Add spices and sugar to boiling water; continue boiling for 5 minutes.

2. Pour hot liquid over tea. Cover; steep 5 minutes.

3. Strain. Add lemon juice.

4. Serve hot. If desired, float thin slice of lemon on top of each cup.

BRAZILIAN CHOCOLATE COFFEE

Yield: approximately 1 gallon

Ingredients

WATER	1 quart
INSTANT DECAFFEINATED COFFEE	12 envelopes
	(6 to 7 tablespoons)
CHOCOLATE, UNSWEETENED	8 1-ounce squares
SUGAR	1 cup
SALT	1/4 teaspoon
MILK, hot	3 quarts
WHIPPED CREAM	as needed
ORANGE RIND, grated	as needed

Procedure

1. Bring water to a boil in heavy saucepan. Reduce heat. Add instant coffee and chocolate; stir until chocolate is melted.

2. Add sugar and salt. Boil about 4 minutes, stirring constantly.

3. Add hot milk gradually, stirring to blend. Beat with a wire whip until light and frothy. Place over hot water to keep hot.

4. Serve in warmed mugs. Top with whipped cream; sprinkle with grated orange rind.

SPICED VIENNESE COFFEE

Yield: 1 gallon

Ingredients

INSTANT COFFEE	1 cup
CLOVES, WHOLE	22
CINNAMON, STICK	4 2-1/2-inch pieces
WATER, hot	1 gallon
SUGAR	1 cup
WHIPPED TOPPING, PREPARED	
or WHIPPED CREAM	2 cups
CINNAMON, GROUND	as needed

Procedure

1. Place coffee powder in large saucepan.

2. Tie cloves and cinnamon sticks in a cheesecloth bag; place in saucepan. Add hot water.

3. Cover pan; bring just to a boil. Remove from heat; let stand 5 to 8 minutes.

4. Remove spice bag. Add sugar; stir until dissolved.

5. Serve at once. Garnish with whipped topping and a sprinkling of ground cinnamon.

Variation:

For Spiced Viennese Float, use above recipe, chilling mixture thoroughly after adding sugar. Serve in tall glasses; top with a No. 20 scoop of vanilla ice cream in place of the whipped topping. Sprinkle with ground cinnamon, if desired.

CAFE DIABLE
(See picture, page 90)

Yield: 4 to 6 portions

Ingredients

ORANGE	1
CLOVES, WHOLE	as needed
SUGAR	4 tablespoons
CINNAMON STICK, broken in half	2 3-inch pieces
LEMON, thinly sliced	1 slice
RUM, JAMAICAN, or COGNAC	1-1/2 cups
COFFEE, DEMITASSE (strong)	2 cups

Procedure

1. Peel orange with knife, keeping peeling in one long, continuous strip.

2. Stud peel with whole cloves, placing about 1 inch apart down full length of peel.

3. Place sugar, 2 additional whole cloves and cinnamon stick in cafe diable dish or upper part of chafing dish.

4. Heat until sugar melts and just begins to turn golden. Drop in lemon slice and orange peel; pour in rum.

5. Dip up a ladleful of the hot rum; set afire and lower the flaming ladle into the dish. Slowly pour in the coffee.

6. Holding peel at one end, with a long handled fork or pair of tongs, ladle the flaming rum mixture over peel until the flame dies.

7. Serve in cafe diable or demitasse cups.

Note

When flaming, lower light in room.

COCOA WITH A HINT OF SPICE

Yield: 50 5-ounce portions

Ingredients

COCOA	2-1/2 cups
SUGAR	2 cups
CINNAMON, GROUND	1-1/2 tablespoons
CLOVES, GROUND	1/2 teaspoon
ALLSPICE, GROUND	1/2 teaspoon
SALT	1 teaspoon
WATER	2-1/2 cups
MILK	7-3/4 quarts
CINNAMON STICKS, 3-inch pieces (optional)	50

Procedure

1. Combine cocoa, sugar, ground spices and salt; mix well. Stir in water. Bring to a boil; cook and stir 5 minutes.
2. Add milk; heat to just below boiling point. Do not boil.
3. Serve hot in cups or mugs with cinnamon stick as a stirrer.

Decorated Roulades with Chaud-Froid,
(Recipe, page 174)

Know Gelatine, Inc.

BANQUETS AND OTHER SPECIAL MEALS

CATERING SPECIAL group functions—whether for more than a thousand or less than ten—is big business. It is good business too, the kind that packs a plus. The possibilities run the full gamut from a simple, refreshing beverage to an elegant full-course meal.

To most people, banquets, special luncheons and other group functions are special occasions. They look forward to them and arrive expecting to have a good time. As such, these affairs have an aura of importance. They are much more likely to be remembered than a casual meal. Thus, they provide a marvelous opportunity to put your best foot forward, your operation on parade.

To begin with, let's have a word about banquets, a term that is frequently used without justification. There are meals that are called "banquets" that fail to measure up. The old-time elaborate dinner with its long procession of courses and impressive complement of white-gloved waiters is something of a rarity in this day and age. Today's banquets do, and should, follow a less lavish pattern.

However, there is danger of too much simplification, of allowing the pendulum to swing too far. The term "banquet" still speaks of ceremony and implies prestige. It promises a special meal, presented with the dignity and grace that raises it a notch or two above the conventional standards of dining.

People who attend a function programmed as a banquet are justified in expecting fine food and a certain finesse. Don't risk disappointing them with anything less. In other words, don't represent a meal as a banquet if the only service that you can offer falls short of the mark.

In an era of rising costs and time-saving requirements, serving a meal in true banquet style may not always be feasible. But less demanding dinners (formal or informal) and other party meals can prove as rewarding. When carried out in a delightful, guest-pleasing fashion, they can play a vital part in your foodservice scheme.

Regardless of the number of people to be served or the extent of the menu, success depends upon meticulous planning and complete instructions to the staff. To insure a smooth-running schedule, make sure that the menu, preparation details, specifications for portions, table set-up and serving procedures are clearly understood by everyone. It is an excellent idea to put all directions in writing to confirm all the plans that you communicate verbally.

There is merit in compiling a small file of menus that prove successful. Kitchen and dining room staffs soon become familiar with menus that they have handled before. The system can save time, first in the initial planning, and then on down the line. In addition, it permits making improvements and ironing out snags.

If your menu is to appear on the table in printed form, use terminology that is honest. Avoid descriptions that sound flowery, but do make an effort to keep any item from sounding everyday-dull. Wording that is unique and appealing keeps guests looking forward to the dishes to come.

Needless to say, the focal point of any party is the food. To cater a function successfully, food needs to radiate excitement and taste especially good. Attractive presentations can also be of enormous value in setting the mood. Pretty dish-ware, colored tablecovers, and a clever way of folding the napkins can provide a world of flair. Candlelight sheds a warm, wonderful glow over any meal.

A delightful wine imparts a certain magic and makes a dinner far more festive. Chosen to complement the food and please the palate, wine service is one of the nuances that can turn the trick and make the meal a memorable event.

In planning the menu, consider the advantages of desserts and other dishes that can be prepared ahead. Weigh the possibility that some items might be better to buy than to make. Make it a firm policy to rule out all dishes that require precise timing, that will not survive delay in prime condition. And one more tip: don't attempt to serve any item to a special group until you are confident that your crew can produce it successfully and serve it forth in style.

LUNCHEON MENUS

*Egg and Lemon Soup
Ripe Olives   Carrot Curls
*Crabmeat-Stuffed Avocado
Crisp-Crusted Rolls   Butter
*Fresh Strawberry Cream Pie

*Vichyssoise
French Bread Slices   Butter
*Turkey in Curried Fruit Sauce with Rice
Green Salad   French Dressing
*Almond Praline Cake

Belvedere Appetizer
Instant Potato Souffle with Shrimp Sauce
Fresh Asparagus Almondine
Torn Leaves of Romaine   Italian Dressing
Frozen Creme   Salty Pretzel Sticks

Celery Victor
*Salmon Mousseline   *Mornay Sauce*
Leaf Spinach   Potatoes Anna
Ice Cream Bombe
Filbert Lace Cookies

Tomato Bouillon
Crisp Crackers
Chicken Roulades Chaud-Froid
Mixed Cooked Vegetable Salad
Tossed with Oil and Vinegar Dressing
Giant Hot Popovers   Butter
Apple Gelatin Jewels with Whipped Cream
Butter Thin Variation of
Many Way Butter Cookies

Hot Dilled Shrimp Shells
Relish Tray
London Broil   Mushroom Souffle
Lyonnaise Green Beans
Coupe Seville

Tossed Green Salad with
Roasted Chopped Almonds
*Chicken Breasts California Style
Steamed Rice
Buttered Broccoli Spears
*Cinnamon Chocolate Swirl Souffle

*Rolled Asparagus Appetizer
*Deviled Crab Cakes
Buttered Carrots with Halved Red Grapes
*Scotch Chocolate Cake with Ice Cream Sauce

*Mint Cooler
Broiled Loin Lamb Chop
Au Gratin Potato
*Baked Tomato Stuffed with Mushroom Cap
*Chocolate Carousel Cake

*Chicken Pimiento Soup
*Crab Divan
Baked Stuffed Potato
Bibb Lettuce Salad with Sliced Cucumber Garnish
Coffee Ice Cream   *Praline Sundae Sauce

DINNER MENUS

*Conchitas

*Wellington Steak
*Cumberland Sauce
Spinach Souffle   Fordhook Limas

Ripe Tomato Slices on Bibb Lettuce
Green Goddess Dressing

French Vanilla Ice Cream
*Oriental Ice Cream Sauce

*Mushroom Paprikash in
Pastry Tart Shells
Crisp Celery Hearts

Roast Young Turkey
*Toasted Rice Stuffing
Sherried Mashed Winter Squash
Buttered Broccoli Spears
Hearts of Romaine
Chiffonade Dressing

*Coconut Snowballs
Sparkling Whole Cranberry Sauce

*Cream of Fresh Tomato Soup
Melba Toast Slices

*Rock Cornish Hen a La Russe
Wild and Tame Rice
Artichoke Bottoms filled with
Creamed Spinach
Bibb Lettuce Salad with
Toasted Sliced Almonds
Sweet-Sour French Dressing

*California Desert Brownies
Topped with Ice Cream and
Brandied Chocolate Sauce

Consomme with *Royale Custard

*Veal Oscar   Delmonico Potatoes

Crisp Salad Greens with Croutons
and Tomato Wedges

Strawberry Ice Cream Pie
*Pineapple Jubilee Sauce

*Crab Paradise with Creamy Lemon Sauce

*Ballotine of Chicken   Veloute Sauce
Lyonnaise Rice   Zucchini Slices

Mimosa Salad
French Dressing with Parsley

*Ice Cream and Candy Cake

*Epicure's Fruit Cocktail

English Lamb Chops
*Baked Tomato with Mushroom Cap
*Peppy Sour Cream Potato

Endive and Watercress Salad
Camembert Cheese
French Bread Slices

*Fresh Lemon Polar Pie

Gazpacho, Diced Fresh Vegetable Garnishes

Baked Pork Chops with Cornbread Stuffing
Cauliflower au Gratin
Carrots with Halved Red Grapes

Hearts of Boston Lettuce
Vinaigrette Dressing

Warm Apple 'N Ice Cream Pie

French Cream of Asparagus Soup
Bread Sticks

Glazed Ham
Pineapple Chunks in Orange Cups
Cinnamon Mashed Louisiana Yams
Almond Buttered Celery
Medley of Salad Greens and Spinach Leaves
Glorious Greens Dressing

Profiteroles with Caramel Sauce

Jellied Tomato Appetizer

Roast Rib of Beef
Ripe Olive Onion Tarts
New Potatoes with Parsley
Frenched Green Beans with Water Chestnuts
Tossed Greens with Avocado
French Dressing

Pear Fantasy   Assorted Miniature Cookies

Consomme with Sherry
Swiss Twists

Danish Fiskebudding with Shrimp Sauce
New Potatoes with Dill

Sauteed Tournedo with *Bordelaise Sauce*
Broiled Tomato Half
Stuffed Mushroom Caps

Belgian Endive and Cress Salad
Vinaigrette Dressing

Nut Torte

Cafe Diable

Table Set for Banquet Service

APPETIZERS-LUNCHEON OR DINNER

AS THE OPENING course of the meal, appetizers hold a favored position to attract the pleasant attention you want. For it is appetizers that give the first impression, extend the "welcome" and set the mood for the rest of the meal to come. Their effect depends upon their originality, appearance and taste.

The vast array of appetizers includes dishes based on fish, seafood, eggs, fruit, vegetables, poultry and meats. Within each of these categories are possibilities for introducing your own special touch. There's ample room for trying new combinations, featuring interesting jellied items, experimenting with crepes and with quiche. To gain additional attention, try creating garnishes that depart from the usual or work out other ideas for presenting your appetizers in fresh, original ways.

Seafood and fruit combinations make up one of the poten-

tials that are not served often enough. You can put shrimp or crabmeat with cubes of avocado and/or citrus sections in a supreme dish to serve with a cocktail sauce. Or, you can arrange the seafood in the hollow of an avocado half. The recipe for Deep Sea Appetizer and others that follow offer appealing variations of the fruit-with-seafood scheme.

This, of course, is only a sampling of the imaginative offerings to be devised with fruit. You can, for example, fill an avocado half with a medley of fresh fruit splashed with rum; serve wedges of melon with paper-thin slices of pros-ciutto (Italian style ham); serve a wedge of honeydew topped with a row of cantaloupe balls held secure with fancy picks; present a small cantaloupe ring heaped with assorted melon balls.   As for fruit cups, you can individualize them by sweetening with grenadine; adding bits of preserved ginger; or, by placing a perky scoop of fruit sherbet on the top

Placing an appetizing green salad in the opening spot can introduce an element of surprise with desired impact.   An addition of anchovy fillets, marinated mushroom slices, garlic croutons or bits of cheese can give your appetizer salad a margin of difference.

The many other appetizers that can be made from raw or cooked vegetables include Celery Victor, stuffed tomatoes, artichoke hearts vinaigrette and piquant mushroom dishes of various kinds.   To give stuffed mushrooms an unusual twist, present the warm stuffed caps in the depressions of an escargot dish.

Jellied appetizers can make an immediate impression as can thin, delicate crepes with a savory filling and other first courses that win their acclaim with an uncommon use of crisp pastry shells.

Cocktail Sauces

SEAFOOD COCKTAIL SAUCE

Yield: 1-1/4 quarts

Ingredients

TOMATO CATSUP	1 quart
CIDER or WINE VINEGAR or LEMON JUICE	1/2 cup
LIQUID HOT PEPPER SEASONING	20 drops
HORSERADISH, FRESH, grated	1/4 cup
CHIVES, minced or ONION, grated	1/2 cup
CELERY, finely chopped	1 cup
WORCESTERSHIRE SAUCE	1 tablespoon
SALT	2 teaspoons
PARSLEY, minced	1/4 cup

Procedure

1. Combine all ingredients; chill thoroughly

CELERY AND ONION COCKTAIL SAUCE

Yield: 1 quart

Ingredients

CELERY, finely diced	2 cups
YOUNG ONIONS or SCALLIONS, finely minced	1/2 cup
CHILI SAUCE	1 cup
CATSUP	1 cup
LEMON JUICE	1/2 cup
WORCESTERSHIRE SAUCE	1 tablespoon
LIQUID HOT PEPPER SEASONING	1 teaspoon
HORSERADISH, grated	2 tablespoons
SALT	1/2 teaspoon

Procedure

1. Combine all ingredients; mix well.

Note

This is a sharp sauce for use with meat or fish cocktails.

CHILLED MUSTARD SAUCE FOR SEAFOOD →

Yield: 1-3/4 quarts

Ingredients

MUSTARD, DRY	3/4 cup
FLOUR	1/2 cup
SUGAR	2 teaspoons
SALT	1 tablespoon
CREAM, LIGHT	1 quart
EGGS, beaten	4
LEMON JUICE, FRESH	1/2 cup
WORCESTERSHIRE SAUCE	1 tablespoon
MAYONNAISE	2 cups

REMOULADE SAUCE
(For Chilled Shrimp, Crabmeat or Lobster)

Yield: 3 quarts

Ingredients

EGG YOLKS, hard-cooked, sieved	8
EGG YOLKS, raw	4
DRY MUSTARD	4 teaspoons
SUGAR	1/4 cup
CAYENNE	1/4 teaspoon
SALT	2 tablespoons
TARRAGON VINEGAR	3/4 cup
LEMON JUICE	3/4 cup
SALAD OIL	2 quarts
PARSLEY, chopped	1/4 cup
ONION, finely chopped	1/2 cup
SWEET PICKLE RELISH	1 cup
CAPERS, drained	3/4 cup

Procedure

1. Beat sieved egg yolks with raw yolks until smooth, using wire whip on mixer.

2. Add mustard, sugar, cayenne and salt; beat until smooth.

3. Combine vinegar and lemon juice. Add to egg mixture in small amounts alternately with oil. Add oil very slowly at first, continuing to beat. (Use mayonnaise procedure.)

4. Fold in parsley, onion, pickle relish and capers. Cover; chill overnight.

Procedure

1. Combine dry ingredients in heavy saucepan, mixing thoroughly. Gradually blend in cream.

2. Cook and stir over medium heat until mixture boils; Reduce heat; simmer 3 to 4 minutes.

3. Add a little hot mixture to beaten eggs; blend. Add to remaining hot mixture; cook 1 minute longer.

4. Remove from heat; stir in lemon juice and Worcestershire. Cool to room temperature.

5. Combine cooled sauce with mayonnaise; chill. Serve cold with lobster, crab or shrimp.

REMOULADE SAUCE CREOLE FOR SHRIMP

Yield: 1-1/2 quarts

Ingredients

PREPARED HORSERADISH MUSTARD	3 cups
PAPRIKA	1/4 cup
GREEN ONIONS, finely chopped	1/2 cup
CELERY, finely chopped	2 cups
OLIVE OIL	2 cups
SALT	2 tablespoons
GARLIC, very finely chopped	2 tablespoons

Procedure

1. Combine ingredients; blend, using a wire whip.

Note

Amount is sufficient for 300 large shrimp. Marinate in sauce overnight. Serve as an appetizer.

Quiche

SHRIMP AND PIMIENTO QUICHE

Yield: 1 (9-inch)

Ingredients

SHRIMP, RAW, shelled, deveined	1/2 pound
ONION, thinly sliced	2/3 cup
OIL, COOKING	3 tablespoons
MUSHROOM PIECES, drained	1 4-ounce can
UNBAKED PIE SHELL,(with high rim) chilled	1 9-inch
CHEESE, SWISS, grated	1 cup (4 ounces)
PIMIENTO, diced	1/3 cup
EGGS	5
MILK	1 cup
CREAM	1 cup
SALT	1 teaspoon
PEPPER, BLACK (COARSE GRIND)	1/8 teaspoon
CAYENNE	dash
NUTMEG	dash

Procedure

1. Split raw shrimp.

2. Saute onion in oil until limp. Add shrimp and mushroom pieces, continue cooking a few minutes until shrimp turns pink. Spread mixture in unbaked pie shell.

3. Top shrimp mixture with cheese and pimiento.

4. Beat eggs with milk, cream and seasonings; pour into pie shell.

5. Bake in oven at 375°F. for 40 minutes or until custard is set and top is brown.

RIPE OLIVE ONION TARTS

Yield: 24 4-inch tarts

Ingredients

PIE PASTRY DOUGH	2 pounds
ONION, thinly sliced	2-1/4 pounds
BUTTER or MARGARINE	1/2 pound
FLOUR	1-1/2 ounces
	(6 tablespoons)
HALF-AND-HALF	1 quart
EGGS, slightly beaten	10 large
SALT	1 tablespoon
PEPPER, WHITE	1/4 teaspoon
NUTMEG	1/4 teaspoon
CAYENNE	dash
RIPE OLIVE HALVES	14 ounces
	(3-1/2 cups)

Procedure

1. Roll out pastry; line 24 4-inch quiche pans about 1 inch deep.

2. Cook onion slowly in butter until soft but not browned.

3. Blend in flour. Add half-and-half; cook and stir until mixture boils and thickens.

4. Cool slightly; stir in eggs. Blend in seasonings and ripe olives.

5. Portion into pastry-lined pans, allowing about 4 ounces per pan. Set on baking sheet.

6. Bake in oven at 375°F. for about 30 minutes, until pastry is browned and filling set.

ALASKA KING CRAB QUICHE

Yield: 6 9-inch quiche

Ingredients

KING CRABMEAT	1-1/2 quarts
ONION, chopped, sauteed	1-1/2 cups
CHEESE, SWISS, grated	3 cups (12 ounces)
PASTRY-LINED 9-INCH PIE PANS	6
EGGS	24 (1-1/4 quarts)
HALF-AND-HALF	2 quarts
VERMOUTH, DRY	3/4 cup
LEMON JUICE	1/2 cup
MUSTARD, DRY	1 tablespoon
CAYENNE	1/4 teaspoon
SALT	1 to 1-1/2 tablespoons

Procedure

1. Divide crabmeat, onion and cheese evenly into pie shells.

2. Beat eggs, half-and-half, vermouth, lemon juice and seasonings until blended. Fill shells with mixture.

3. Bake in oven at 350°F. for 45 minutes or until custard is browned and set.

4. Cut into wedges. Serve warm.

High Style Service

Fruits

BELVEDERE APPETIZER

Yield: 50 portions

Ingredients

ORANGE SECTIONS, FRESH, drained	3 quarts
PINEAPPLE CHUNKS, CANNED IN JUICE, drained	3 quarts
AVOCADO BALLS	1 quart
PINEAPPLE AND ORANGE JUICE	1-1/4 quarts
LIME JUICE	3/4 cup
SUGAR	1/2 cup

Procedure

1. Combine orange sections, pineapple chunks and avocado balls.
2. Combine pineapple juice and orange juice drained from fruit. Add orange juice, if necessary, to make up required amount. Add lime juice. Add sugar; stir until dissolved. Pour over fruit; chill thoroughly.

EPICURE'S FRUIT COCKTAIL

Yield: 48 portions

Ingredients

PINEAPPLE, FRESH PACK IN GLASS or	1/2 gallon
FRESH PINEAPPLES, cubed	2 medium
STRAWBERRIES, FRESH or	2 quarts
STRAWBERRIES, FROZEN	2-1/2 pounds
MELON BALLS, FRESH	1-1/2 quarts
MARASCHINO CHERRIES, quartered	2 cups
MARASCHINO CHERRY JUICE	1 quart
SIMPLE SYRUP	as needed
MARASCHINO CHERRIES, WHOLE	48
FRESH MINT SPRIGS	48

Procedure

1. Combine fruits and maraschino cherry juice. Let stand at room temperature for 1 hour to blend flavors.
2. Add simple syrup, if desired.
3. Chill at least 4 hours. Serve in sherbets or supreme cups.
4. Garnish with a whole maraschino cherry and a sprig of mint. Serve very cold.

CANTALOUPE SURPRISE

Yield: 48 portions

Ingredients

CANTALOUPES	24
HONEYDEW MELONS	2
STRAWBERRIES, sliced	4 quarts
ORANGES, sectioned, diced	3 quarts
APPLES, unpeeled, diced	2 quarts
MINT, chopped	1-1/2 bunches
ORANGE JUICE, FRESH	2 cups
LEMON JUICE, FRESH	1/2 cup
SUGAR	1 cup
KIRSCH (optional)	1/2 cup
SHERBET, ORANGE OR RASPBERRY	1 gallon
THOMPSON SEEDLESS GRAPES	1 quart

Procedure

1. Cut melons in half; remove seeds. Scoop out fruit with melon baller. Reserve cantaloupe shells.

2. Combine melon balls, strawberries, oranges and apples.

3. Combine mint, orange and lemon juice, sugar and kirsch; stir well; pour over fruit. Refrigerate at least 3 hours.

4. Fill cantaloupe shells with mixed fruit. Top with sherbet. Garnish with grapes.

PINEAPPLE GOLD AND GREEN APPETIZER

Yield: 24 portions

Ingredients

AVOCADOS, large	6
SALT	as needed
PINEAPPLE CHUNKS, chilled, drained	1 No. 10 can
SOUR CREAM	3 cups
LEMON JUICE	1/3 cup
SYRUP DRAINED FROM PINEAPPLE	1/2 cup
CURRY POWDER	2 teaspoons
BACON, crisp, cooked	12 slices
WATERCRESS	as needed

Procedure

1. Halve avocados; remove seed. Cut into balls or peel halves and dice the fruit. Sprinkle lightly with salt.

2. Combine drained pineapple chunks and avocado in individual serving dishes.

3. Blend sour cream, lemon juice, pineapple syrup and curry powder. Spoon over chilled pineapple and avocado.

4. Crumble bacon. Sprinkle on top of appetizers. Garnish with watercress.

Fruit Arranged for Contrast

Jellied Appetizers

JELLIED SHRIMP COCKTAIL

Yield: 50 1/2-cup portions

Ingredients

GELATIN, LEMON	1-1/2 pounds (3-1/2 cups)
SALT	2 tablespoons
CAYENNE	1/4 teaspoon
TOMATO JUICE, hot	3 quarts
WATER, hot	1 quart
LEMON JUICE	1/4 cup
HORSERADISH	3 tablespoons
ONION, grated	3 tablespoons
SHRIMP, cooked, diced	2 pounds (1-1/2 quarts)
CELERY, chopped	1 quart

Procedure

1. Dissolve gelatin, salt and cayenne in hot tomato juice and water. Add lemon juice. Chill until slightly thickened.

2. Fold in horseradish, grated onion, shrimp and celery.

3. Pour into individual molds or shallow pans. Chill until firm.

4. Unmold or cut into squares. Serve on crisp greens. Garnish with mayonnaise blended with sour cream, if desired.

BLEU CHEESE MOUSSE

Yield: 50 1/2-cup portions

Ingredients

GELATINE, UNFLAVORED	1-3/4 ounces (7 tablespoons)
WATER, cold	1-3/4 cups
COTTAGE CHEESE, CREAMED	3-1/2 quarts
SOUR CREAM	3-1/2 quarts
BLEU CHEESE SALAD DRESSING	
MIX	1 10-ounce jar

Procedure

1. Soften gelatine in cold water; dissolve over hot water.

2. Mix cottage cheese and sour cream together thoroughly. Add bleu cheese dressing mix; blend well.

3. Add melted gelatine. Pour into individual molds or in shallow pans. Chill until firm.

4. Unmold or cut into squares. Garnish with radishes and cress. Serve with assorted crackers or Melba toast.

JELLIED TOMATO APPETIZER

Yield: 24 portions

Ingredients

TOMATO JUICE	3 46-ounce cans
ONION, sliced from	2 onions
CELERY LEAVES	2 cups
BAY LEAF	3
SUGAR	1 tablespoon
SALT	1 tablespoon
PEPPER	1/4 teaspoon
WORCESTERSHIRE SAUCE	1 tablespoon
GELATINE, UNFLAVORED	3 ounces
WATER, cold	1-1/2 cups

Procedure

1. Simmer tomato juice with seasonings 20 minutes; strain.

2. Soften gelatine in cold water; dissolve in hot seasoned tomato juice. Chill until set to the consistency of jellied soup.

3. Serve in chilled bouillon or punch cups. Top with sour cream and chopped chives.

SUNSHINE SALAD WEDGES ⟶

Yield: 8 9-inch pies, 48 portions

Ingredients

ORANGE AND GRAPEFRUIT SECTIONS,	
FRESH OR CANNED, with juice	2 quarts
GELATIN, ORANGE	1-1/2 pounds (3-1/2 cups)
SUGAR	2 cups
WATER, hot	2 quarts
WATER, cold and FRUIT JUICE	2 quarts
BAKED 9-INCH PIE SHELLS, cooled	8

CHEESE-TOPPED TOMATO ASPIC
IN FLAKY HERB SHELL

Yield: 6 9-inch salad pies

Ingredients

PASTRY MIX	2-1/2 pounds
CELERY SEED or POULTRY SEASONING	1-1/2 to 2 tablespoons
GELATIN, LEMON	1-1/2 pounds (3-1/2 cups)
SALT	2 tablespoons
CAYENNE	1/2 teaspoon
TOMATO JUICE, hot	2 quarts
TOMATO JUICE, cold	2-1/2 quarts
PREPARED HORSERADISH	3 tablespoons
ONION, grated	3 tablespoons
COTTAGE CHEESE	3 pounds

Procedure

1. Combine pastry mix and celery seed or poultry seasoning. Make pastry; roll, make up and bake 6 9-inch pie shells.

2. Combine gelatin, salt and cayenne. Add hot tomato juice; stir until gelatin is completely dissolved. Add cold tomato juice, horseradish and onion. Chill until well thickened.

3. Pour into shells, allowing about 3 cups filling per shell. Chill until firm. Spread or border with cottage cheese, allowing 8 ounces per shell. Garnish with chopped parsley or chives, if desired.

Procedure

1. Drain fruit, reserving juice. Dice fruit, if desired. Add cold water to juice to make required amount.

2. Dissolve gelatin and sugar in hot water. Add cold liquid. Chill until slightly thickened.

3. Fold in fruit. Pour into cooled pie shells allowing 3 cups per pie. Chill until firm.

4. Using a pastry bag, border pies with softened cream cheese, if desired.

To serve: cut into wedges; arrange on salad greens.

DEVILED TONGUE MOLD

Yield: 24 1/2-cup portions

Ingredients

GELATINE, UNFLAVORED	3 tablespoons
WATER, cold	1 cup
WATER, boiling	1 quart
SEASONED SALT	1 teaspoon
SALT	1-1/2 teaspoons
MAYONNAISE	1 cup
LIQUID HOT PEPPER SEASONING	1/2 teaspoon
LEMON JUICE	2 tablespoons
HORSERADISH	1/4 cup
ONION, finely cut	2 tablespoons
TONGUE, cooked, diced	2 pounds
EGGS, hard-cooked, diced	4
DILL PICKLE, finely cut	1-1/2 cups
CELERY, finely cut	1 cup
PIMIENTO, chopped	2 tablespoons

Procedure

1. Soften gelatine in cold water. Add boiling water; stir to dissolve. Add seasoned salt and salt. Cool until slightly thickened.

2. Mix mayonnaise, hot pepper seasoning, lemon juice, horseradish and onion; combine with remaining ingredients.

3. Fold tongue mixture into slightly thickened gelatine. Turn into individual molds; chill until firm.

Celery Victor *(Recipe, page 126)*

Spanish Green Olive Commission

Vegetable Appetizers

SESAME EGGPLANT APPETIZER

Yield: 1-1/4 quarts

Ingredients

EGGPLANTS (1 POUND SIZE)	3
SALT	1 tablespoon
BLACK PEPPER, GROUND	1/2 teaspoon
INSTANT GARLIC POWDER	1/2 teaspoon
CAYENNE	1/8 teaspoon
SESAME SEED, toasted	1/3 cup
SOUR CREAM	1/3 cup
LEMON JUICE	1-1/2 teaspoons

Procedure

1. Prick eggplant skins with fork.
2. Bake unpeeled in oven at 400°F. for 1 hour, 15 minutes or until eggplants are very soft and partially collapse.
3. Cool slightly. Remove pulp from skins.
4. Beat eggplant pulp until smooth. Add remaining ingredients; mix well.
5. Chill thoroughly.

TOMATO JUICE COCKTAIL

Yield: 24 4-ounce portions

Ingredients

TOMATO JUICE	1 No. 10 can
ONION, grated	1 tablespoon
CELERY SALT	1-1/2 teaspoons
HORSERADISH	1 tablespoon
LEMON JUICE	3 tablespoons
SALT	1-1/2 teaspoons
BLACK PEPPER	dash
WORCESTERSHIRE SAUCE	1 tablespoon

Procedure

1. Mix ingredients thoroughly. Chill.

CELERY VICTOR
(See picture, page 124)

Yield: 24 portions

Ingredients

CELERY HEARTS (APPROXIMATELY 6 OUNCES EACH)	12
CHICKEN STOCK	as needed
OIL AND VINEGAR DRESSING	1 quart
ICEBERG LETTUCE (LEAVES)	1-1/2 pounds
ICEBERG LETTUCE, shredded	3 pounds
OLIVES, GREEN, PIMIENTO-STUFFED, sliced	2 cups
OLIVES, WHOLE	24

Procedure

1. Trim celery; tie securely.
2. Poach in stock until tender but not limp. Cool.
3. Marinate in dressing. Cut lengthwise into halves.
4. Line serving dishes with lettuce leaves. Fill with shredded lettuce. Arrange celery on lettuce.
5. Spoon about 1 ounce of sliced olives over celery. Garnish with whole olives. Serve with dressing used for marinade.

ROLLED ASPARAGUS APPETIZER

Yield: 24 portions

Ingredients

MAYONNAISE	1/2 cup
HORSERADISH MUSTARD	1 tablespoon
BOILED HAM, sliced 1/16-inch thick	24 slices
ASPARAGUS STALKS, cooked	24

Procedure

1. Combine mayonnaise and horseradish mustard.
2. Spread each slice of ham with mixture, allowing 1 teaspoon per slice.
3. Place a stalk of cooked asparagus along one edge of ham slice; roll up the ham around the asparagus. Chill until quite firm.
4. Cut into bite-size pieces; arrange on lettuce.
5. Serve with 2 or 3 large potato chips, cheese straws or corn chips.

MUSHROOMS AND EGGPLANT ITALIENNE

Yield: 48 portions

Ingredients

MUSHROOMS, FRESH, SMALL*	8 pounds
OLIVE OIL	3 cups
CELERY, diced	2 quarts
ONION, sliced	2 quarts
EGGPLANT, peeled, diced	1 gallon
TOMATO SAUCE	2 quarts
WINE VINEGAR	2 cups
WATER	2 cups
OLIVES, STUFFED, sliced	2 cups
SUGAR	1 cup
SALT	3 tablespoons
BLACK PEPPER, GROUND	1 teaspoon
LETTUCE	as needed

Procedure

1. Rinse mushrooms; pat dry. Trim stem ends.

2. Heat oil. Add celery and onion; saute until tender but not brown.

3. Add eggplant. Cover; cook until eggplant is almost tender.

4. Add tomato sauce, vinegar, water, olives, sugar, salt and pepper. Bring to boiling.

5. Add mushrooms. Reduce heat; cook 5 minutes or until mushrooms and eggplant are tender.

6. Cool. Refrigerate. Serve on lettuce as appetizer.

*Or, one No. 10 can whole mushrooms.

TOMATO CUP ──────────▶

Yield: 25 portions

Ingredients

TOMATOES, SMALL (4 to pound)	25
CELERY, sliced	3 cups
AVOCADO, diced	3 cups
FRENCH DRESSING	3/4 cup
WATERCRESS or CURLY ENDIVE	as needed

MUSHROOM PAPRIKASH

Yield: 48 portions

Ingredients

MUSHROOMS, FRESH*	8 pounds
BUTTER or MARGARINE	1/2 pound
ONION, finely chopped	2 cups
FLOUR	1/4 cup
PAPRIKA	1/4 cup
LEMON JUICE	2 tablespoons
SALT	4 teaspoons
RED PEPPER, GROUND	1/4 to 1/2 teaspoon
SOUR CREAM	1 quart

Procedure

1. Rinse mushrooms; pat dry. Slice.

2. Melt butter; add onion. Saute until tender but not brown. Add mushrooms; saute 3 minutes, stirring occasionally.

3. Stir in flour, paprika, lemon juice, salt and red pepper. Cook 3 minutes, stirring constantly.

4. Add sour cream. Heat but do not boil.

5. Serve in baked pastry tart shells or over toast points, if desired.

*Or, one No. 10 can sliced mushrooms.

Procedure

1. Peel tomatoes; remove centers to form cups. Drain thoroughly.
2. Marinate celery and avocado in French dressing. Drain.
3. Fill tomato cups with celery and avocado mixture. Arrange in a nest of curly endive or watercress.
4. Garnish with mayonnaise and one of the following: shredded chicken, green pepper ring, cheese ball, section of grapefruit or pineapple chunk.

MUSHROOM SALAD APPETIZER

Yield: 48 portions

Ingredients

MUSHROOMS, FRESH	6 pounds
WATER	as needed
CELERY, thinly sliced	1-1/2 quarts
CARROTS, thinly sliced	3 cups
GREEN OLIVES, STUFFED, sliced	3 cups
ONION, chopped	1-1/2 cups
CAPERS	1/2 cup
SWEET PICKLE JUICE	1-1/2 quarts
VINEGAR, WHITE	1-1/2 cups
SALAD OIL	1-1/2 cups

Procedure

1. Rinse mushrooms; pat dry. Slice.
2. Place two inches of water in a large pot; bring to boiling point. Add mushrooms; return to boiling point. Drain in colander.
3. Put mushrooms in ice water to cover. When thoroughly chilled, drain again.
4. Combine mushrooms with remaining ingredients. Cover; refrigerate.
5. Serve in lettuce cups. Garnish with parsley, if desired.

Seafood Appetizers

LOBSTER PECAN COCKTAIL

Yield: 28 portions

Ingredients

LOBSTER MEAT, cooked	3 quarts
PECANS, chopped	2 cups
HARD-COOKED EGG WHITES, chopped	18
SALT	1 teaspoon
SALAD DRESSING	1 quart
LETTUCE CUPS	28
HARD-COOKED EGG YOLKS, sieved	18
WHOLE PECAN HALVES	28

Procedure

1. Combine lobster, pecans, egg whites and salt. Add salad dressing; toss lightly to mix. Chill.

2. Arrange in lettuce cups. Top with sieved egg yolks. Garnish with pecan halves.

HOT DILLED SHRIMP SHELLS

Yield: 28 portions

Ingredients

BUTTER or MARGARINE	6 ounces
ONION, chopped	1/3 cup
WHITE WINE (DRY)	1 quart
WHITE SAUCE, medium, well-seasoned	2 quarts
DILL, chopped	1/3 cup
SHRIMP, cleaned, cooked	6 pounds
BAKED PASTRY TART SHELLS	28

Procedure

1. Melt butter; add onion and wine. Simmer until reduced to 1/3 of original volume.

2. Add white sauce and dill; blend.

3. Add shrimp; heat through.

4. Serve in baked tart shells.

ESCARGOT

Yield: 48 snails

Ingredients

BUTTER	1 pound
SHALLOTS, chopped	4 ounces
PARSLEY, chopped	1 ounce
GARLIC, minced	5 cloves
SNAIL SHELLS	48
SNAILS	48

Procedure

1. Combine butter, shallots, parsley and garlic; blend to form a paste.
2. Put a small amount of mixture in snail shell; insert snail; close shell with butter mixture.
3. Heat in oven at 400°F. just until butter bubbles. Do not allow butter to brown. Serve hot.

CRAB PARADISE WITH CREAMY LEMON SAUCE

Yield: 24 portions

Ingredients

CRABMEAT	3 pounds
PINEAPPLE CHUNKS, drained	3 cups
ORANGE SECTIONS	2 cups
AVOCADO, cut into cubes or balls	2 cups
SOUR CREAM	2 cups
LEMON JUICE	1/3 cup
PARSLEY, chopped	1/3 cup
SALT	as needed
LETTUCE	as needed

Procedure

1. Combine crabmeat, pineapple, orange and avocado.
2. Combine sour cream, lemon juice and parsley. Season with salt.
3. Pour sauce over crabmeat mixture; toss lightly to mix. Chill.
4. Serve in lettuce-lined sherbet glasses or supreme cups.

CONCHITAS

Yield: 24 portions (3 shells each)

Ingredients

BAY SCALLOPS	2 pounds
LEMON JUICE	1/3 cup
PARMESAN CHEESE, grated	3/4 cup
BUTTER or MARGARINE	1/4 pound

Procedure

1. Divide scallops into 72 scallop shells.
2. Sprinkle with lemon juice and cheese. Top each with a small piece (1/3 teaspoon) butter.
3. Broil 3 to 5 minutes or until bubbly and scallops are just tender. Do not overcook.
4. Serve hot as an appetizer.

KING CRAB-CELERY VICTOR

Yield: 12 portions

Ingredients

CRABMEAT*	1-1/2 pounds
CELERY HEARTS	6
STOCK, well seasoned	as needed
OIL AND VINEGAR DRESSING	1-1/2 cups
CRISP SALAD GREENS	as needed
WHITE GRAPES, small clusters	12
MINT	12 sprigs

Procedure

1. Thaw or drain crabmeat. Remove any remaining shell or cartilage. Cut crabmeat into 1-inch pieces. Refrigerate.
2. Wash celery hearts; trim. Lay in shallow pan; add stock to almost cover. Cook gently until just tender.
3. Let celery cool in stock; drain.
4. Cut hearts in half lengthwise. Place in oil and vinegar dressing. Marinate, refrigerated, for several hours.
5. Remove celery hearts from dressing; drain.
6. For each portion, arrange about 1/4 cup crabmeat and half a celery heart on salad greens. Garnish with grapes and mint.

*King or other crabmeat, fresh, frozen, or pasteurized or canned crabmeat.

AVOCADO AND SEAFOOD COCKTAIL

Yield: 48 portions

Ingredients

SHRIMP (25 to 30 COUNT)	4 pounds
LOBSTER MEAT, diced	1 quart
CRABMEAT	1 quart
AVOCADO, diced	2 quarts
LIME JUICE, FRESH	1/3 cup
SALT	1-1/2 tablespoons
ICEBERG LETTUCE, shredded	as needed
ZESTY COCKTAIL SAUCE*	1-1/2 quarts

Procedure

1. Cook, peel and devein shrimp. Combine shrimp, lobster and crab-meat.

2. Toss avocado with lime juice. Add avocado and salt to seafood. Toss lightly to mix.

3. Line supreme cups or sherbets with lettuce. Top with seafood mixture. Spoon Zesty Cocktail Sauce* on top.

*ZESTY COCKTAIL SAUCE

Yield: 1-1/2 quarts

Ingredients

CATSUP	1-1/2 quarts
LIME JUICE, FRESH	1/2 cup
HORSERADISH	3 tablespoons
SALT	2 teaspoons
GARLIC, finely minced	1 teaspoon
ONION JUICE	4 teaspoons
CAYENNE	few grains

Procedure

1. Combine ingredients; mix well. Chill.

TUNA CRANBERRY COCKTAIL ⟶

Yield: 60 portions

Ingredients

TUNA, SOLID, WHITE MEAT	1 60 to 66-1/2 ounce can
ROMAINE LEAVES, SMALL	as needed
ORANGE SECTIONS, FRESH, drained	2-1/4 quarts
CRANBERRY SAUCE, WHOLE BERRY	1-3/4 quarts
CREAM, HEAVY (for whipping)	2-1/4 cups
HORSERADISH, FRESH or FROZEN, grated	3 tablespoons

TOP HAT RAISIN LOBSTER CURRY

Yield: 12 5-ounce portions

Ingredients

RAISINS, SEEDLESS	8 ounces
CURRY POWDER	1-1/2 teaspoons
PAPRIKA	3/4 teaspoon
BUTTER	3 ounces
FLOUR	3 tablespoons
SEASONED SALT	1-1/2 teaspoons
CHICKEN BROTH	1-1/2 cups
EGG YOLKS	3
CREAM, LIGHT	1-1/2 cups
PIMIENTO, chopped	3 tablespoons
LOBSTER, cooked, cubed	2 pounds
SHERRY (optional)	3 tablespoons
PUFF PASTRY CASES, baked	12

Procedure

1. Lightly saute raisins, curry powder and paprika in butter.

2. Blend in flour and salt. Add broth; cook and stir until sauce begins to thicken.

3. Beat egg yolks lightly with cream. Add to hot mixture; continue to cook 2 to 3 minutes more.

4. Add pimiento, lobster and sherry. Heat through. Serve in pastry cases.

Procedure

1. Drain tuna; break into large sized pieces.

2. Stand a few small romaine leaves against one side of each sherbet glass. Place pieces of tuna and orange sections in each glass, allowing about 1/4 cup of the combination for each portion.

3. Spoon cranberry sauce over tuna and oranges.

4. Whip cream; blend in horseradish. Top cocktails with mixture. Garnish with whole cranberry placed on top of horseradish whipped cream.

INDIVIDUAL SCALLOP CASSEROLES

Yield: 24 portions

Ingredients

SCALLOPS	8 pounds
EGG YOLKS, slightly beaten	4
CREAM, LIGHT	2 cups
DRY WHITE WINE	1 cup
LEMON JUICE	2 tablespoons
INSTANT CHOPPED ONION	3 tablespoons
WHITE PEPPER, GROUND	1/2 teaspoon
GINGER, GROUND	1/2 teaspoon
SALT	1 tablespoon
BREAD CRUMBS, SOFT	1 quart
BUTTER or MARGARINE, melted	1/2 cup
CHEESE, PARMESAN, grated	1/2 cup

Procedure

1. Arrange scallops in individual coquille shells or baking dishes. (If scallops are large, cut in bite-size pieces.)

2. Combine beaten egg yolks, cream, wine, lemon juice and seasonings; mix well. Pour equal amounts (about 2 tablespoons) of mixture over each portion of scallops.

3. Combine bread crumbs, melted butter and cheese. Sprinkle over scallops. Bake in oven at 425°F. for 10 to 12 minutes or until scallops are done and topping browned. Do not allow sauce to boil.

AVOCADO DILLED SHRIMP SALAD ➤

Yield: 24 portions

Ingredients

SALAD OIL	2 cups
WHITE WINE VINEGAR	1 cup
DILL WEED	1 tablespoon
SALT	1 tablespoon
SEASONED PEPPER	1 teaspoon
GARLIC, mashed	1 clove
SHRIMP, LARGE, cooked, shelled, deveined	72 (about 1-1/2 pounds, cooked weight)
AVOCADOS, large	12
LEMON JUICE	as needed

CRAB COCKTAIL ELEGANTE

Yield: 30 portions

Ingredients

CATSUP	1-1/2 cups
CHILI SAUCE	3/4 cup
GRAPEFRUIT JUICE	3/4 cup
LEMON JUICE	1/3 cup
CELERY, finely diced	1 cup
GREEN ONIONS, finely sliced	3 onions
HORSERADISH	2 teaspoons
LIQUID HOT PEPPER SEASONING	4 drops
AVOCADO, cut into cubes or balls	3 cups
LEMON JUICE	as needed
CRABMEAT	1-1/2 quarts
GRAPEFRUIT SECTIONS, chilled	3 cups
LETTUCE CUPS (optional)	as needed
LEMON WEDGES	30

Procedure

1. Combine catsup, chili sauce, grapefruit juice, lemon juice, celery, onions, horseradish and liquid hot pepper seasoning. Chill several hours to blend flavors.

2. Dip avocado in lemon juice. Arrange with crabmeat and grapefruit sections in lettuce cups or in seafood cocktail dishes.

3. Top with chilled sauce; garnish with lemon wedges.

Procedure

1. Combine oil, vinegar, seasonings and garlic.
2. Pour over shrimp; marinate in refrigerator at least 8 hours.
3. Cut avocados in half; remove seeds. Brush cavities with lemon juice.
4. Arrange 3 shrimp in each avocado half. Drizzle with a small amount of the marinade.
5. Serve as salad or appetizer.

DEEP SEA APPETIZER

Yield: 24 portions

Ingredients

SCALLOPS	2 pounds
WHITE WINE	2 cups
PINEAPPLE CHUNKS, CANNED	2-1/2 quarts
PINEAPPLE SYRUP	1 cup
CHERRY TOMATOES	1 quart
SALAD OIL	1 cup
LIME PEEL, grated	1-1/2 tablespoons
LIME JUICE	1 cup
PARSLEY, chopped	1 cup

Procedure

1. Combine scallops and wine. Bring to a boil. Reduce heat; simmer 6 to 8 minutes. Cool. Drain. Slice.
2. Drain pineapple, reserving required amount of syrup.
3. Combine sliced scallops, pineapple chunks, pineapple syrup and remaining ingredients.
4. Marinate, refrigerated, for at least 1 hour.
5. Arrange in scallop shells.

AMBASSADOR SEAFOOD SAMPLER

Yield: 1 portion

Ingredients

For each portion allow:

CLAM, RAW	1
CRABMEAT	1/2 ounce
LOBSTER	1/2 ounce
SHRIMP	2
KING CRAB	1/2 ounce
COCKTAIL SAUCE	1-1/2 ounces
LEMON	1/2

Procedure

1. Place chilled seafood individually into 5 clam shells. Arrange shells in a bed of crushed ice around container of cocktail sauce.
2. Garnish with lemon.

SHRIMP SEA ISLAND
(Appetizer)

Yield: 25 4-ounce portions, 4 to 6 whole shrimp, 1-1/2 ounces sauce

Ingredients

SHRIMP, peeled, deveined	6 pounds
ONIONS, medium	3
CATSUP	1/2 cup
CHILI SAUCE	1/2 cup
MAYONNAISE	1-1/2 cups
PICKLE RELISH	1/2 cup
MIXED SEASONING	1 teaspoon

Procedure

1. Cook and chill shrimp.
2. Shred onions or cut in very thin rings.
3. Combine catsup, chili sauce, mayonnaise, pickle relish and seasoning; blend well. Add shrimp and onions. Chill 2 to 3 hours before serving.
4. Serve on lettuce in cocktail glass, in sea shells or in avocado half.

Meat and Poultry Appetizers

CHICKEN-FILLED CREPES

Yield: 30 portions (2 crepes)

Ingredients

ONION, chopped	1 small
CELERY, diced	1 cup
BUTTER or MARGARINE	2 tablespoons
MUSHROOMS, diced	1 cup
BUTTER or MARGARINE, melted	8 ounces
FLOUR	1 cup
SALT	1-1/2 teaspoons
CREAM, 12%	3 cups
CHICKEN BROTH	3 cups
WINE, DRY, WHITE	1-1/2 cups
CHEESE, SHARP CHEDDAR, grated	3 cups (12 ounces)
PARSLEY, FRESH, minced	1/3 cup
CHICKEN, boned, finely chopped	1 36-ounce can
CREPES, baked (6-inch)	60

Procedure

1. Saute chopped onion and celery in first amount of butter until tender but not browned. Set aside.

2. Brown mushrooms in part of the melted butter. Remove mushrooms from pan.

3. Add remaining butter to pan; blend in flour and salt. Add cream and chicken broth. Cook and stir until thickened and smooth.

4. Add wine and half the cheese; stir until cheese melts. Combine reserved onion mixture and parsley with chicken.

5. Add about 1/4 cup of the sauce to chicken mixture or enough to moisten to spreading consistency.

6. Add mushrooms to remaining sauce.

7. Roll crepes with filling. Place two filled crepes in each individual ovenware serving dish. Top with sauce, allowing 1/4 to 1/3 cup per portion.

8. Sprinkle with remaining cheese; place under broiler to thoroughly heat and brown.

HAM TARTS WITH SOUR CREAM-HORSERADISH SAUCE

Yield: 36

Ingredients

HAM, baked, ground	1-1/2 pounds
CELERY, finely chopped	3/4 cup
PICKLE RELISH	1/3 cup
SOUR CREAM	1-1/2 cups
MUSTARD, PREPARED	2 teaspoons
PASTRY TART SHELLS, baked	36
SOUR CREAM	2-1/4 cups
HORSERADISH	1/3 cup
SALT	3/4 teaspoon

Procedure

1. Combine ham, celery, pickle relish, first amount of sour cream and mustard; mix well.
2. Fill each tart shell with about 2 tablespoons of mixture.
3. Bake in oven at 400°F. for about 5 minutes.
4. Combine remaining sour cream, horseradish and salt.
5. Top each tart with a tablespoon of mixture.
6. Bake 5 minutes longer. Serve hot.

CHOPPED CHICKEN LIVERS

Yield: 20 portions (No. 20 scoop)

Ingredients

LIVER (CHICKEN, CALVES OR BEEF), sauteed	1 pound
ONION, browned	1 cup
BEEF, boiled	1/2 pound
EGGS, hard-cooked	3
SALT	1 teaspoon
SUGAR	1/2 teaspoon
PEPPER	1/4 teaspoon
WORCESTERSHIRE SAUCE	1/2 teaspoon
MONOSODIUM GLUTAMATE	1 teaspoon
CHICKEN FAT	1/2 cup

Procedure

1. Grind liver, onion, beef and eggs; add seasonings and chicken fat; mix thoroughly.
2. Chill. Garnish with red radish.

CHICKEN AND AVOCADO COCKTAIL

Yield: 50 portions

Ingredients

CHICKEN MEAT, cut into 3/4-inch cubes	2 quarts (2-1/2 pounds)
AVOCADO, cut into 3/4-inch cubes	3 cups
LETTUCE, small leaves	as needed
CELERY, diced	1-1/2 quarts
COCKTAIL SAUCE	1-1/4 quarts
LEMON WEDGES	50

Procedure

1. Cut chicken meat from simmered or steamed chicken that has been allowed to stand (refrigerated) in broth overnight. Remove all skin and bits of gristle.

2. Combine chicken cubes and avocado, mixing lightly.

3. Chill diced celery.

4. Line individual chilled cocktail cups with lettuce. Place 2 tablespoons celery in bottom of each cup. Spoon chicken and avocado mixture on top of celery. Top each portion with about 1-1/2 tablespoons cocktail sauce. Garnish with lemon wedge.

TURKEY COCKTAIL

Yield: 50 1/2-cup portions

Ingredients

TURKEY, roasted, boned, chopped	2 quarts
SOUR CREAM	1 quart
YOGHURT	1-1/2 quarts
RIPE OLIVES, pitted, sliced	2 cups
CHIVES, chopped	1 cup
ONION, chopped	1 cup
CUCUMBERS, unpeeled, chopped	4 medium
TOMATOES, FRESH, chopped	4 large
SALT	1-1/2 tablespoons
LETTUCE	as needed

Procedure

1. Combine cold chopped turkey meat, sour cream, yoghurt, ripe olives, chives, onion, cucumber, tomatoes and salt. Mix lightly but well.

2. Chill. Serve on lettuce leaves on small plates or on shredded lettuce in sherbet or supreme dishes. Serve with crackers or cheese straws.

Chilled Soups Styled for Special Occasions

American Spice Trade Association

SOUPS

BRACING, COMFORTING, satisfying, refreshing—that's how patrons remember a good soup. There's probably no other dish as varied or that is nearly as capable of meeting so many moods or pleasing so many tastes.

Soups range from the kinds that are simply clear, well-flavored broths to those of the thick, meaty type that are much too filling to eat with a full-course meal. In between, there is a wonderful galaxy of cream soups, vegetable soups and bisques. Soups also are classified as hot or chilled with a few that are equally pleasing when presented steaming hot or frosty cold.

The matter of temperature is of vital importance. There's no middle road, nothing that comes near to perfection between the two extremes. Soups that are meant to be hot should be served piping hot, the hotter the better. Equally, the success of a cold soup depends on its being served chilled through and through.

Soups have a further plus. There's plenty of leeway for original thinking. Make the time to give your soups original touches and presentations that take them away from the beaten path.

A dash of sherry adds zest to chicken soups. Madeira does something special for cream of mushroom. Chicken soup can also benefit from a bit of curry powder or a whisper of mace. A little chopped mint enhances green pea soup, while basil performs much the same magic for soups that are tomato.

The soup course can be a remembered part of the meal when it's granted a little extra attention and presented with drama. The dishware and other accessories that you bring into play can delight the eye, complement the character of the soup and assist in getting it to the customer at the optimum temperature.

There is a wonderful assortment of serving equipment available in attractive shapes and colors that can add a world of charm to your soup service. An abalone shell set in a bed of rock salt can emphasize the nature of a soup that features seafood. Similarly, compatible tableware can identify with the famous soups of other countries and strengthen their impact at serving time.

Covered soup bowls, tureens and similar containers draw favorable attention and at the same time help the soup to retain its heat. For the same practical reason, deep cups or bowls are favored for consomme and other soups that tend to cool quickly. Shallow soup plates work out best for the thicker soups that do not have this rapid cooling tendency. In any case, make it a cardinal rule always to have thoroughly warm dishware for serving hot soups.

Many cold soups make the most of their eye-catching advantage when presented in glassware that permits the color to show through. Jellied madrilene is effective when layered with sour cream, parfait fashion, in tall, slender glasses. Fruit soups look especially well in glass nappies or iced supreme dishes. Punch cups are a nice conceit for liquid soups that people find pleasant to sip.

A garnish can often spell the difference between a routine soup and one that is remembered as special. Clear soups take on importance with a garnish of diced avocado, toasted almonds, thinly sliced cucumber or small mushroom caps. A slice of lemon or lime floating on a cup of hot broth can add appetizing aroma and heighten appearance and taste.

The list of garnishing ideas is long and exciting. A dollop of lightly salted whipped cream makes an attractive topping for many cream soups. A small twisted pretzel; croutons cut in matchstick lengths; buttered, toasted crumbs; diced or shredded American cheese; grated Parmesan; and crisp Chinese noodles take into account only a few of the possibilities.

Offering a choice of trimmings can inject an element of novelty. The iced salad soup, gazpacho, lends itself to this type of service, with an array of diced cucumber, green pepper, chopped hard-cooked egg and green onion offered as "extras." Other soups can easily subscribe to the impression that this ritual makes.

Crisp crackers are a natural accompaniment for soups with manufacturers today providing an almost bewildering assortment of kinds. However, don't overlook the merits of bread sticks, Swiss twists and Melba toast. There's also the exciting potential of taste-teasing go-alongs such as olives, radishes, carrot sticks, celery and other appropriate relishes.

Cold Soups

SUMMER SALAD SOUP

Yield: 20 5-ounce portions

Ingredients

CREAM OF CELERY SOUP, CONDENSED	1 50-ounce can
COTTAGE CHEESE	1 cup
MILK	1-1/4 quarts
CUCUMBERS, finely chopped	1/2 cup
GREEN PEPPER, finely chopped	1/2 cup
ONION, finely chopped	2 tablespoons

Procedure

1. Blend soup into cottage cheese, using a wire whip. Add remaining ingredients.
2. Refrigerate, covered, 4 to 6 hours or overnight.
3. Serve in chilled cups.

CHICKEN AND AVOCADO SOUP

Yield: 48 1/2-cup portions

Ingredients

AVOCADOS, peeled	6 large
CREAM OF CHICKEN SOUP, CONDENSED	2 51-ounce cans
MILK	1 quart
GROUND ALLSPICE	1 teaspoon
MILK or CREAM	1 quart

Procedure

1. Remove stones from avocado. Mash 5 avocados in mixer using the whip attachment. (Approximately 5 cups pulp).
2. Cut remaining avocado into 6 pieces lengthwise. Cut sections crosswise into thin slices.
3. Add fruit to soup; blend in 1 quart milk and allspice. Heat to boiling. Turn into glass jars; chill overnight.
4. When ready to serve, stir soup well, blending in remaining quart of milk or cream. Serve in cup set in bed of ice.

MINT COOLER

Yield: 8 portions

Ingredients

GREEN PEA SOUP, CONDENSED	1 11-1/4-ounce can
MILK	2 cups
MINT LEAVES, FRESH	5 to 6
or MINT SYRUP	1/2 teaspoon
GREEN PEPPER RING	1
WATERCRESS or PARSLEY	as needed

Procedure

1. Blend soup, milk, mint and green pepper in blender. Strain. Add more milk, if necessary, to give consistency desired. Chill.
2. Serve in stemmed glass. Garnish with watercress or parsley.

VICHYSSOISE

Yield: 2 gallons

Ingredients

LEEKS, chopped (white part only)	2 pounds
ONION, finely chopped	8 ounces
BUTTER or MARGARINE	8 ounces
CHICKEN FLAVORED SOUP BASE	4 ounces
WATER	1-1/4 gallons
INSTANT MASHED POTATOES	1-1/2 pounds
MILK	1 quart
CREAM, LIGHT	1 quart
CREAM, HEAVY	1 quart
CHIVES, chopped	as needed

Procedure

1. Cook leeks and onion in butter until tender.
2. Add soup base and water. Cover; simmer until vegetables are thoroughly cooked.
3. Stir in potatoes gradually; cook a few minutes more.
4. Force through a fine sieve. Cool.
5. Add milk, light cream and heavy cream. Chill several hours.
6. Serve garnished with chives.

CURRIED AVOCADO SOUP ⟶

Yield: 1 gallon

Ingredients

BUTTER or MARGARINE	4 ounces
WATER	1/2 cup
ONION, chopped	2 cups
CELERY, chopped	2 cups
CURRY POWDER	2 tablespoons
APPLES, peeled, chopped	1 quart
BAY LEAVES	2
SALT	1 tablespoon
CHICKEN STOCK	2 quarts ·
CREAM, LIGHT	1 quart
AVOCADO, sieved	1 quart

BLUEBERRY SOUP

Yield: 50 1-cup portions

Ingredients

BLUEBERRY PUREE*	6-3/4 quarts
SUGAR	2-1/2 cups
RASPBERRY ICE CREAM TOPPING	
or RASPBERRY PRESERVES, beaten	3/4 cup
LEMON JUICE	1/2 cup
NUTMEG	1-1/2 teaspoons
BUTTERMILK	5 quarts
SALT	1 teaspoon
ORANGE SLICES, thin	50
BLUEBERRIES, FRESH, WHOLE	1 quart

Procedure

1. Combine blueberry puree, sugar, raspberry topping or preserves, lemon juice, nutmeg, buttermilk and salt. Chill thoroughly.

2. Serve icy cold. Garnish each portion with an orange slice and a few fresh blueberries.

*Use approximately 2 No. 10 cans of blueberries in syrup or approximately 16 pounds of frozen blueberries in syrup to make blueberry puree.

Procedure

1. Melt butter; stir in water, onion, celery, curry, apples, bay leaves and salt. Cover; simmer 20 to 30 minutes or until vegetables are cooked.

2. Remove bay leaves; puree vegetable mixture. Stir in chicken stock. Cool.

3. Combine cooled mixture, cream and avocado. Whip or beat until smooth. Chill.

4. Serve in iced supreme cups. Garnish with small avocado crescents, if desired.

VICHY POIS
(Chilled Frozen Pea Soup)

Yield: 25 portions

Ingredients

ONION, diced	3 cups
CELERY, diced	3 cups
GARLIC, cut	4 to 6 cloves
CHICKEN SOUP BASE	2 tablespoons
SALT	2 tablespoons
CURRY POWDER	1-1/2 tablespoons
GROUND WHITE PEPPER	1/4 teaspoon
WATER	3 cups
FROZEN GREEN PEAS, cooked	5 pounds
MILK, chilled	3 quarts

Procedure

1. Combine onion, celery, garlic, chicken soup base, salt, curry powder, white pepper and water. Simmer, covered, 10 minutes.

2. Pour half of the vegetable mixture with half of the cooked peas into a blender; chop until very fine. Repeat with remainder.

3. Add chilled milk. Refrigerate. Serve garnished with sour cream and cut chives or paprika and/or a few cooked frozen peas, if desired.

BORSCHT ⟶

Yield: 50 1-cup portions

Ingredients

ONION, grated	1/2 cup
LEMON JUICE	1/2 cup
GARLIC SALT	1-1/2 tablespoons
SALT	3 tablespoons
GROUND WHITE PEPPER	1 teaspoon
SUGAR	1/2 cup
BEET PUREE*	1-1/2 gallons
BUTTERMILK	1-1/2 gallons
SOUR CREAM	1 quart
DILL or CHIVES, cut	1 cup

*Use approximately 2 No. 10 cans sliced beets and liquid to make puree.

FRUIT SOUP

Yield: 32 1/2-cup portions

Ingredients

TAPIOCA, QUICK COOKING	5 ounces (1 cup)
WATER	2 quarts
SUGAR	1/2 cup
SALT	1/4 teaspoon
ORANGE JUICE, FROZEN, CONCENTRATED	2 cups
ORANGE SECTIONS, FRESH, diced (WITH JUICE)	2 cups
SLICED PEACHES, FROZEN, thawed	1 quart (2-1/4 pounds)
BANANAS, sliced	3 cups (1-1/4 pounds)
SOUR CREAM	2-1/2 cups

Procedure

1. Add tapioca to water; bring to a boil, stirring often.

2. Remove from heat. Add sugar, salt and concentrated orange juice. Cover; chill.

3. Fold fruit into chilled mixture.

4. Garnish portions with sour cream.

Procedure

1. Add onion, lemon juice, garlic salt, white pepper and sugar to beet puree; mix well.

2. Stir in buttermilk gradually. Chill.

3. Serve icy cold, each portion garnished with a rounded tablespoon sour cream and a sprinkling of fresh dill or chives.

GAZPACHO

Yield: 50 portions

Ingredients

ONION, finely chopped	3 cups
GARLIC, minced	3 cloves
GREEN PEPPER, chopped	3 cups
CELERY, diced	1-1/2 cups
TOMATOES, FRESH, diced	2 quarts
PEPPER	1 teaspoon
PAPRIKA	3 tablespoons
BEEF CONSOMME, CANNED	2 quarts
TOMATO JUICE	2 quarts
LEMON JUICE	1-1/2 cups
SALT	as needed
CUCUMBERS, thinly sliced	1 quart
ICE CUBES	as needed
TOMATO SLICES	50

Procedure

1. Combine onion, garlic, green pepper, celery, diced tomato, pepper and paprika. Stir in consomme, tomato juice and lemon juice. Season with salt.

2. Chill several hours or overnight.

3. Add cucumbers.

4. Serve each portion over 2 or 3 ice cubes. Garnish with a slice of tomato.

Hot Soups

SHRIMP BISQUE

Yield: 48 portions

Ingredients

SHRIMP, RAW, IN SHELL	8 pounds
COURT BOUILLON or WATER, boiling	1 gallon
BUTTER or MARGARINE	1-1/2 pounds
FLOUR	12 ounces
PAPRIKA	2 tablespoons
CHICKEN STOCK, boiling	1 gallon
TOMATO PUREE	1 cup
ONION FLAKES	1/2 cup
CELERY FLAKES	1/4 cup
SALT	3 tablespoons
BAY LEAVES	4
THYME LEAVES	1 tablespoon
INSTANT MINCED GARLIC	2 teaspoons
WHITE PEPPER, GROUND	1 teaspoon
CAYENNE	1/2 teaspoon
MILK, hot	2 quarts
CREAM, LIGHT, hot	2 cups

Procedure

1. Add raw shrimp to boiling court bouillon or water; cook 5 minutes.

2. Remove shrimp from liquid, reserving liquid.

3. Cool shrimp; peel and devein, saving shells. Cut shrimp in 1/2-inch pieces.

4. Melt butter, blend in flour and paprika. Cook over low heat 3 to 4 minutes.

5. Add reserved liquid from shrimp, the shells, chicken stock, tomato puree and seasonings. Bring to boil. Reduce heat; simmer 30 minutes.

6. Gradually add hot milk and cream. Simmer 15 minutes longer. Strain.

7. Add shrimp. Heat through.

EGG AND LEMON SOUP

Yield: approximately 3 quarts

Ingredients

CHICKEN STOCK	3 quarts
RICE	3/4 cup
EGGS	4
WATER	2 tablespoons
LEMON JUICE, FRESH, strained	1/2 cup

Procedure

1. Bring chicken stock to boil; add rice. Simmer, covered, 25 to 30 minutes or until rice is tender.

2. Beat eggs with water; add lemon juice, beating to blend well.

3. Add some of the hot mixture to egg mixture; blend. Gradually add to remainder of hot broth, stirring constantly.

FRENCH CREAM OF ASPARAGUS SOUP

Yield: 4-1/2 gallons

Ingredients

ASPARAGUS, FRESH, trimmed	18 pounds
RICE	10-1/2 ounces
ONION, sliced fine	1-1/2 pounds
BUTTER or MARGARINE	6 ounces
CARROTS, grated or chopped	1 pound
LIQUID FROM ASPARAGUS	3-1/2 quarts
SODA	1/4 ounce (1-1/2 teaspoons)
MILK, hot	2-1/3 gallons
CREAM, hot	2/3 quart
SALT	as needed

Procedure

1. Cook asparagus. Drain, saving the liquid. Puree asparagus.

2. Steam rice.

3. Saute onions in butter until glossy in appearance; add carrots; cook until tender.

4. Combine pureed asparagus, asparagus liquid and vegetables; heat.

5. Add soda; blend. Add hot milk, hot cream and cooked rice. Taste; add salt to season.

MINTED CREAM OF GREEN PEA SOUP
WITH POTATO ROSETTES

Yield: 50 portions

Ingredients

ONION, chopped	1-1/2 pounds
MINT, FRESH, chopped	1/4 cup
BUTTER or MARGARINE	1 pound
FLOUR, ALL-PURPOSE	1 pound
CHICKEN STOCK, hot	1 gallon
PEAS, FROZEN	5 pounds
CHICKEN STOCK, hot	1 gallon
CREAM, HEAVY, hot	2 quarts
SUGAR	1/4 cup
CAYENNE PEPPER	dash
SALT	as needed
POTATO-CHEESE ROSETTES	50 garnishes

(Recipe, facing page)

Procedure

1. Saute onion and mint in butter until tender, but do not allow to brown.

2. Add flour; blend. Cook 5 minutes.

3. Add first amount of chicken stock. Cook and stir until blended and smooth.

4. Cook peas in remaining stock. Put peas and liquid through food mill. Add to thickened stock.

5. Strain mixture through a china cap.

6. Add cream; blend. Season with sugar, cayenne and salt.

7. Garnish with potato-cheese rosettes and fresh mint leaves, if desired.

Note

This is a thick cream soup. If thinner soup is desired, add hot milk or cream.

POTATO-CHEESE ROSETTES

Yield: 50 garnishes

Ingredients

INSTANT MASHED POTATOES	12 ounces
WATER, boiling	3 cups
SALT	1-1/2 teaspoons
BUTTER or MARGARINE	2 ounces
MILK, hot	2 cups
EGG YOLKS	4
CHEESE, PARMESAN or CHEDDAR, grated	6 ounces

Procedure

1. Prepare mashed potatoes according to label directions, using above proportions of water, salt, butter and hot milk.

2. Add egg yolks, one at a time, beating to blend.

3. Force through pastry tube onto greased baking sheet making small rosettes or rings. Top with cheese.

4. Brown lightly in oven at 425°F.

CHICKEN PIMIENTO SOUP

Yield: 25 1-cup portions

Ingredients

CELERY, chopped	1 quart
ONION, chopped	1/4 cup
BUTTER or MARGARINE	6 ounces
FLOUR, ALL-PURPOSE	8 ounces (2 cups)
SALT	2 tablespoons
PEPPER	3/4 teaspoon
CHICKEN BROTH	3-1/4 quarts
CHICKEN, cooked, chopped	1 pound (3 cups)
MILK, hot	2 quarts
PIMIENTO, chopped	1/3 cup

Procedure

1. Saute celery and onion in butter until golden.

2. Blend in flour, salt and pepper. Gradually stir in chicken broth. Cook over low heat, stirring occasionally, until slightly thickened. Add chicken; continue cooking 15 minutes.

3. Add milk and pimiento; reheat. Serve with a garnish of chopped parsley, if desired.

Curried Chicken Soup (Recipe, facing page)

American Spice Trade Association

CURRIED CHICKEN SOUP
(See picture, facing page)

Yield: 48 portions

Ingredients

INSTANT MINCED ONION	1-1/2 cups
WATER	1-1/2 cups
BUTTER or MARGARINE	1 pound
CARROTS, diced	1 quart
APPLES, diced	2 cups
CURRY POWDER	1 cup
FLOUR	3 cups
CHICKEN STOCK, hot	3 gallons
SALT	1/4 cup
INSTANT GARLIC POWDER	1 tablespoon
BLACK PEPPER, GROUND	1 teaspoon
CREAM	2 cups
RICE, cooked	1-1/2 quarts
CHICKEN, cooked, diced	1 quart
FREEZE DRIED CHIVES or PARSLEY FLAKES	1/3 cup

Procedure

1. Rehydrate onion in water 10 minutes.

2. Heat butter; add onion, carrots, apples and curry powder. Saute 5 minutes.

3. Blend in flour; cook and stir 5 minutes longer.

4. Add stock and seasonings; mix well. Bring to boiling point. Reduce heat; simmer, covered, 35 to 45 minutes.

5. Strain soup through a china cap. Gradually add cream. Heat, but do not boil.

6. Add rice and chicken. Check seasonings. Serve hot.

7. Sprinkle chives or parsley over each portion. Garnish with toast croutons cut in matchstick lengths, if desired.

CREAM OF POTATO SOUP AMANDINE

Yield: 50 portions

Ingredients

ONION, chopped	2 cups
CELERY, chopped	2 cups
BUTTER or MARGARINE	8 ounces
CHICKEN STOCK	2 gallons
CHERVIL	1-1/2 teaspoons
SALT	as needed
PEPPER	as needed
POTATOES, FROZEN, SHREDDED	5 pounds
CREAM SAUCE, light	2-1/2 quarts
CHICKEN, cooked, diced	1 quart
GREEN OLIVES, STUFFED, sliced	2 cups
ALMONDS, SLIVERED, toasted	1 cup

Procedure

1. Saute onion and celery in butter.
2. Add stock and seasonings; bring to a boil.
3. Add potatoes; cook until tender.
4. Puree mixture; add cream sauce, stirring until blended.
5. Add chicken and olives. Adjust seasoning and consistency.
6. Serve hot, garnished with almonds.

CREAM OF FRESH MUSHROOM AND TOMATO SOUP

Yield: 24 portions

Ingredients

BUTTER or MARGARINE	1 pound
ONION, finely chopped	1-1/2 cups
GARLIC, minced	1/4 teaspoon
MUSHROOMS, FRESH, sliced	2 quarts
LEMON JUICE	1 tablespoon
FLOUR	1-1/2 cups
MILK	1-1/2 quarts
CHICKEN STOCK*	1-1/2 quarts
BAKING SODA	1/2 teaspoon
SALT	2 tablespoons
BLACK PEPPER, GROUND	1/2 teaspoon
TOMATOES, FRESH, diced	1-1/2 gallons

Procedure

1. Melt butter. Add onion, garlic, mushrooms and lemon juice; saute until onion is golden.

2. Blend in flour. Add milk, stock, soda, salt and pepper; cook and stir until sauce is well blended.

3. Add tomatoes; cook over very low heat for 20 minutes, stirring occasionally. Serve hot.

*If desired, omit stock and increase milk to 3 quarts.

CREAM OF FRESH TOMATO SOUP

Yield: 1-1/2 gallons

Ingredients

TOMATOES, CANNED	2 quarts
TOMATOES, FRESH, chopped	1 quart
HALF AND HALF	3 quarts
FLOUR	1/2 cup
BUTTER	1/2 pound
SUGAR	1/4 cup
SALT	2 tablespoons and 1 teaspoon
WHITE PEPPER	1/2 teaspoon
TOMATOES, FRESH, finely chopped	1 cup

Procedure

1. Mix tomatoes and half and half while cold. Heat slowly to a simmering temperature. Do not boil.

2. Rub flour and butter together until blended. Add a little of the hot mixture; blend. Add to remainder of hot mixture. Cook and stir over hot, not boiling, water until thickened.

3. Add sugar, salt and pepper. Strain.

4. Add remaining fresh tomatoes. Serve garnished with whipped cream seasoned with curry powder, if desired.

Garnishes

EGG THREADS

Yield: for 2 quarts consomme

Ingredients

EGGS (at room temperature)	2
FLOUR	1/4 teaspoon
CONSOMME	2 quarts

Procedure

1. Beat eggs with a fork just long enough to combine yolks and whites. Add flour.

2. Bring consomme to a boil; pour in the egg mixture slowly in a fine stream. At the same time, hold a fork in the other hand and stir wide circles on surface of the simmering consomme to catch the egg as it strikes the hot liquid and draw it out in long threads.

ROYALE CUSTARD

Yield: for 2 quarts consomme

Ingredients

EGGS	2
EGG YOLKS	2
MILK	1 cup
SALT	1/8 teaspoon
PAPRIKA	1/8 teaspoon
NUTMEG	1/8 teaspoon

Procedure

1. Beat eggs and egg yolks together. Add milk and seasonings.

2. Pour into a well-buttered, shallow, straight-sided mold. Set in a pan of water. Bake in oven at 325°F. about 30 minutes or until set.

3. Cool thoroughly. Cut into cubes or fancy shapes. Add to consomme just before serving.

Plated for Party Fare

Cling Peach Advisory Board

ENTREES

THE ENTREE SETS the standard for the meal. It determines the prestige of the menu, establishes the cost, and provides the cue for other items on the menu.

The usual choice for special dinners is either meat or poultry. Fish offers another possibility, although it appears more often at noontime functions than at the dinner hour. At the more elaborate banquets, fish is sometimes featured as a special course preceding the piece de resistance of the meal, the entree.

Beef, lamb, pork and veal all offer a diversity of cuts with the tenderest, choicest ones—steaks, roasts and chops—unquestionably among the top choices. Chicken, turkey, duckling and the gamey Rock Cornish hens are held in high esteem though long gone are the days when these poultry products—particularly chicken and turkey—were regarded as luxury items. To be ranked as specialties today they must be presented with special flair.

Within the wide range of possibilities, it is wise to select an entree that most people like. Make it one that is quickly and easily served and presents no problem to eat. Cost limits the choices as do the factors of equipment, the number to be served and the time element, i.e., whether the dish requires last minute preparation or can withstand a waiting period if there is a delay in service.

When the choice narrows down to a dish that is well-liked but a bit common-place, the challenge lies in presenting the item in an original way. Look to tasty sauces and glazes; to companionable stuffings and garnishments. Consider the glorious galaxy of go-alongs that can be produced from fruit, vegetables, relishes, and similar items. One pleasing nuance, as long as it is unexpected, can turn the trick and set the meal apart as a memorable one.

The entree recipes are grouped as luncheon and dinner selections. There may be occasions when serving an entree from the dinner group at a luncheon may be desirable. Or an opposite switch may seem in order. Such flexibility in entree selection can be an important step in preparing the most effective menu for a special occasion.

Luncheon Entrees

BY TRADITION, luncheon is a less formal meal than dinner, The menu usually has fewer courses and can feature main dish salads, seafood specialties, fruited curries and many other attractive entrees that are not regularly served at the dinner hour.

Many noon-time functions are attended by women who welcome a "lighter" luncheon—perhaps one planned around an unusual salad, omelet or souffle—in place of the heartier, less frilly fare that suits the tastes of men.

INSTANT POTATO SOUFFLE

Yield: 32 portions

Ingredients

INSTANT MASHED POTATOES, prepared	2 quarts
COTTAGE CHEESE	1 quart
SOUR CREAM	2 cups
ONION, very finely chopped	1 cup
PARSLEY, finely chopped	1 tablespoon
GARLIC SALT	1 teaspoon
EGG YOLKS, slightly beaten	12 (1 cup)
SALT	as needed
PEPPER	as needed
EGG WHITES	12 (1-1/2 cups)

Procedure

1. Combine instant mashed potatoes (prepared according to package directions) with cottage cheese, sour cream, onion, parsley, garlic salt and egg yolks; blend. Season with salt and pepper.

2. Beat egg whites until stiff but not dry. Fold into potato mixture.

3. Divide equally into 4 2-quart souffle dishes.

4. Bake in oven at 350°F. for 40 to 45 minutes.

Serve with Shrimp Sauce*

*SHRIMP SAUCE

Yield: 32 portions

Ingredients

WHITE SAUCE, medium (prepared with fish stock)	2 quarts
NUTMEG	1 to 2 teaspoons
SHRIMP, VERY SMALL, cooked	4 pounds

Procedure

1. Season white sauce with nutmeg.

2. Add shrimp; heat through.

CRABMEAT-STUFFED AVOCADO

Yield: 48 portions

Ingredients

AVOCADOS	48
LEMON JUICE	as needed
CRABMEAT	12 pounds
CELERY, diced	3 quarts
ONION, finely minced	1 cup
MAYONNAISE	1-1/2 quarts
LEMON JUICE	1/2 cup
SALT	2 tablespoons
PEPPER, WHITE, GROUND	1 teaspoon
LETTUCE CUPS, SMALL	as needed
TOMATOES, cut in wedges	8 pounds
EGGS, hard-cooked	24
ANCHOVY FILLETS	96

Procedure

1. Cut avocados in half lengthwise. Remove stones; peel one half of each avocado. Brush cut areas with lemon juice.

2. Combine crabmeat and celery.

3. Combine onion, mayonnaise, measured amount of lemon juice, salt and pepper; mix well. Pour over crabmeat and celery; toss lightly to mix.

4. Fill unpeeled halves of avocado with salad mixture. Top with peeled halves.

5. Place on luncheon plates. Arrange small lettuce cups on either side. Fill cups with tomato wedges and egg as garnish. Crisscross two anchovy fillets over top of each stuffed avocado.

TURKEY IN CURRIED FRUIT SAUCE
(See picture, page 168)

Yield: 6-1/2 quarts, 40 portions

Ingredients

BUTTER or MARGARINE	6 ounces
ONION, chopped	3 cups
PINEAPPLE JUICE	1-1/2 quarts
CHICKEN BROTH	1-1/2 quarts
CORNSTARCH	3/4 cup
SALT	2-1/2 tablespoons
CURRY POWDER	2-1/2 tablespoons
GREEN PEPPER, cut in thin strips	3 cups
TURKEY, cooked, cut in strips	5 pounds
MANDARIN ORANGE SECTIONS, drained	2 quarts
PINEAPPLE SLICES, grilled	40
RICE, cooked	6-1/2 quarts
COCONUT	1 quart

Procedure

1. Melt butter; add onion; saute until tender but not brown.

2. Combine pineapple juice and broth.

3. Combine cornstarch, salt and curry powder; stir to a thin smooth paste with part of the liquid.

4. Add remainder of liquid and green pepper to the sauteed onion; heat. Add cornstarch mixture; cook and stir until sauce thickens.

5. Add turkey, heat through. Add drained orange sections.

6. To serve: Place a slice of grilled pineapple on a portion (about 2/3 cup) of rice. Top with sauce allowing approximately 2/3 cup per portion. Sprinkle with coconut.

Turkey in Curried Fruit Sauce (Recipe, page 167)

SALMON MOUSSELINE

Yield: 24 portions, approximately 6 ounces, 1-1/2 ounces sauce

Ingredients

SALMON, CANNED, skin and bones removed	4 pounds
EGG WHITES	1 cup
SALT	2 tablespoons
PEPPER, WHITE	1/2 teaspoon
TARRAGON, DRIED, finely crumbled	1-1/4 teaspoons
CREAM, HEAVY	2 quarts
TOMATO PASTE	3/4 cup
RIPE OLIVES, coarsely chopped	3 cups
PARSLEY, chopped	1/2 cup
MORNAY SAUCE (Recipe facing page)	4-1/2 cups

Procedure

1. Grind salmon using fine blade of grinder. Chill thoroughly.

2. Place ground salmon in mixer bowl. Beat in egg whites gradually. Add salt, pepper and tarragon.

3. Blend in cream slowly, mixing thoroughly.

4. Add tomato paste; mix well. Stir in olives and parsley.

5. Fill greased timbale molds with mixture, allowing 6 ounces per portion. Set in steam table pan, add hot water to half the depth of molds.

6. Bake in oven at 350°F. for 20 to 25 minutes, until firm.

7. Unmold; cover each with 1-1/2 ounces Mornay sauce.

MORNAY SAUCE

Yield: 4-1/2 cups

Ingredients

BUTTER or MARGARINE	2 ounces
FLOUR	6 tablespoons
SALT	1-1/2 teaspoons
PEPPER, WHITE	1/8 teaspoon
MILK, scalded	1 quart
LIQUID RED PEPPER SEASONING	1/16 teaspoon
PARMESAN CHEESE, grated	1 cup

Procedure

1. Combine butter and flour. Cook together slowly 3 to 4 minutes.

2. Add salt, pepper and hot milk. Cook and stir until sauce boils and thickens.

3. Add red pepper seasoning and cheese; heat slowly until cheese melts and sauce is smooth.

CRAB-STUFFED SHRIMP (IN SHELL)

Yield: 16 to 20 portions

Ingredients

SHRIMP, RAW, unshelled, size 16 to 20	5 pounds
CRABMEAT	3/4 pound
EGG, lightly beaten	1
DILL, FRESH, finely chopped	1 tablespoon
SALT	as needed
BREAD CRUMBS, soft	1 cup
BUTTER, melted	as needed

Procedure

1. Cook unshelled shrimp in boiling salted water 3 to 5 minutes. Drain. Remove feelers from inner curve of shell leaving tail and shell on shrimp. Make a slit down back of shell to devein.

2. Shred crabmeat; mix with egg. Add dill and salt. Mix with crumbs; add melted butter to moisten.

3. Stuff crabmeat mixture into slit along back of shrimp.

4. Arrange stuffed shrimp in heat proof serving dish with melted butter; place under broiler until thoroughly heated.

PRAWNS 'N PINEAPPLE

Yield: 25 entree portions or 50 portions hors d'oeuvres

Ingredients

SHRIMP, RAW	7-1/2 pounds
SHERRY	1-1/4 cups
SOY SAUCE	1-1/4 cups
LEMON JUICE	1/3 cup
GINGER	2-1/2 teaspoons
MUSTARD, DRY	2 tablespoons
FLOUR, sifted	3-3/4 cups
SALT	2-1/2 teaspoons
BAKING POWDER	1-1/4 teaspoons
EGGS, slightly beaten	5
WATER	3-3/4 cups
PINEAPPLE SWEET-SOUR SAUCE (Recipe, facing page)	1 recipe

Procedure

1. Shell and devein shrimp, leaving tails on. Butterfly shrimp by splitting along back curve, cutting almost to inner edge. Open and press flat.

2. Combine sherry, soy sauce, lemon juice, ginger and mustard; pour over shrimp. Cover; refrigerate several hours, turning 2 or 3 times.

3. Sift flour, salt and baking powder together. Combine eggs and water; add to dry ingredients; beat lightly.

4. Drain shrimp well. Holding by tail, dip each shrimp in batter; drain off excess batter.

5. Fry in 2 to 3 inches of hot oil at 365°F. until golden brown. Keep hot.

6. Combine with pineapple sweet-sour sauce before serving.

PINEAPPLE SWEET-SOUR SAUCE

Yield: for 25 portions

Ingredients

PINEAPPLE, SLICED (52 COUNT)	1 No. 10 can
PINEAPPLE SYRUP	2-1/2 cups
SUGAR, BROWN	10 ounces
VINEGAR	1-2/3 cups
WATER	2-1/2 cups
SOY SAUCE	1/3 cup
MONOSODIUM GLUTAMATE	2-1/2 teaspoons
SALT	1/2 teaspoon
CORNSTARCH	1/2 cup
GREEN ONIONS, sliced	2/3 cup

Procedure

1. Drain pineapple, reserving required amount of syrup.

2. Combine syrup, brown sugar, vinegar, water, soy sauce, monosodium glutamate and salt. Stir to dissolve sugar. Blend a small amount of mixture with cornstarch to form a smooth paste; stir into remaining liquid.

3. Heat, stirring, until sauce boils and thickens.

4. Add drained pineapple slices (cut in half, if desired) and onions. Heat 5 minutes.

COQUILLES COMMERCE TOWERS

Yield: 24 portions (48 shells)

Ingredients

SAUTERNE	2 quarts
BOUQUET GARNI	1
SCALLOPS, BAY	8 pounds
MUSHROOMS, minced	2 pounds
SHALLOTS, finely chopped	24 (1/2 pound)
ONION, finely chopped	1/2 medium
BUTTER	4 ounces
LEMON JUICE	2 tablespoons
BUTTER	8 ounces
FLOUR	8 ounces
CREAM, HEAVY	1 cup
EGG YOLKS, beaten	8
PARSLEY, chopped	1/4 cup
CRUMBS, buttered	as needed

Procedure

1. Combine sauterne and bouquet garni; bring to a boil. Add scallops; cook until tender. Remove scallops from wine. Discard garni.

2. Braise mushrooms, shallots and onion in first amount of butter. Add lemon juice. Cover; cook about 10 minutes.

3. Strain mushroom mixture. Add liquid to wine mixture. Add the vegetable portion of the mixture to scallops.

4. Make a roux of remaining butter and flour. Add combined liquids gradually; cook and stir until sauce is thick and smooth. Simmer a few minutes.

5. Combine cream and beaten egg yolks, add a little of the hot sauce; blend. Add egg mixture to remaining sauce, stirring constantly.

6. Add parsley and scallop mixture. Remove from heat.

7. Fill coquille shells. Top with buttered crumbs. Bake in oven at 375°F. until brown.

8. Garnish with lemon and parsley.

MINI-ROLLS PARMIGIANA

Yield: 48 portions

Ingredients

BROILER-FRYER CHICKEN THIGHS, boned*	96
SEASONED SALT	as needed
INSTANT MINCED ONION	2 cups
PARSLEY, FRESH, chopped	2 cups
MOZZARELLA CHEESE, cut in 2-1/2-inch strips	3 pounds
TOMATO SAUCE	2 No. 10 cans
BASIL, DRIED LEAF	2 tablespoons
OREGANO, DRIED LEAF	2 tablespoons
SPAGHETTI or LINGUINI	6 pounds
PARMESAN CHEESE, grated	as needed

Procedure

1. Place boned thighs, skin side down. Sprinkle with seasoned salt, then sprinkle with instant minced onion and parsley.

2. Place piece of cheese on each boned thigh; fold sides over cheese; fasten with skewer. Place skewered side down, in foil-lined shallow pan.

3. Bake in oven at 400°F. for 40 minutes.

4. Combine tomato sauce and herbs. Simmer about 15 minutes. Strain.

5. Cook spaghetti according to package directions.

6. Serve mini-rolls on spaghetti. Top with sauce. Serve with Parmesan cheese.

*To bone thighs, cut along thinner side of thigh to the bone, slashing thigh the length of the bone. Holding one end of the bone, scrape the meat away until bone is free. Cut off rounded piece of cartilage.

VEAL OR CHICKEN ROULADES CHAUD-FROID

(See picture, page 96)

Yield: 24 portions

Ingredients

VEAL CUTLETS or CHICKEN BREASTS, 4-ounce	24
SALT	1 tablespoon
MONOSODIUM GLUTAMATE	1 tablespoon
PARSLEY, chopped	3 cups
PIMIENTO, chopped, drained	1-1/2 cups
MUSHROOMS, CANNED, chopped, drained	1-1/2 pounds
CHICKEN BROTH	3 quarts
INSTANT MINCED ONION	3/4 cup
CHAUD-FROID GLAZE (Recipe, facing page)	1-1/3 quarts

Procedure

1. Flatten veal slices or chicken breasts; sprinkle with salt and monosodium glutamate.

2. Combine parsley, pimiento and mushrooms. Spread mixture on meat. Fold over filling; roll lightly. Fasten with skewers. Combine chicken broth and minced onion. Add rolls. Cover; simmer 25 to 30 minutes or until tender.

4. Remove rolls from broth. Chill.

5. Place rolls on rack. Spoon glaze over meat, using long fast strokes. Garnish as desired. Refrigerate.

CHAUD-FROID GLAZE

Yield: 1-1/3 quarts

Ingredients

ROUX	4 ounces
CHICKEN BROTH	1 quart
GELATINE, UNFLAVORED	1 ounce
WATER, cold	1 cup
EGG YOLKS	2
CREAM, HEAVY	1/2 cup

Procedure

1. Stir roux into broth; cook and stir until mixture thickens and comes to a boil. Cook over very low heat 5 minutes.

2. Soften gelatine in cold water. Stir into hot mixture until dissolved.

3. Beat egg yolks with cream; blend with sauce. Heat and stir 2 minutes. *Do not boil.*

4. Remove from heat. Chill until mixture thickens sufficiently to adhere to meat and give a smooth even glaze. (If glaze becomes too thick and forms thick patches on meat, heat slightly to regain proper consistency.)

PARMESAN TOAST STRIPS

Yield: 80 strips

Ingredients

CORN FLAKE CRUMBS	1 cup
PARMESAN CHEESE, grated	3/4 cup
BREAD, toasted	16 slices
BUTTER or MARGARINE, melted	12 ounces
ONION SALT	2 teaspoons

Procedure

1. Mix corn flake crumbs and cheese.

2. Cut crusts from toast slices. Cut each slice in 5 narrow strips.

3. Combine butter and onion salt. Roll strips in butter, then in corn flake mixture. Place on ungreased baking sheet.

4. Bake in oven at 400°F. about 5 minutes or until crisp.

5. Serve at once as soup or salad accompaniment.

DANISH FISKEBUDDING WITH SHRIMP SAUCE

Yield: 16 portions

Ingredients

COD FILLETS,* cut into small pieces	1-1/2 pounds
MILK	1 quart
EGGS	4
CORNSTARCH	1/2 cup
SALT	2 teaspoons
PEPPER, WHITE	1/2 teaspoon
BUTTER, soft	4 ounces
PEAS, TINY, FROZEN, cooked	1 quart
WHITE SAUCE, MEDIUM**	1 quart
NUTMEG	1 teaspoon
SHRIMP, small, cooked	2 pounds

Procedure

1. Combine fish and milk in 1-gallon food blender. Cover; blend 10 seconds at low speed. Scrape down; blend another 10 seconds.

2. Add eggs, cornstarch, salt, pepper and butter; blend together at low speed 10 seconds.

3. Pour into well-buttered 2-quart ring mold or into 2 1-quart molds.

4. Set mold in pan of warm water. Bake in oven at 350°F. for 1-1/4 to 1-1/2 hours, or until set.

5. Remove from oven; allow to stand for 10 minutes.

6. Unmold onto serving platter; mound hot cooked peas in center.

7. Season white sauce with nutmeg. Add shrimp; heat through.

8. Pour sauce around top edges of mold or serve sauce on side.

*Or other lean fish fillets.

**Or white sauce prepared with fish stock.

CRAB DIVAN

Yield: 48 portions

Ingredients

CRABMEAT, FRESH, FROZEN or PASTEURIZED*	8 pounds
BROCCOLI SPEARS, FROZEN	4 2-1/2-pound packages
FLOUR	4 ounces
SALT	2-1/2 tablespoons
PEPPER	2 teaspoons
BUTTER or MARGARINE, melted	8 ounces
MILK or HALF-AND-HALF	1 quart
CHEESE, AMERICAN, grated	8 ounces
TOMATOES, CANNED	1 gallon
CORN FLAKES, crushed	1 cup

Procedure

1. Thaw crabmeat, if frozen. Drain crabmeat; remove any remaining shell or cartilage. Cut crabmeat into 1-inch pieces.

2. Cook broccoli just to crisp tender stage. Drain thoroughly. Arrange in greased steam table pans or individual casseroles.

3. Blend flour, salt and pepper into melted butter; add milk gradually. Cook and stir until thickened and smooth.

4. Add cheese; stir until melted. Stir in tomatoes.

5. Ladle sauce over crabmeat; sprinkle with corn flakes.

6. Bake in oven at 400°F. for 20 to 25 minutes or until lightly browned.

*Or 24 6-1/2 ounce cans crabmeat.

DEVILED CRAB

Yield: 20 crab cakes

Ingredients

FLOUR	3/4 cup
CREAM, COFFEE	2 cups
BUTTER	1/4 pound
EGG YOLKS, slightly beaten	2
PARSLEY, chopped	4 teaspoons
WORCESTERSHIRE SAUCE	1 teaspoon
SALT	1 teaspoon
CELERY SALT	1/2 teaspoon
PEPPER	1/4 teaspoon
CRABMEAT, flaked	1 pound

Procedure

1. Make a smooth paste of the flour and cream, heat slowly until warm; add the butter. Cook until thick, stirring constantly.

2. Add a little of the hot mixture to the slightly beaten egg yolks; blend. Add to the remainder of the hot mixture. Add the remaining ingredients.

3. Chill 2 to 3 hours. Shape into 20 patties or croquettes.

4. Dip into fine bread crumbs. Allow to warm to room temperature. Fry in deep fat at 350°F. until golden brown.

Stuffed Boned Squab Spectacular

Squab separated by mushroom mounds, garnished with artichoke bottoms, cherry tomato halves.

Buffet Entree Items

BUFFETS OFFER unusual potential for catering special functions. You can adapt a buffet to suit the occasion or hour of day. Use it to expedite service, create a mood, dramatize the whole menu or highlight a specialty.

You can make your offerings simple or elaborate according to the tastes of your clientele and the capabilities of your staff. The variety can run the gamut from a table d'hote menu where everyone takes the same thing, to a lavish display of full smorgasbord proportions.

In any case, a buffet does not necessitate a highly trained crew. On the other hand, it is smart to take advantage of the things they do exceptionally well. Buffets provide a natural theater for an expert at carving. They also offer a marvelous opportunity to show off talents for garnishing or sculpturing in ice.

With a no-choice menu, the entree can feature a popular hot item or—during the warmer months—one that is chilled. When the buffet is planned to offer more freedom of choice, it is common practice to provide at least one hot entree and a variety of cold meats, seafood and salads.

When a skillful carver is in command, a standing rib roast makes an impressive hot entree. So does a handsome roast turkey or a glazed baked ham. When people are expected to serve themselves, hot entrees such as a curry, goulash or a similar item prepared in sauce can be offered in a twin chafing dish alongside its accompaniment of noodles or rice.

Cold entrees provide the greatest leeway for artistic displays with dishes such as aspic-coated hams; tastefully decorated molds; garnished, chaud-froid coated items and eye-catching arrays of sliced cheeses and meats.

Cold Buffet Items

HAM IN SPINACH ASPIC

Yield: approximately 3-1/2 quarts aspic

Ingredients

HAMS, CANNED (PULLMAN LOAVES) 7 to 7-1/2 pound*	3
GELATINE, UNFLAVORED	3-1/4 ounces
WATER, cold	2 cups
WATER, hot	2 quarts
VINEGAR	2 cups
SUGAR	2 cups
SALT	2 tablespoons
SPINACH, RAW, finely chopped	3 quarts (1-3/4 pounds)
GREEN ONIONS, finely cut	1/3 cup

Procedure

1. Remove hams from can as label directs. Trim away gelatine and fat. Trim each ham on sides and top, if necessary, to make piece about 1/2 inch smaller, all around, than straight-sided 10-inch by 5-inch by 4-inch loaf pan.

2. Roughen top and sides of ham slightly with a fork. Set hams squarely in loaf pans.

3. Soften unflavored gelatine in cold water.

4. Combine hot water, vinegar, sugar and salt; bring to a boil. Dissolve gelatine in hot liquid.

5. Chill until slightly thickened; fold in spinach and onions.

6. Pour enough gelatine mixture over ham to fill sides and make a 1/2-inch layer on top. Chill until firm.

7. Unmold; turn, aspic side up, on serving platter.

*Pullman hams are available in various weights and lengths. Purchase to correspond with the size loaf pans which are to be used.

CANNED HAM IN JELLIED MUSTARD SAUCE

Yield: approximately 50 portions

Ingredients

HAM, CANNED	1 10-pound size
BUTTER, melted	2 ounces
FLOUR	1/4 cup
WATER	2 cups
SALT	1 teaspoon
MUSTARD, PREPARED	1 tablespoon
SUGAR	1 teaspoon
VINEGAR	1 tablespoon
PAPRIKA	1 tablespoon
GELATINE, UNFLAVORED	2 tablespoons
WATER, cold	1/2 cup
OLIVES, STUFFED	as needed
PARSLEY	as needed

Procedure

1. Remove ham from can; scrape off all jelly. Cut in 1/8-inch slices. Reassemble slices to form original shape; tie firmly into shape with string. Place on rack set on foil or waxed paper.

2. Blend melted butter and flour; cook until mixture bubbles. Remove from heat. Stir in water gradually; cook and stir until sauce thickens.

3. Add salt, mustard, sugar, vinegar and paprika. Remove from heat.

4. Combine gelatine and cold water. Blend with hot sauce. Cool until lukewarm but not set.

5. Pour mustard sauce over ham to give a thin smooth surface which shows ham is sliced. Press sliced olives and parsley sprigs into a design on top before sauce is entirely cooled.

6. Heat remaining sauce with any that has dripped from ham onto foil. Cover sides of ham, spreading with spatula.

7. Press chopped stuffed olives and chopped parsley against sides before sauce is set. Chill until serving time.

8. Arrange on serving tray. Snip string in four places and remove.

MOLDED CHICKEN SALAD ⟶

Yield: 6 quarts

Ingredients

CHICKEN STOCK, well-seasoned	2-1/2 quarts
GELATINE, UNFLAVORED	1-1/2 ounces
MAYONNAISE	1-1/2 quarts
MONOSODIUM GLUTAMATE	1 tablespoon
LEMON JUICE	1/2 cup
CHICKEN, finely diced or minced	3 quarts
CELERY, finely chopped	1 quart
PIMIENTO, chopped	3/4 cup
ONION, finely chopped	1/2 cup

TUNA MOUSSE

Yield: 2 gallons

Ingredients

GELATIN, LEMON	1-1/2 pounds
WATER, hot	3-1/2 quarts
LEMON JUICE	1/2 cup
VINEGAR	1/2 cup
CAYENNE	1/4 teaspoon
WHIPPED TOPPING, prepared*	3 cups
MAYONNAISE	3 cups
TUNA, finely flaked	2-1/2 pounds
CELERY, finely chopped	2 quarts
DILL PICKLES, chopped	1 cup
PIMIENTO, chopped	1/2 cup

Procedure

1. Dissolve gelatin in hot water. Add lemon juice, vinegar and cayenne. Chill until slightly thickened.

2. Blend whipped topping and mayonnaise into gelatin mixture, using a wire whip.

3. Mix in remaining ingredients.

4. Pour into shallow pans or large ring molds. Chill until firm.

5. Cut into portions. Serve on crisp salad greens. Garnish as desired.

*Prepare topping without sugar and vanilla.

Procedure

1. Put stock in a saucepan. Sprinkle gelatine over top. Place over low heat; stir until gelatine dissolves.

2. Stir into mayonnaise. Add monosodium glutamate and lemon juice; blend smooth.

3. Chill, stirring frequently, until mixture mounds slightly when dropped from spoon.

4. Fold in chicken, celery, pimiento and onion.

5. Turn into 4 loaf pans 10-inch by 5-inch or one 12-inch by 20-inch by 2-1/2-inch pan. Chill until firm.

6. Unmold loaves (or cut pan into squares). Serve on salad greens.

SALMON A LA RITZ

Yield: 32 portions

Ingredients

SALMON, 1-POUND CANS	8
GELATINE, UNFLAVORED	1 ounce
WATER, cold	1 cup
MAYONNAISE	1 quart
MUSTARD, PREPARED	2 tablespoons
LEMON JUICE	1 tablespoon
CAPERS	as needed
PIMIENTO	as needed

Procedure

1. Chill cans of salmon thoroughly.

2. Sprinkle gelatine over water to soften; dissolve over hot water. Cool.

3. Combine cooled gelatine, mayonnaise, mustard and lemon juice; mix. Cool until slightly thickened.

4. Remove both ends from cans of salmon. Ease from can without breaking. Drain on paper towels.

5. Place salmon from two cans end to end, making four cylinder-shaped forms. Arrange on serving platters.

6. Spread with mayonnaise chaud-froid. Decorate with capers and pimiento, as desired. Chill. Garnish with greens and lemon wedges.

PINEAPPLE-WINE GLAZED HAM

Yield: approximately 3-1/2 quarts gelatin glaze

Ingredients

HAMS, CANNED (PULLMAN LOAVES)	
7 to 7-1/2 pound*	3
GELATINE, UNFLAVORED	2 tablespoons
WATER, cold	1/2 cup
GELATIN, ORANGE FLAVOR	12 ounces
WATER, boiling	1-1/4 quarts
LEMON JUICE	1 cup
SAUTERNE	2 cups
PINEAPPLE, CRUSHED (with syrup)	1-1/4 quarts

Procedure

1. Remove ham from can as label directs. Trim away gelatine and fat. Trim each ham on sides and top, if necessary, to make piece about 1/2 inch smaller, all around, than straight-sided 10-inch by 5-inch by 4-inch loaf pan.

2. Roughen top and sides of ham slightly with a fork. Set hams squarely in loaf pans.

3. Soften unflavored gelatine in cold water.

4. Dissolve orange gelatin in boiling water. Add softened unflavored gelatine; stir to dissolve.

5. Add lemon juice, wine and undrained pineapple. Chill until slightly thickened.

6. Pour enough of the pineapple mixture over each ham to fill sides and make a 1/2-inch layer on top. Chill until firm.

7. Unmold; turn, aspic side up, on serving platter.

8. Decorate as desired. To make flower, center a slice of pineapple with cherry tomato; make stem and leaves of green pepper.

9. Use a very sharp, thin blade knife for slicing. *Do not slice thin.*

*Pullman hams are available in various weights and lengths. Purchase to correspond with the size loaf pans which are to be used.

DEEP SEA MOLD

Yield: 12 portions

Ingredients

GELATINE, UNFLAVORED	1 ounce
WATER, cold	2 cups
SOUR CREAM	2 cups
SALAD DRESSING	2 cups
DILL WEED, DRIED	2 teaspoons
SALT	1-1/2 teaspoons
LEMON JUICE	1/3 cup
WORCESTERSHIRE SAUCE	2 teaspoons
ONION, minced	1 teaspoon
LIQUID HOT PEPPER SEASONING	1/4 teaspoon
TUNA, drained, flaked	4 7-ounce cans
SHRIMP, cooked, finely chopped	2-1/2 cups
CELERY, chopped	1-1/2 cups
GREEN PEPPER, chopped	1/2 cup
PIMIENTO, diced	1/4 cup

Procedure

1. Sprinkle gelatine over water in saucepan. Place over low heat; stir until gelatine dissolves, 3 to 5 minutes.

2. Remove from heat. Cool.

3. Combine sour cream and salad dressing; stir in seasonings. Blend mixture into cooled gelatine.

4. Fold in remaining ingredients.

5. Turn into a 3-quart mold. Chill until firm.

BEEF IN ASPIC

Yield: 32 portions

Ingredients

GELATINE, UNFLAVORED	2-1/4 ounces
STOCK, seasoned, cold	2 cups
STOCK, seasoned, hot	1 quart
TOMATOES, CANNED	1-1/2 quarts
ONION, minced	1/2 cup
GREEN PEPPER, finely chopped	1/3 cup
SALT	2 tablespoons
PEPPER	1 teaspoon
BEEF, cooked, chopped	2-1/2 pounds

Procedure

1. Soften gelatine in cold stock. Add to hot stock; stir until gelatine is dissolved. Cool.

2. Add tomatoes, onion, green pepper, salt and pepper. Fold in meat. Correct seasoning.

3. Chill until slightly thickened, stirring occasionally.

4. Turn into aspic-lined, decorated large molds or into loaf pans. Chill until firm.

Glazed Ham Prepared for Buffet Service

Cling Peach Advisory Board
California Prune Advisory Board

GLAZED CORNED BEEF BRISKET

Yield: approximately 48 portions

Ingredients

CORNED BEEF BRISKET	20 pounds
WATER	as needed
APPLESAUCE	1 cup
APRICOT NECTAR	1/2 cup
LEMON JUICE	1-1/2 tablespoons
SUGAR, BROWN	1/2 cup
SALT	1/2 teaspoon
WHOLE CLOVES	as needed

Procedure

1. Simmer meat in water to cover 4 to 5 hours or until tender.

2. Remove meat; place pieces, fat side up, on rack in open roasting pan.

3. Combine applesauce, nectar, lemon juice, brown sugar and salt. Spread over brisket. Stud with cloves. Bake in oven at 350°F. for 20 to 25 minutes or until glaze is set. Serve hot or cold.

Hot Buffet Items

ORIENTAL BEEF WITH APPLES ON RICE

Yield: 2 gallons, 32 1-cup portions, 1/2 cup rice

Ingredients

ONION, sliced	1 pound, 2 ounces
SHORTENING	7 ounces (1 cup)
GREEN PEPPER, cut in strips	2 pounds, 10 ounces
CANNED APPLE SLICES	1 No. 10 can
BEEF, ROUND OR CHUCK, trimmed and cubed	4-1/2 pounds
WATER	1-1/4 quarts
WORCESTERSHIRE SAUCE	3 tablespoons
SOY SAUCE	4-1/2 tablespoons
SALT	2 tablespoons
PEPPER	1 teaspoon
MONOSODIUM GLUTAMATE	1 tablespoon
CORNSTARCH	3 ounces (1/2 cup + 1 tablespoon)
WATER, cold	2/3 cup
RICE, cooked	1 gallon

Procedure

1. Saute onion in shortening until soft. Add green pepper, apples and beef.

2. Combine water, Worcestershire sauce, soy sauce, salt, pepper and monosodium glutamate. Pour over meat mixture. Cover; simmer for 2 to 2-1/2 hours or until meat is tender.

3. Blend cornstarch with cold water; stir into hot mixture; cook until thickened, stirring constantly.

4. Serve over hot cooked rice.

VEAL GOULASH

Yield: 50 6-ounce portions

Ingredients

VEAL, LEAN	11-1/2 pounds
SALT	1/2 cup
BLACK PEPPER	2 teaspoons
MONOSODIUM GLUTAMATE	4 teaspoons
ONION, finely chopped	1/2 pound
CELERY, cut fine	1/2 pound
FLOUR	1-1/4 pounds
OIL or MELTED CLEAR FAT	2 cups
TOMATOES	1 No. 2-1/2 can
	(3-1/2 cups)
GARLIC CLOVES, crushed	2 large
BAY LEAF, crushed	1
CLOVES, WHOLE	6
WATER	1-1/2 gallons

Procedure

1. Cube veal to 3/4-inch pieces. Or, cut in strips 1 inch by 1/2 inch. Spread in 12-inch by 20-inch pan. Stir salt, pepper and monosodium glutamate together; sprinkle 1/2 of it over meat.

2. Add onion and celery to meat; mix.

3. Sift flour over meat; mix well until all flour is taken up. Pour oil over; mix thoroughly again.

4. Brown in oven at 450°F. for 35 to 40 minutes. Stir frequently for even browning and to separate pieces. When meat is well browned, reduce oven heat to 350°F.

5. Simmer tomatoes with garlic, bay leaf and cloves for 10 to 15 minutes. Remove cloves.

6. Add tomatoes, water and remainder of seasonings (from step 1) to meat. Continue cooking in oven, stirring occasionally, until meat is very tender, about 1 hour. Replace water lost in cooking as needed.

QUICK CHICKEN STROGANOFF

Yield: 24 portions

Ingredients

BROILER-FRYER HALF-BREASTS, boned, skinned	24
COOKING OIL or RENDERED CHICKEN FAT	10 ounces
SALT	1/4 cup
ONION, finely chopped	1-1/2 pounds
MUSHROOMS, sliced	2 pounds
SHERRY or WATER	1-1/4 cups
THYME, POWDERED	1-1/2 teaspoons
PAPRIKA, SWEET	1 tablespoon
CORNSTARCH	1/4 cup
WATER, cold	1/2 cup
SOUR CREAM	1 quart

Procedure

1. Cut each half-breast into 10 or 12 strips.

2. Heat oil in skillet over high heat. Add chicken and salt. Cook, stirring constantly, 3 minutes.

3. Add onion and mushrooms; cook and stir 4 minutes longer.

4. Add sherry, thyme and paprika. Reduce heat to medium. Cover; cook 4 minutes more.

5. Blend cornstarch and water. Stir into mixture; cook until thickened.

6. Blend in sour cream. Heat, but do not boil.

7. Serve with hot cooked noodles or rice.

LAMB FRUIT CURRY

Yield: 24 portions

Ingredients

LAMB SHOULDER, LEAN	12 pounds
WATER	4 to 5 quarts
SALT	4 teaspoons
ONION, chopped	2 cups
CELERY, chopped	2 cups
GARLIC, minced	4 cloves
BUTTER or MARGARINE	2 ounces
SALT	4 teaspoons
PEPPER	1 teaspoon
CURRY POWDER	2 tablespoons
RAISINS	1/2 cup
APPLES, peeled, diced	4
COCONUT, FLAKED	1 cup
LAMB BROTH	1 gallon
FLOUR	1 cup
WATER, cold	1 cup
RICE, cooked, hot	1 gallon

Procedure

1. Wipe lamb shoulder; add to water; add salt. Simmer gently until tender.

2. Cool; skim fat from broth. Remove meat; cut into cubes.

3. Cook onion, celery and garlic in butter until tender. Add seasonings, fruit, coconut and lamb broth. Cook over low heat 30 to 40 minutes.

4. Blend flour and cold water to make a smooth paste. Stir into broth; cook and stir until thickened.

5. Add cubed lamb to sauce; heat thoroughly.

6. Serve over hot rice.

Roast Turkey Circled by Savory Stuffing

American Spice Trade Association

HUNGARIAN GOULASH

Yield: 50 portions

Ingredients

BEEF, BONELESS, cut in 1-1/2-inch pieces	16 pounds
FLOUR	2 cups
SHORTENING	3 ounces
GARLIC, finely chopped	2 cloves
ONION, chopped	3 pounds
CARAWAY SEEDS	1-1/2 tablespoons
BAY LEAF	1
MARJORAM	1/2 teaspoon
PAPRIKA	2 tablespoons
BEEF STOCK	1-1/2 gallons
TOMATO PUREE	2 No. 2-1/2 cans
SALT	1/4 cup
PEPPER	1 teaspoon

Procedure

1. Dredge meat with flour. Brown in fat.

2. Add garlic and onion; saute 10 minutes.

3. Soak caraway seeds in hot water for 30 minutes. Add bay leaf and marjoram; tie spices in muslin.

4. Add to meat with paprika, beef stock, tomato puree, salt and pepper. Simmer 2-1/2 hours, covered.

5. Skim off fat. Remove spice bag. Serve goulash on cooked flat noodles.

SCALLOPS ESPANOL

Yield: 6 quarts, 36 2/3-cup portions

Ingredients

SCALLOPS, FRESH or FROZEN	5 pounds
ONION, chopped	2 cups
GREEN PEPPER, chopped	1 cup
BUTTER or MARGARINE	12 ounces
SALT	1-1/2 tablespoons
SUGAR	1/4 cup
CAYENNE	1/2 teaspoon
MUSHROOMS, CANNED, sliced	1 cup
TOMATOES, CANNED, with juice	2 quarts
TAPIOCA, QUICK COOKING	1/4 cup

Procedure

1. Partially thaw frozen scallops, placing in colander to drain.
2. Saute onion and green pepper in butter until tender.
3. Add salt, sugar, cayenne, mushrooms, tomatoes and tapioca.
4. Bring to boil. Reduce heat; simmer 15 minutes, stirring frequently.
5. Add scallops; simmer just until scallops are done, approximately 10 minutes.
6. Serve over rice.

Note

If thicker sauce is desired, adjust thickening with cornstarch blended with tomato juice or water.

CACCIATORE CHICKEN CHUNKS

Yield: 16 3/4-cup portions

Ingredients

GARLIC CLOVES	4 medium
SALT	1/2 teaspoon
MUSHROOMS, CANNED, SLICED, drained	2-1/2 cups
BUTTER or MARGARINE	2 tablespoons
ONION, thinly sliced	1 pound
GREEN PEPPER, diced	1 cup
TOMATO SOUP, CONDENSED	1 51-ounce can
MUSHROOM LIQUID	1 cup
LEMON JUICE	2 tablespoons
OREGANO LEAF, crushed	1 teaspoon
CHICKEN, cooked, cut in 1-inch cubes	2 pounds

Procedure

1. Mince garlic with salt.

2. Drain mushrooms, reserving required amount of liquid.

3. Melt butter; add garlic, onion, green pepper and drained mushrooms. Saute until onion is tender.

4. Add soup, mushroom liquid, lemon juice and oregano. Simmer 10 minutes, stirring occasionally to avoid sticking.

5. Add chicken. Heat.

6. Serve over cooked rice, spaghetti or noodles.

DINNER ENTREES

Rosy Barbecued Chicken to Serve with Rice

The Rice Council

Fish and Seafood

FILLET OF SOLE WITH WHITE WINE

Yield: 48 portions

Ingredients

FILLETS OF SOLE or FLOUNDER	12 pounds
SALT	as needed
PEPPER	as needed
MONOSODIUM GLUTAMATE	1 tablespoon
BUTTER or MARGARINE	6 ounces
ONION, finely chopped	1/4 cup
PARSLEY, chopped	1/4 cup
MUSHROOMS, chopped	12 large
CELERY, finely chopped	1 quart
BAY LEAVES	4
SAUTERNE or RHINE WINE	2-1/2 quarts
WATER	1-1/4 quarts
BOUILLON CUBES	12
CREAM, LIGHT	1 cup
CHEESE, PARMESAN, grated	as needed

Procedure

1. Sprinkle fillets on both sides with salt, pepper and monosodium glutamate. Let stand while preparing sauce.

2. Melt butter in a large skillet, add onion, parsley, mushrooms, celery, bay leaves, wine, water and bouillon cubes. Heat thoroughly.

3. Lay seasoned fillets, a few at a time, in hot liquid; simmer until barely cooked. Remove carefully to shallow baking pans.

4. Reduce liquid to about half original quantity. Add cream; heat but do not boil.

5. Correct seasoning. Strain sauce over fish. Sprinkle with cheese.

6. Bake in oven at 450°F. until top is lightly browned, about 10 minutes.

LOBSTER THERMIDOR

Yield: 24 portions

Ingredients

WHITE TABLE WINE	1 4/5-quart bottle
WATER	1 quart
ONION, chopped	1-1/2 cups
CELERY, chopped	1-1/2 cups
CARROT, chopped	1 cup
PARSLEY	4 sprigs
SALT	1 tablespoon
TARRAGON	2 teaspoons
PEPPERCORNS, WHOLE	1/2 teaspoon
BAY LEAVES	2
LOBSTER TAILS, 8-OUNCE	24
STOCK FROM COOKING LOBSTER	1-1/2 quarts
BUTTER or MARGARINE	10 ounces
FLOUR	6 ounces (1-1/2 cups)
MUSTARD, DRY	2 tablespoons
CAYENNE PEPPER	dash
CREAM, HEAVY	2 cups
RIPE OLIVES, sliced	3 cups
CHEESE, GRUYERE, grated	1 cup

Procedure

1. Combine wine, water, vegetables, salt, tarragon, peppercorns and bay leaves. Cover; simmer 10 minutes.

2. Add lobster tails; simmer 20 minutes.

3. Remove lobster tails; cool sufficiently to handle.

4. Carefully remove meat from shells, keeping shells intact   Dice lobster meat.

5. Strain stock, reserving required amount.

6. Melt butter; blend in flour. Cook over low heat. Blend in mustard and cayenne. Gradually blend in stock and cream. Cook and stir until sauce thickens. Add olives.

7. Reserve 1-1/2 cups sauce for tops of lobsters.

8. Add diced lobster meat to remaining sauce; heap into shells.

9. Spoon reserved sauce over filled shells; sprinkle with cheese.

10. Place under broiler until thoroughly heated and lightly browned.

Ham and Pork

GLAZED HAM

Yield: 2-1/2 quarts glaze (for 3 to 4 hams)

Ingredients

SMOKED or CANNED HAMS	3 or 4
	(30 to 40 pounds)
GELATIN, ORANGE FLAVOR	1-1/2 pounds
SALT	1-1/2 teaspoons
WATER, hot	1 quart
CORN SYRUP, LIGHT	1 quart
CLOVES, WHOLE (optional)	as needed

Procedure

1. Bake ham according to label directions.

2. Dissolve gelatin and salt in hot water. Add corn syrup; stir until blended. Cool. (If mixture becomes too thick, stir over hot water until just slightly thick.)

3. To glaze hams, remove from oven 30 to 40 minutes before done; pour off drippings. If hams have rind, remove it at this time. Score fat; stud with whole cloves, if desired.

4. Spoon 1/3 of the slightly thickened gelatin mixture over tops of hams. Return to finish baking, spooning rest of glaze over ham in two additions.

Note

If glazing less than the full number of hams, store leftover glaze in refrigerator for future use. Or, make *Raisin Sauce*: Combine 1 quart of glaze with 1 cup raisins and 1 cup drained mandarin oranges.

GOURMET HAM SLICE

Yield: 12 portions

Ingredients

HAM (FULLY COOKED) CENTER SLICES cut 2-inches thick	2
CLOVES, WHOLE	as needed
PINEAPPLE TIDBITS, CANNED	1-1/4 quarts
SYRUP DRAINED FROM PINEAPPLE	1/2 cup
MUSTARD, PREPARED	2 tablespoons
SUGAR, BROWN	1/4 cup
VINEGAR	2 tablespoons
CELERY, finely chopped	1/2 cup
ONION, finely chopped	1/2 cup
BUTTER or MARGARINE	2 ounces
CORNBREAD or CORN MUFFIN CRUMBS	3 cups
SALT	1/2 teaspoon
PEPPER	1/8 teaspoon
SAGE, POWDERED	1/2 teaspoon
MILK (optional)	1/4 cup
PARSLEY, chopped	as needed

Procedure

1. Stud sides of ham with whole cloves; place in shallow baking pan.

2. Drain pineapple. Measure required amount of syrup; reserve fruit.

3. Pour pineapple syrup over ham. Cover; bake in oven at 350°F. for 1 hour.

4. Remove from oven. Spread top of ham with mustard. Arrange pineapple tidbits over top. Sprinkle with brown sugar; drizzle with vinegar.

5. Saute celery and onion in butter until tender but not brown. Add cornbread crumbs and seasonings. Moisten with milk, if desired.

6. Spoon stuffing on pineapple, pressing down lightly to shape.

7. Mark diagonal lines in top with knife. Cover; continue baking 15 minutes. Uncover; bake 15 minutes longer or until lightly browned.

8. Fill in diagonal lines with chopped parsley.

Ham with Party Garnish

Pickle Packers International, Inc.

BAKED HAM WITH PEANUT BUTTER CRUST

Yield: 1 ham

Ingredients

HAM, SMOKED, 12-to 14-POUND SIZE	1
SUGAR, BROWN	1/2 cup
PEANUT BUTTER	1/2 cup
MUSTARD, DRY	1/2 teaspoon

Procedure

1. Place ham, fat side up, on rack in open roasting pan. Insert meat thermometer so bulb reaches the center of thickest part and does not rest in fat or on bone. Do not add water.

2. Bake, uncovered, in oven at 300°F. until thermometer registers 160°F. Allow 18 to 20 minutes per pound for baking.

3. Combine brown sugar, peanut butter and mustard. About 30 minutes before end of baking time, spread ham with peanut butter mixture. Return to oven to finish baking.

ORANGE-RAISIN STUFFED PORK CHOPS ➤

Yield: 25 portions

Ingredients

PORK RIB CHOPS, CUT 3/4 to 1 INCH THICK	25 (6 to 8 pounds)
BREAD CRUMBS, dry	2 quarts
NUTMEG, GROUND	2 teaspoons
ORANGE PULP, diced	1 quart
SEEDLESS RAISINS	2 cups
LARD or DRIPPINGS	1/2 pound (1 cup)
SALT	as needed
PEPPER	as needed
ORANGE JUICE	1 cup
WATER	1 cup

HUNGARIAN PORK CHOPS

Yield: 25 portions

Ingredients

PORK CHOPS, LEAN, 5-OUNCE	25
FLOUR	3/4 cup
SALT	1 tablespoon
PEPPER, WHITE	1/2 teaspoon
SHORTENING	1/2 cup
CREAM OF MUSHROOM SOUP, CONDENSED	1 50-ounce can
WATER	1 cup
THYME	1 teaspoon
ONION, thinly sliced	1-1/2 cups (6 ounces)
PARSLEY, chopped	1 cup
SOUR CREAM	1 cup

Procedure

1. Dip chops in seasoned flour. Brown in shortening. Arrange in steam table pans.

2. Pour off fat from skillet in which chops were browned. Blend soup, water and thyme in the skillet. Heat.

3. Add onion, parsley and sour cream. Mix thoroughly.

4. Pour sauce over browned chops.

5. Cover; bake in oven at 350°F. for 1 hour or until tender.

6. Garnish with additional parsley, if desired.

Procedure

1. Make a pocket in each chop by cutting into the chop along the bone. (Chops cut from this side hold the stuffing better.)

2. Combine bread crumbs, nutmeg, orange pulp and raisins. Mix well.

3. Fill the pockets with the stuffing mixture.

4. Brown the chops on both sides in lard or drippings (chops may be browned in deep fat if preferred). Drain.

5. Arrange chops in baking pan. Season with salt and pepper; add orange juice and water.

6. Cover tightly; cook slowly on top of range or in oven at 350°F. for 45 minutes to 1 hour, or until done.

PORK STEAKS IN SPANISH SAUCE

Yield: 40 portions

Ingredients

SHORTENING, melted	1 cup
ONION, chopped	1 quart
CELERY, chopped	1 quart
GREEN PEPPER, chopped	2 cups
FLOUR	1/2 cup
TOMATOES	1 No. 10 can
SALT	4 teaspoons
SUGAR	1 tablespoon
BAY LEAVES	2
PORK STEAKS	40
SHORTENING	as needed

Procedure

1. Combine melted shortening, onion, celery and green pepper. Cook until tender but not brown.

2. Blend flour into vegetable mixture.

3. Add tomatoes and seasonings, cook and stir until thickened. Continue cooking until vegetables are tender. Remove bay leaves.

4. Brown pork steaks in a small amount of shortening. Remove to baking pan.

5. Pour sauce over steaks. Cover; bake in oven at 350°F. for 1-1/2 hours or until done.

Jelly Glaze Adds Flair to Pork

Concord Grape Association

BAKED STUFFED PORK CHOPS

Yield: 30 portions

Ingredients

PORK CHOPS, CUT 3 TO POUND	30
CORNBREAD DRESSING *(Recipe, facing page)*	3 pounds
SALT	1-1/2 tablespoons
PEPPER	2 teaspoons
FLOUR	as needed

Procedure

1. Split pork chops through center to bone; stuff with cornbread dressing.

2. Season with salt and pepper.

3. Arrange in baking pan. Sprinkle lightly with flour.

4. Bake in oven at 350°F. until well done.

CORNBREAD DRESSING

Yield: 7 pounds

Ingredients

CORNBREAD, baked, dry	
(use unsweetened type of cornbread)	12 ounces
WHITE BREAD or ROLLS, dry	1-1/2 pounds
CHICKEN STOCK, hot	1-1/2 quarts
ONION, finely chopped	1/2 pound
CELERY, finely chopped	1/2 pound
BUTTER or CHICKEN FAT or FAT	
FROM MEAT TO BE USED	12 ounces
THYME	1-1/2 teaspoons
SAGE	1-1/2 teaspoons
SALT	1-1/2 tablespoons
PEPPER	1-1/2 teaspoons

Procedure

1. Grind dry (staled) cornbread and white bread fine on machine.

2. Pour hot chicken stock over crumbs; steam 10 minutes.

3. Saute onion and celery in butter or other fat until just golden; add to bread mixture.

4. Add seasonings; mix well.

Note

To bake dressing separately: place in a baking pan; bake in oven at 350°F. for 30 to 45 minutes. Cover pan with foil, if desired, to avoid formation of crust.

CURRIED PORK CHOPS

Yield: 25 portions

Ingredients

PORK CHOPS (6-OUNCE)	25
FLOUR	3/4 cup
SHORTENING or OIL	1/4 cup
MUSHROOMS, sliced	1-1/2 pounds
BUTTER or MARGARINE	1/4 pound
ONION, chopped	1-1/2 cups
FLOUR	3/4 cup
MILK, hot	1-1/2 quarts
WATER	3/4 cup
SALT	2-1/2 tablespoons
PEPPER	3/4 teaspoon
CURRY POWDER	1 tablespoon
RICE, cooked (plain or with parsley or raisins)	1 gallon

Procedure

1. Dredge chops with flour. Brown both sides in shortening.

2. Place chops in single layer in baking pans. Cover with mushrooms.

3. Melt butter; add onion. Cook over low heat until golden brown. Stir in flour.

4. Add milk, water and seasonings. Cook over low heat, stirring constantly, until thickened.

5. Pour sauce over chops. Cover; bake in oven at 350°F. for 1-1/2 hours or until chops are tender.

6. Skim off surface fat. Serve with plain, parsley or raisin rice.

ORANGE PORK CHOPS

Yield: 24 portions (1 chop, 1 ounce sauce)

Ingredients

PORK CHOPS, CENTER CUT, 3 TO A POUND	24
SALT	as needed
PEPPER	as needed
PAPRIKA	as needed
SUGAR	1-1/2 cups
CORNSTARCH	1/2 cup
SALT	1 teaspoon
CINNAMON	1-1/2 teaspoons
CLOVES, WHOLE	2 tablespoons
ORANGE RIND, grated from	1 large orange
ORANGE JUICE, FRESH or FROZEN ORANGE JUICE CONCENTRATE, reconstituted	3 cups 1 6-ounce can
ORANGE SLICES, halved or ORANGE SECTIONS, chilled, drained	24 2 quarts

Procedure

1. Sprinkle chops with salt, pepper and paprika. Braise until tender.

2. Combine sugar, cornstarch, salt, cinnamon, cloves, grated orange rind and orange juice; cook and stir until thickened and clear.

3. Add orange slices or sections. Cover; remove from heat.

4. Spoon sauce carefully over chops to retain shape of orange pieces.

FESTIVE HAWAIIAN PORK

Yield: 48 portions

Ingredients

GREEN PEPPER	2-1/2 pounds
TOMATOES, RIPE, FIRM	4 pounds
PINEAPPLE CHUNKS	1/2 No. 10 can
EGGS, beaten	12
FLOUR	2 cups
SALT	2-2/3 tablespoons
PEPPER	2 teaspoons
PORK, boneless, cut in 1/2-inch cubes	12 pounds
LARD FOR DEEP-FAT FRYING	as needed
SUGAR	1 quart
CORNSTARCH	2 cups
SOY SAUCE	2 cups
VINEGAR	1 quart
PINEAPPLE JUICE	2 quarts
RICE or CHINESE NOODLES	48 portions

Procedure

1. Wash peppers; trim. Cut into strips 1/4-inch by 2-inches. Blanch in salted boiling water about 5 minutes; drain.

2. Peel tomatoes; cut into wedges; remove seeds.

3. Drain pineapple, reserving juice. Measure juice; add additional juice to make required amount.

4. Combine beaten eggs, flour, salt and pepper. Mix well.

5. Coat pork in egg batter. Fry in deep fat at 350°F. until golden brown, about 6 to 8 minutes. Drain.

6. Mix sugar and cornstarch. Add soy sauce, vinegar and pineapple juice. Cook, stirring until thickened and clear.

7. Add meat to sauce; simmer until meat is done, about 15 to 20 minutes.

8. Add green pepper, tomatoes and pineapple chunks. Cook until just heated through, about 5 minutes.

9. Serve over hot cooked rice or Chinese noodles.

Lamb

ENGLISH LAMB CHOPS WITH CURRY SAUCE

Yield: 25 portions

Ingredients

BUTTER or MARGARINE	1/2 pound
ONION, sliced from	5 large onions
APPLES, peeled, chopped	3-3/4 quarts
FLOUR	1-1/4 cups
CURRY POWDER	1/2 to 1 cup
SALT	1-1/2 tablespoons
PEPPER	1/2 teaspoon
STOCK or BOUILLON	2-1/2 quarts
LEMON JUICE	1/3 cup
ENGLISH LAMB CHOPS, CUT 1-INCH THICK	25
COCONUT, FLAKED	2 cups

Procedure

1. Melt butter; add onion and apples. Cook over low heat, stirring occasionally, 5 minutes.

2. Add flour, curry powder, salt and pepper; blend. Gradually add stock and lemon juice.

3. Cook and stir over low heat until thickened. Cover; simmer over low heat 20 minutes, stirring frequently.

4. Broil lamb chops to desired doneness. Serve with curry sauce; sprinkle with coconut.

RACK OF LAMB WITH STRAWBERRY GLAZE

Yield: 24 portions

Ingredients

MINT LEAVES, chopped	2 tablespoons
SALT	1 tablespoon
PEPPER	3/4 teaspoon
LAMB RACKS (8-RIBS EACH)	6
STRAWBERRY JELLY or JAM	1-1/2 quarts
FROZEN ORANGE JUICE CONCENTRATE, thawed	1-1/2 cups
LEMON JUICE	2 tablespoons
CINNAMON	3/4 teaspoon
WORCESTERSHIRE SAUCE	1 tablespoon
PARSLEY, coarsely chopped	as needed

Procedure

1. Combine mint leaves, salt and pepper; rub mixture into lamb racks.

2. Place lamb, meat side up, on racks in roasting pans. Insert thermometers in meatiest part of roasts. Place in oven at 325°F.

3. Combine jelly or jam, orange juice, lemon juice, cinnamon and Worcestershire sauce; bring to a boil. Brush lamb racks with strawberry mixture frequently. Roast until meat thermometers register 145°F.

4. Serve 2 ribs per portion. Garnish with chopped parsley. Heat any surplus basting mixture and serve as a sauce, if desired.

ROAST LAMB TORTOLA

Yield: approximately 50 portions

Ingredients

GARLIC CLOVES, sliced	4
LAMB SHOULDER ROASTS, BONELESS, NETTED	4
GINGER, GROUND	1-1/2 tablespoons
MUSTARD, DRY	1-1/2 tablespoons
COFFEE, strong, hot	1 quart
SUGAR	3 tablespoons
CREAM or NON-DAIRY CREAMER	3/4 cup
PORT WINE	3/4 cup
PAN JUICES AND WATER	1-1/2 quarts
FAT (FROM PAN)	1/2 cup
FLOUR	1/2 cup
CURRANT JELLY	1-1/3 cups

Procedure

1. Insert garlic slices into lamb.

2. Combine ginger and mustard; rub over lamb.

3. Place in baking pan. Roast in oven at 325°F. allowing 40 minutes per pound or until meat thermometer registers 175°F.

4. After 1 hour of roasting, combine coffee, sugar, cream and wine; pour over lamb. Continue roasting, basting occasionally with mixture in pan, for remainder of roasting time.

5. Remove meat; keep warm.

6. Skim fat from pan juices. Reserve required amount of fat. Add water to pan juices to make required amount.

7. Blend fat with flour; add pan juice liquid and jelly. Cook and stir until thickened and smooth.

8. Serve sauce with lamb.

Veal

VEAL CUTLETS ROMANA

Yield: 50 portions

Ingredients

VEAL CUTLETS, pounded thin	20 pounds
FLOUR	10 ounces (2-1/2 cups)
SHORTENING	1-1/4 pounds
MUSHROOMS, FRESH, sliced	2-1/2 pounds
ONION, chopped	8 ounces
WATER, hot	2 quarts
SAUTERNE WINE	1-1/4 quarts
PARSLEY, chopped	1 cup
LEMON JUICE	2/3 cup
CHICKEN SOUP BASE	5 ounces (2/3 cup)
PEPPER	1 teaspoon
BROCCOLI SPEARS, FROZEN	12-1/2 pounds
BREAD CRUMBS, buttered	1 quart

Procedure

1. Dust cutlets with flour. Brown in shortening. Transfer to baking pan.

2. Saute mushrooms and onion until lightly browned.

3. Add water, wine, parsley, lemon juice, soup base and pepper. Bring to a boil; simmer 2 to 3 minutes.

4. Pour sauce over cutlets. Cover; bake in oven at 350°F. for about 45 minutes, or until cutlets are tender. If desired, thicken sauce with additional flour.

5. Cook broccoli until crisp tender.

6. To serve, arrange portions of veal with broccoli; top with buttered crumbs.

VEAL CACCIATORE

Yield: 80 portions

Ingredients

GREEN PEPPER, chopped	1-1/2 quarts
ONION, finely chopped	2 quarts
GARLIC, INSTANT GRANULATED	1 tablespoon
COOKING OIL	1-1/2 cups
MUSHROOMS, sliced, undrained	6 8-ounce cans
TOMATOES	1 No. 10 can
TOMATO PUREE	1-1/4 quarts
VINEGAR	1/2 cup
BAY LEAF, crumbled	1 small
SALT	1/4 cup
PEPPER	2 tablespoons
FLOUR	2 pounds, 12 ounces
SALT	1/4 cup
PEPPER	4 teaspoons
VEAL, BONELESS, 1/8-INCH SLICES (3-OUNCES EACH)	30 pounds
PARMESAN CHEESE (optional)	as needed

Procedure

1. Saute green pepper, onion, and garlic in oil until tender.

2. Add mushrooms, tomatoes, tomato puree, vinegar, bay leaf and first amount of salt and pepper. Cover; simmer 30 minutes, stirring occasionally.

3. Combine flour and remaining salt and pepper. Dredge veal.

4. Grill meat on a well-greased grill until browned on both sides and meat is done. Place cutlets in steam table pans or arrange in serving dishes. Pour sauce over meat.

5. Sprinkle portions with Parmesan cheese, if desired.

VEAL OSCAR

Yield: 1 portion

Ingredients
For each portion allow:

VEAL CUTLET, 8-ounce	1
SALT	as needed
PEPPER	as needed
BUTTER	as needed
ASPARAGUS SPEARS, cooked, hot	3
LOBSTER MEAT, chopped	1 ounce
BUTTON MUSHROOMS, heated	2
BEARNAISE SAUCE *(Recipe, facing page)*	1 ounce

Procedure

1. Season veal with salt and pepper. Saute in butter until just done.
2. Place on hot serving dish.
3. Top with hot cooked asparagus. Place a layer of lobster meat (heated) on top of asparagus; the button mushrooms on top of lobster. Pour Bearnaise sauce over all.

Elegant Arrangement for Entree

Cling Peach Advisory Board

BEARNAISE SAUCE

Yield: 1 quart

Ingredients

DRY WHITE WINE	2 cups
EGG YOLKS, well-beaten	6
VINEGAR, TARRAGON	1/4 cup
PARSLEY, chopped	2 tablespoons
SHALLOTS, chopped	2 tablespoons
TARRAGON, GROUND	1-1/2 teaspoons
CHERVIL	1-1/2 teaspoons
SALT	1 teaspoon
BLACK PEPPER, FRESHLY GROUND	as needed
BUTTER, melted	1 pound

Procedure

1. Beat 1/4 cup of wine into the beaten egg yolks; set aside.

2. Combine remaining wine with vinegar, parsley, shallots, 1/2 teaspoon of the tarragon, 1/2 teaspoon of the chervil, salt and pepper; simmer slowly 15 minutes, stirring occasionally.

3. Remove from heat. Add egg yolks, stirring briskly. Add butter, 2 tablespoons at a time, beating thoroughly after each addition. Strain through a fine sieve.

4. Add remaining tarragon and chervil; blend well.

Stuffings

TOASTED RICE STUFFING

Yield: 9 quarts (for 2 24-pound turkeys)

Ingredients

RICE, UNCOOKED	1-1/2 quarts
WATER	3 quarts
SALT	1-1/2 tablespoons
ONION, chopped	1 cup
CELERY, chopped	1-1/2 cups
MARGARINE	1 pound
BREAD CRUMBS, fine toasted	3 quarts
EGGS, slightly beaten	12
POULTRY SEASONING	1 tablespoon
PECANS, broken (optional)	1 quart
SALT	as needed
PEPPER	as needed

Procedure

1. Spread uncooked rice in shallow pan; bake in oven at 350°F. for 20 to 30 minutes or until light brown. Stir rice occasionally to insure uniform browning.

2. Place toasted rice in saucepan; add water and salt; bring to boil. Cover with tight-fitting lid; lower heat; simmer until tender. Remove lid to permit rice to steam dry.

3. Saute onion and celery in margarine until onion is transparent but not brown.

4. Combine with rice and remaining ingredients. Season with salt and pepper.

5. Stuff lightly into turkey prepared for roasting. Or, turn into baking pan; bake in oven at 375°F. until thoroughly heated through.

Fruited Stuffing in Special Portions

Cling Peach Advisory Board

CARROT BREAD STUFFING

Yield: 3 quarts (48 1/4-cup portions)

Ingredients

SHORTENING or BACON FAT, melted	1-1/2 cups
BREAD CUBES, soft	3 gallons (3-3/4 pounds)
CARROTS, grated	2 quarts (2 pounds)
ONION, finely chopped	2 cups
EGGS, beaten	1 quart (2 pounds)
SALT	2 tablespoons
BOUILLON	1 quart

Procedure

1. Combine melted shortening, bread cubes, carrots, onion, beaten eggs and salt. Add bouillon; mix thoroughly.

Note

This stuffing may be used with any variety of meat, poultry or fish. Or, it may be baked separately in a greased 12-inch by 20-inch by 2-1/2-inch pan in oven at 375°F. for 1 hour. Use a No. 16 scoop to portion stuffing.

FABULOUS APPLE STUFFING   ⟶

Yield: 48 portions (3/4 cup)

Ingredients

BUTTER or MARGARINE	12 ounces
ONION, chopped	1-1/4 pounds
CELERY, chopped	1 pound, 2 ounces
SAUSAGE MEAT, broken up	1-1/2 pounds
HERB SEASONED STUFFING	3 pounds
APPLE JUICE	2 quarts
APPLE SLICES, drained, chopped	1 No. 10 can
POULTRY SEASONING	2-1/2 teaspoons
SALT	1-1/2 teaspoons
PARSLEY, chopped	1/3 cup

CHICKEN-ALMOND BREAD STUFFING
(for Roast Turkey)

Yield: 48 1/2-cup portions

Ingredients

BREAD CUBES, soft, 1/2 inch	3 pounds, 12 ounces
WATER	4-1/2 cups
CREAM OF CHICKEN SOUP, CONDENSED	1 50 or 51 ounce can
ALMONDS, SLIVERED, BLANCHED	1-1/2 cups
ONION, INSTANT MINCED	2 tablespoons
ROSEMARY, crushed	1 teaspoon

Procedure

1. Toast bread cubes.

2. Gradually blend water with undiluted soup in a 1-gallon measure; stir until smooth with a wire whip.

3. Combine toasted bread cubes, soup mixture, almonds, onion and rosemary in a 4-gallon mixing bowl, using 2 large forks to blend ingredients.

4. Place in a greased 12-inch by 20-inch by 2-1/2-inch steam table pan. Bake in oven at 350°F. for 30 to 35 minutes or until browned.

5. Portion with a No. 8 scoop, or cut pan into 48 portions.

Procedure

1. Melt butter. Add onion and celery; saute until onion is transparent.

2. Add sausage meat; cook until lightly browned.

3. Combine remaining ingredients; add sausage mixture. Mix lightly but well.

4. Turn into two 12-inch by 20-inch by 2-1/2-inch pans. Cover with foil. Bake in oven at 375°F. for 40 minutes.

5. Serve topped with sliced turkey, roast pork, oven fried chicken or roast duck and gravy.

FRUITED RICE, DRESSING OR STUFFING

Yield: 50 2/3-cup portions

Ingredients

CELERY, diced	1 pound
ONION, finely chopped	10 ounces
BUTTER or MARGARINE	1-1/2 pounds
ORANGE PEEL, coarsely grated	1-1/2 cups
SALT	4 tablespoons
POULTRY SEASONING	1 tablespoon
ORANGE JUICE	3 quarts
WATER	3 quarts
RICE, UNCOOKED	3 quarts (5-1/4 pounds)

Procedure

1. Saute celery and onion in butter until tender. Add orange peel, salt, poultry seasoning, orange juice, water and rice.

2. Bring to a boil; stir well. Reduce heat; cover tightly; simmer about 25 minutes, or according to package directions.

Variations

1. Add 1-1/4 pounds currants with the uncooked rice. When done, add 1 pound slivered toasted almonds; toss lightly.

2. Substitute chicken broth for orange juice and water. Add 2-1/2 pounds snipped dried apricots with the uncooked rice. Or, add 2 pounds diced fresh apples when rice is done.

Game

VENISON RAGOUT

Yield: 12 3/4-cup portions

Ingredients

VENISON, cut in 1-1/2-inch cubes	5 pounds
MARINADE *(Recipe, facing page)*	5 cups
SHORTENING	1/2 cup
FLOUR	1/2 cup
TOMATO PUREE	1 cup
BOUILLON	2 cups
JUNIPER BERRIES, crushed (optional)	3
HERB BOUQUET OF PARSLEY, SAGE AND THYME	1
MUSHROOMS, sliced	1 pound
GREEN ONIONS WITH TOPS, chopped	1 cup
BUTTER	2 ounces
FLOUR	1/2 cup

Procedure

1. Place venison in an earthenware bowl. Add marinade; cover; refrigerate 24 hours, turning meat several times in marinade.

2. Drain meat; pat dry. Reserve 1 cup of the marinade.

3. Saute meat in shortening until seared on all sides. Sprinkle meat with first amount of flour; continue cooking until brown.

4. Add reserved marinade, tomato puree, bouillon, juniper berries and herb bouquet. Bring to a boil; cover. Reduce heat; simmer 1-1/2 hours or until meat is tender. Add additional bouillon if needed. Cool; skim off fat.

5. Saute mushrooms and green onions in butter 5 minutes. Blend in remaining flour; cook until lightly browned.

6. Add flour mixture to meat; simmer until thickened.

7. Serve over Almondine rice. *(Recipe, facing page)*

MARINADE FOR VENISON

Yield: 5 cups

Ingredients

DRY RED WINE	1 bottle (4/5 qt.)
RED WINE VINEGAR	1/4 cup
CARROTS, sliced	1 cup
ONION, sliced	1 cup
WHOLE PEPPERCORNS	1 teaspoon
WHOLE CLOVES	1/2 teaspoon
JUNIPER BERRIES (optional)	1/2 teaspoon
THYME	1/2 teaspoon
PARSLEY, chopped	1 tablespoon
BAY LEAVES	2
SALT	1 tablespoon

Procedure

1. Combine all ingredients.

RICE ALMONDINE

Yield: 12 3/4-cup portions

Ingredients

BUTTER or MARGARINE	3 ounces
RICE, UNCOOKED	3 cups
GREEN ONIONS WITH TOPS, chopped	3 cups
BEEF or CHICKEN BROTH	1-1/2 quarts
SALT	1 tablespoon
ALMONDS, UNBLANCHED, sliced	1-1/2 cups

Procedure

1. Melt butter; add rice and chopped green onions; saute until golden but not brown.

2. Add broth and salt. Bring to a boil; stir once. Cover; simmer for 14 minutes or until rice is tender.

3. Remove from heat. Add almonds; toss lightly.

Poultry

CHICKEN KIEV

Yield: 12 portions

Ingredients

BUTTER, softened	3/4 cup (6 ounces)
GARLIC, minced	1 clove
PARSLEY, minced	2 tablespoons
CHIVES, minced	2 tablespoons
SALT	2 teaspoons
PEPPER	1/2 teaspoon
ROSEMARY, GROUND	1-1/2 teaspoons
CHICKEN BREASTS (BROILER-FRYER), boned	12
FLOUR	1-1/2 cups
SALT	1 teaspoon
EGGS, slightly beaten	3
WATER	3 tablespoons

Procedure

1. Combine softened butter with garlic, parsley, chives, first amount of salt, pepper and rosemary. Form into a log. Freeze until hard. Cut into 12 equal pieces.

2. Remove skin from chicken. Pound each breast to 1/4-inch thickness.

3. Place 1 piece of hardened butter mixture on each flattened piece of chicken. Roll chicken around butter; secure edges with wooden picks or skewers.

4. Combine flour and remaining salt. Combine eggs and water. Roll chicken in flour; dip in egg mixture; roll again in flour.

5. Fry chicken in deep fat at 375°F. using a fry basket. Caution: do not prick or pierce chicken. Cook 15 to 18 minutes or until golden brown and tender.

BALLOTINE OF CHICKEN

Yield: 25 portions

Ingredients

BREAD CRUMBS, WHITE, soft	5 ounces
MILK, hot	1-1/4 cups
BUTTER or MARGARINE	4-1/2 ounces
EGG	1 large
EGG YOLKS	2
SALT	1-1/2 teaspoons
PEPPER, WHITE	1/8 teaspoon
NUTMEG	1/8 teaspoon
VEAL, ground	1 pound, 5 ounces
DRY SHERRY WINE	1/4 cup
RIPE OLIVE HALVES	8 ounces
BONED CHICKEN LEGS WITH THIGHS	25 large
BUTTER or MARGARINE, melted	as needed

Procedure

1. Combine bread crumbs and milk. Cook and stir over low heat until mixture is so thick it leaves sides of pan and forms a ball.

2. Turn out into shallow pan. Cover closely to prevent surface drying. Chill.

3. Cream butter, add bread crumb mixture, egg and egg yolks; beat until smooth.

4. Add seasonings, veal and sherry; mix well.

5. Stir in olives. Chill.

6. Pound out chicken legs slightly. Portion approximately 2 ounces filling on each leg (rounded No. 24 scoop). Fold meat over stuffing, shaping into a ball. Skewer.

7. Arrange stuffed legs in shallow pan; brush with melted butter.

8. Bake in oven at 400°F. for 30 minutes. Reduce heat to 350°F.; bake 20 minutes longer or until chicken is tender. Remove skewers before serving.

CHICKEN AND HAM, NEW ORLEANS

Yield: 30 portions

Ingredients

CHICKEN BREASTS, boned, split in half	15
FLOUR	2-1/2 cups
SALT	1-1/2 tablespoons
PEPPER	1/2 teaspoon
CELERY SALT	1-1/2 teaspoons
PAPRIKA	2-1/2 teaspoons
HAM, COOKED BONELESS ROLL	30 1/4-inch slices
EGGS, beaten	2 cups
MILK	2-1/2 cups
CLOVES, GROUND	3/4 teaspoon
SALT	1-1/2 teaspoons
CORNMEAL, YELLOW	3 cups
SANDWICH BREAD	30 slices
CREAM OF CHICKEN SOUP, CONDENSED	1-1/2 quarts
MUSHROOMS, drained	3-1/3 cups
PIMIENTO, chopped, drained	1/2 cup
MILK	1 cup
SHERRY	1 cup

Procedure

1. Wash chicken breasts; dry.

2. Combine flour, first amount of salt, pepper, celery salt and paprika. Dredge chicken in seasoned flour, coating all surfaces.

3. Place chicken, skin side down, in hot fat in a heavy, deep skillet; brown on both sides. Cover tightly; simmer 15 to 20 minutes or until tender.

4. Fry or grill ham slices, browning both sides.

5. Combine eggs, first amount of milk, cloves and remaining salt.

6. Place cornmeal in shallow pan.

7. Dip bread slices, one at a time, into egg mixture, then in cornmeal, turning to coat both sides. Brown on both sides on a medium hot, well-greased griddle.

8. Combine soup, mushrooms, pimiento and remaining milk. Heat, stirring to keep smooth. Add sherry just before serving.

9. To serve: put ham slice on each slice of corn toast. Top with a piece of fried chicken. Pour 2-2/3-ounce ladle of sauce over serving.

CORNISH HEN A LA RUSSE

Yield: 25 portions

Ingredients

CORNISH HENS, 1-POUND SIZE	25
SALT	3 tablespoons
CELERY LEAVES from	1 stalk
LEMONS, cut in wedges	3 lemons
BUTTER or MARGARINE, melted	1 pound
LEMON JUICE	1/2 cup

Procedure

1. Season hens inside and out with salt. Place a few celery leaves and a lemon wedge inside each hen.
2. Place breast side up, in shallow roasting pan.
3. Combine melted butter and lemon juice. Brush hens well with mixture.
4. Roast, uncovered, in oven at 350°F. for 1 hour or until tender, basting occasionally with butter mixture.
5. Serve with Russian Sour Cream Sauce.*

*RUSSIAN SOUR CREAM SAUCE

Yield: 25 portions

Ingredients

SOUR CREAM	1-1/2 quarts
CHICKEN STOCK	1-1/2 cups
SAUTERNE WINE	1-1/2 cups
DEHYDRATED ONION, MINCED	3/4 cup
MUSHROOMS, sliced	3 pounds
BUTTER	12 ounces
SUGAR	2 tablespoons
GREEN OLIVES, PIMIENTO STUFFED, sliced	1-1/2 quarts

Procedure

1. Combine sour cream, chicken stock and wine.
2. Saute onion and sliced mushrooms in butter 5 minutes.
3. Add sour cream mixture, sugar and sliced olives; heat.

Baked Chicken with Rice and Corn Dressing
(Recipe, facing page)

The Rice Council

BAKED CHICKEN WITH RICE AND CORN STUFFING
(See picture, facing page)

Yield: 48 portions

Ingredients

BUTTER or MARGARINE, melted	8 ounces
LEMON JUICE	1/3 cup
BROILER-FRYERS, QUARTERED	12
SALT	2 tablespoons
PEPPER	1 teaspoon
PORK SAUSAGE, BULK	2 pounds
GREEN ONIONS (WITH TOPS), chopped	1-1/2 quarts
CELERY, chopped	1-1/2 quarts
RICE, hot (cooked in chicken broth)	1-1/2 gallons
CORN, WHOLE KERNEL, drained	1 No. 10 can
SALT	as needed
PEPPER	as needed

Procedure

1. Combine butter and lemon juice. Brush chicken pieces. Sprinkle with salt and pepper. Arrange in baking pans, skin side up.

2. Bake in oven at 375°F. for 45 minutes.

3. Saute sausage, chopped onions and celery until vegetables are tender. Add rice and corn. Season with salt and pepper.

4. Turn rice mixture into a baking pan. Arrange partially cooked chicken on top.

5. Bake 30 minutes longer or until chicken is done.

BREAST OF CHICKEN BEARNAISE

Yield: 24 portions

Ingredients

CHICKEN, HALF-BREASTS, boned, skinned	24 large
CHICKEN BROTH or WATER, salted	as needed
ASPARAGUS	96 large spears*
ONION, minced	4 teaspoons
TARRAGON WINE VINEGAR	1/3 cup
TARRAGON, DRIED	2 teaspoons
EGG YOLKS, large	7 (5 ounces)
BUTTER, melted	14 ounces
LEMON JUICE	4 teaspoons
CAYENNE	generous dash
RIPE OLIVES, sliced, drained	6 ounces (1-1/4 cups)
PARSLEY, finely chopped	2 tablespoons
PIMIENTO, cut in strips	as needed

Procedure

1. Poach chicken breasts in broth or salted water until done, about 25 minutes. Keep warm until ready to serve.

2. Trim asparagus; cook until just tender. Drain well.

3. Combine onion, vinegar and dried tarragon; cook rapidly until reduced to 1/2 its original volume. Strain into heavy saucepan. Cool to lukewarm.

4. Add egg yolks, beat briskly with wire whisk. Place over hot water or very low heat; gradually add butter, whisking until sauce thickens.

5. Remove from heat; blend in lemon juice and cayenne. Add olives and parsley.

6. Mask chicken breasts with a thin coating of the sauce. Serve with asparagus tips. Garnish asparagus with pimiento strips.

*Approximately 15 pounds fresh asparagus, as purchased.

COUNTRY CAPTAIN

Yield: 16 portions

Ingredients

CHICKEN, BROILER-FRYERS, cut in serving pieces	12 pounds
SALT	as needed
PEPPER	as needed
BUTTER or MARGARINE	4 ounces
SHORTENING	4 ounces
ONION, chopped	2 cups
GREEN PEPPER, chopped	2 cups
GARLIC, crushed	3 cloves
CURRY POWDER	2 tablespoons
THYME, LEAF	1-1/2 teaspoons
SEASONED STEWED TOMATOES (CANNED)	2 quarts
CURRANTS or RAISINS	1 cup
RICE, hot, cooked	3 quarts
ALMONDS, toasted	2 cups

Procedure

1. Season chicken pieces with salt and pepper.

2. Melt butter with shortening. Saute chicken pieces in melted fat turning to brown all sides.

3. Transfer chicken to baking pan.

4. Saute onion, green pepper, garlic, curry powder and thyme in fat remaining in skillet, cooking until onion is tender but not brown.

5. Add stewed tomatoes and currants. Pour over chicken. Cover; cook in oven at 350°F. for 30 minutes or until chicken is tender.

6. Serve over rice. Garnish with almonds. Accompany with chutney, if desired.

CHICKEN BREASTS CACCIATORE

Yield: 20 portions

Ingredients

INSTANT DEHYDRATED SLICED ONION	2-1/2 cups
INSTANT DEHYDRATED CHOPPED	
GREEN PEPPER	1-3/4 cups
CHICKEN BREASTS	20
SEASONED FLOUR	as needed
SHORTENING	as needed
MUSHROOMS, CANNED, sliced, drained	2-1/2 cups
COOKING OIL	1/4 cup
MUSHROOM LIQUID AND WATER	1-1/2 cups
LEMON JUICE	1/4 cup
TOMATO SOUP, CONDENSED	1 50-ounce can
SALT	1-1/2 teaspoons
INSTANT GRANULATED GARLIC	1/2 teaspoon
THYME	1/2 teaspoon
LIQUID HOT PEPPER SEASONING	few drops

Procedure

1. Rehydrate onion and green pepper.

2. Coat chicken in seasoned flour. Brown in shortening in skillet or deep fat fryer. Place in steam table pans or individual casseroles.

3. Cook onion, pepper and mushrooms in oil until just tender.

4. Add water to mushroom liquid to make required amount. Combine with lemon juice, soup, salt, garlic, thyme and liquid hot pepper seasoning. Add vegetable mixture; bring just to boiling.

5. Pour sauce over chicken. Cover; cook in oven at 350°F. for 1 hour or until chicken is tender, basting occasionally with sauce.

6. Serve with hot noodles or rice, as desired.

SOUTHERN BAKED CHICKEN

Yield: 32 portions, 1/4 chicken, 2 ounces sauce

Ingredients

MILK	2-1/2 quarts
CHICKEN STOCK	2-1/2 quarts
MARGARINE	8 ounces
FLOUR	8 ounces
SALT	1-1/4 ounces
PEPPER, WHITE, GROUND	3/4 teaspoon
CHICKENS, QUARTERED,	
(2 POUNDS, 5 OUNCES TO	
2 POUNDS, 8 OUNCES EACH)	8
FLOUR	1 pound
SALT	2 ounces
PEPPER, BLACK, GROUND	2 teaspoons
MUSHROOMS, sliced	1 pound
MARGARINE	2 ounces
GREEN ONIONS, thinly sliced	5 ounces

Procedure

1. Combine milk and stock; heat.

2. Make a roux of first amount of margarine and flour. Cook over low heat 20 minutes. Add to hot liquid, stir until smooth. Cook until thickened. Add first amount of salt and white pepper. Keep hot.

3. Wash chickens; drain.

4. Mix remaining flour, salt and black pepper. Dredge chicken pieces in seasoned flour.

5. Fry in deep fat until lightly browned. Drain thoroughly. Arrange in baking pan.

6. Saute mushrooms in remaining margarine. Spread mushrooms and onions over chicken.

7. Pour sauce over chicken. Cover. Bake in oven at 300°F. until chicken is tender. (Higher temperature causes sauce to break.) Arrange chicken in hot table pans, pour sauce over. Serve additional sauce, if necessary.

PHEASANT (OR CHICKEN) MUSCATEL

Yield: 24 portions

Ingredients

BROILER PHEASANTS or BROILER CHICKENS, 1-1/2-POUND SIZE, split in half	12
LEMONS	2
SALT	as needed
PEPPER	as needed
BUTTER or MARGARINE	12 ounces
ORANGE JUICE from	12 oranges
WHITE RAISINS	1 quart
LEMON RIND, grated	1-1/2 tablespoons
MUSCATEL WINE	1-1/3 cups
CHICKEN STOCK	1 quart

Procedure

1. Rinse pheasants inside and outside with warm water. Drain well.

2. Rub inside of pheasants with lemon. Season with salt and pepper. Place in a baking pan, breast side up. Spread with butter.

3. Ream out oranges for juice. Save shells.

4. Add orange juice, raisins, lemon rind, wine and chicken stock to the baking pan. Bake in oven at 350°F. for 45 minutes or until done, basting about every 10 minutes.

5. Serve with Pecan Rice in Fluted Orange Cups. *(Recipe, facing page)*

PECAN RICE IN FLUTED ORANGE CUPS

Yield: 24 portions

Ingredients

CHICKEN STOCK	2 quarts
RICE, UNCOOKED	1 quart
SALT	1 tablespoon
BUTTER or MARGARINE	4 ounces
PECANS, chopped	2-1/2 cups
PARSLEY, chopped	1/2 cup
ORANGE CUPS (from reamed-out oranges)	24

Procedure

1. Combine chicken stock, rice and salt in a 2 gallon stock pot. Bring to a boil. Stir well.
2. Cover; cook over low heat 14 minutes. Remove from heat.
3. Add butter, pecans and parsley. Mix gently, but well.
4. Flute orange cups. Spoon hot rice into the shells.

CHICKEN QUARTER, WINE BAKED

Yield: 24 portions, 1/4 chicken each

Ingredients

BROILER-FRYER CHICKEN, quartered	6 (12 pounds)
MONOSODIUM GLUTAMATE	2 tablespoons
WHITE WINE	1-1/2 cups
BUTTER or MARGARINE, melted	3 ounces
SALT	2 tablespoons
PEPPER, GROUND	3/4 teaspoon
TARRAGON, GROUND or finely minced	2 tablespoons

Procedure

1. Wash chicken; drain. Pat dry.
2. Sprinkle with monosodium glutamate. Place 12 pieces, skin side up, in each of two steam table pans 12-inch by 20-inch by 2-1/2-inch.
3. Combine wine, melted butter and seasonings. Spoon evenly over chicken in both pans.
4. Bake in oven at 375°F. for 1 hour, basting every 15 minutes with pan juices.

CHICKEN BREASTS CALIFORNIA STYLE

Yield: 16 portions

Ingredients

CHICKEN HALF-BREASTS, boned	16
SALT	as needed
PEPPER, WHITE	as needed
SHORTENING or COOKING OIL	as needed
ORANGES, peeled	4
ORANGE RIND, grated	1 tablespoon
ORANGE JUICE, freshly squeezed	2 cups
ALLSPICE	1/2 teaspoon
SUGAR, LIGHT BROWN	1/4 cup (packed)
CORNSTARCH	1 tablespoon
WATER, cold	2 tablespoons

Procedure

1. Sprinkle chicken pieces with salt and pepper. Brown in shortening. Place in baking pan.

2. Slice oranges into 4 slices each. Place a slice on each piece of chicken.

3. Combine orange rind, orange juice, allspice and brown sugar. Pour over chicken.

4. Bake in oven at 375°F. for 45 minutes or until chicken is tender.

5. Remove chicken from pan.

6. Blend cornstarch and water. Thicken sauce in baking pan.

7. Serve sauce over chicken.

ORANGE-GLAZED DUCK
WITH MINCEMEAT RICE STUFFING

Yield: 24 portions

Ingredients

DUCKS (ABOUT 4-POUND SIZE)	6
SALT	as needed
PEPPER	as needed
ONION, quartered	6 small onions
BUTTER or MARGARINE, melted	4 ounces
ORANGE JUICE CONCENTRATE	12 ounces
ORANGE RIND, grated	1/3 cup
HONEY	1-1/2 cups
ONION, chopped	3 cups
BUTTER or MARGARINE	2 ounces
SALT	1 tablespoon
RICE, cooked	5 quarts
MINCEMEAT, brandied	1 quart

Procedure

1. Season cavities of duck with salt and pepper. Place 4 pieces of onion in each.

2. Place on racks in baking pan. Roast in oven at 325°F. until beginning to brown.

3. Combine melted butter, orange juice concentrate, grated orange rind and honey. Brush duck with mixture.

4. Continue to roast duck until done, brushing occasionally with glaze.

5. Saute chopped onion in butter until softened but not brown. Add salt.

6. Combine with rice and mincemeat; toss together lightly to mix. Heat gently until thoroughly hot.

7. Cut duck into quarters, discarding onion from inside. Serve over stuffing.

ALMOND-CRUSTED CHICKEN
WITH ORANGE-KUMQUAT SAUCE ⟶

Yield: 24 portions

Ingredients

CHICKEN, LEGS AND THIGHS or HALF BREASTS	24
BOTTLED BROWNING SAUCE (optional)	as needed
FLOUR	1 cup
SALT	3 tablespoons
PEPPER	1/2 teaspoon
PAPRIKA	1 tablespoon
EGGS, slightly beaten	6
MILK	1/2 cup
ALMONDS, NATURAL, CHOPPED	4-1/2 cups
BUTTER or MARGARINE, melted	2-1/4 cups
JELLY, CRABAPPLE	4-1/2 cups
ARROWROOT	1 cup
SALT	2 tablespoons
SAVORY	1-1/2 teaspoons
ORANGE JUICE	2-1/2 quarts
SYRUP FROM CANNED MANDARIN ORANGES	2 cups
WHITE VINEGAR	1/2 cup
BUTTER or MARGARINE or DRIPPINGS	3/4 cup
MANDARIN ORANGE SECTIONS, CANNED, drained	4-1/2 cups
KUMQUATS, sliced, seeded	2-1/4 cups

Procedure

1. If brown skin is desired on chicken, brush pieces with bottled browning sauce diluted with a little water.

2. Mix flour and seasonings. Combine eggs and milk.

3. Coat chicken with seasoned flour; dip in egg mixture.

4. Coat skin side of chicken with almonds. Place, skin side up, in shallow baking pans. Drizzle with 2/3 of the first amount of butter. Bake in oven at 375°F. for 30 minutes. Drizzle with remaining 1/3 of butter; continue baking 35 minutes longer, basting twice.

5. Blend jelly, arrowroot, salt and savory with wire whisk. Add orange juice and orange syrup. Cook and stir over medium heat until mixture comes to a boil and is thickened.

6. Add vinegar, butter or drippings and fruit. Heat gently.

7. Serve chicken pieces with sauce, allowing 3/4 cup sauce per portion. Garnish with a maraschino cherry on stem, and watercress or parsley, as desired.

Beef

WELLINGTON STEAK

Yield: 1 portion

Ingredients
For each portion allow:

BEEF TENDERLOIN, well trimmed	5 ounces
SIRLOIN, GROUND	2 ounces
PATE DE FOIE GRAS	1/3 ounce
PIE PASTRY	as needed
EGG WASH*	as needed
CUMBERLAND SAUCE *(Recipe, facing page)*	

Procedure
1. Grill tenderloin steak, cooking to very rare stage. Cool.
2. Mix ground sirloin and pate de foie gras. Place on top of steak.
3. Roll out pie pastry. Wrap steak in pastry, sealing completely.
4. Brush with egg wash. Bake in oven at 400°F. to rare, medium or well done stage, as desired.
5. Garnish plate with cress. Serve with Cumberland sauce on side.

*EGG WASH

Yield: 1 quart

Ingredients

MILK, WHOLE	1 quart
EGGS, slightly beaten	3
or EGGS, WHOLE FROZEN	4 ounces
SALT	1/2 teaspoon

Procedure
1. Combine ingredients; mix well.

CUMBERLAND SAUCE

Yield: approximately 1 gallon

Ingredients

BROWN SAUCE	1-1/4 quarts
RED CURRANT JELLY	2-1/2 quarts
ORANGE JUICE, from	3 oranges
ORANGE RIND, from	3 oranges
LEMON RIND, from	3 lemons

Procedure

1. Combine brown sauce, currant jelly and orange juice. Heat and stir until jelly melts.

2. Peel oranges and lemons very thin, using a very sharp knife. Cut peeling into very small, thin strips.

3. Allow sauce to cool; add rind. (Adding to cool sauce holds color and essence of the rind.)

ALOHA STEAK

Yield: 120 portions

Ingredients

SOY SAUCE	1 gallon
SUGAR	2 quarts
GINGER, FRESH, crushed	2 ounces
GARLIC, finely minced	6 cloves
PEPPER	1/2 teaspoon
MONOSODIUM GLUTAMATE	3 tablespoons
SHERRY	1 cup
SIRLOIN STEAKS (PRIME), trimmed	120 (12 to 16-ounce)
MACADAMIA NUTS, chopped or bits	as needed

Procedure

1. Mix soy sauce, sugar, ginger, garlic, pepper, monosodium glutamate and sherry.

2. Marinate steaks in sauce for not more than 15 minutes.

3. Broil steaks to desired doneness. Sprinkle with a dash of macadamia nuts.

TOURNEDO BORDELAISE GARNI

Yield: 1 portion

Ingredients

For each portion allow:

TOURNEDO, 5 to 6 ounces	1
TOMATO TOPPED WITH GREEN BEANS	1
ARTICHOKE BOTTOM WITH CAULIFLOWER	1
POTATOES, shaped, small	4
BORDELAISE SAUCE*	2-1/2 ounces

Procedure

1. Grill tournedo or saute quickly in butter or oil until browned but still rare.

2. Garnish with partially baked tomato topped with cooked, buttered green beans; artichoke bottom topped with cooked, buttered cauliflower; and small shaped potatoes.

3. Serve with Bordelaise sauce.

*BORDELAISE SAUCE

Yield: 20 portions

Ingredients

RED DINNER WINE	1 quart
SHALLOTS, chopped	8 ounces
PEPPER, crushed	1 tablespoon
THYME	pinch
BAY LEAF	1/2 leaf
BROWN SAUCE (DEMI-GLACE)	1-1/2 quarts
LEMON JUICE	1/2 ounce
SALT	as needed
MARROW, diced, poached	6 ounces

Procedure

1. Combine wine, shallots, pepper, thyme and bay leaf. Simmer to reduce by one-half.

2. Add brown sauce and lemon juice; bring to a boil. Strain through very fine sieve or cheese cloth. Season with salt.

3. Add diced marrow. Serve over tournedos or steaks.

Note

If richer sauce is desired, incorporate soft butter. Do not boil after butter is added.

BROCHETTE OF BEEF RINALDO

Yield: 15 portions

Ingredients

SAUTERNE WINE, DRY	1 gallon
PEPPER, COARSELY GROUND	2 ounces
MONOSODIUM GLUTAMATE	2 ounces
SWEET BASIL	1/2 ounce
SALT	3 ounces
GARLIC CLOVES, crushed	2 ounces
FRESH GINGER ROOT, sliced	3 ounces
BEEF, TOP SIRLOIN, cut in 1-inch cubes	5 pounds
GREEN PEPPER, cut in 1-inch squares from	2 large peppers
ONION, WHOLE	2 No. 2-1/2 cans
BUTTON MUSHROOMS	1 1-pound can
TOMATOES, cut into six wedges each	5 large

Procedure

1. Combine wine, pepper, monosodium glutamate, basil, salt, garlic and ginger root. Pour over beef cubes. Aliow to marinate overnight.

2. Thread marinated beef cubes on a 9-inch skewer, alternating meat with green pepper, onion, mushroom and tomato. (Allow 4 cubes of meat per skewer.)

3. Broil. Serve on a bed of rice. Accompany with Mustard Sauce Rinaldo.*

*MUSTARD SAUCE RINALDO

Yield: 15 portions

Ingredients

SAUTERNE WINE	2 cups
BROWN GRAVY (medium thickness), boiling	2 quarts
MUSTARD, DRY	1/4 pound
BUTTER, cut in 1/2-inch slices	3/4 pound

Procedure

1. Bring wine to boil; reduce to 1/2 cup. Add to boiling brown gravy.

2. Whip in the dry mustard; remove from heat.

3. Add slices of butter gradually, whipping constantly until all is blended together.

BEEF STROGANOFF I

Yield: 50 6-ounce portions

Ingredients

BEEF TENDERLOIN TIPS, cut 1-1/2-inch by 1/2-inch by 1/2-inch	14 pounds
SEASONED FLOUR*	2 quarts
MARGARINE	1-1/3 pounds
MARGARINE	1 pound
ONION, 1/4-inch dice	1-3/4 quarts
GARLIC CLOVES, FRESH, crushed with salt	6 medium
MUSHROOMS, sliced	4 pounds
FLOUR	2 cups
TOMATO PASTE	1 cup
BEEF STOCK	4-1/2 quarts
SOUR CREAM (DAIRY)	2-1/2 quarts
SHERRY	1 cup

Procedure

1. Dredge meat in seasoned flour. Brown meat in first amount of margarine using a heavy bottomed pan over high heat. Turn often to brown all sides.

2. Remove meat. Add second amount of margarine to pan. Add onion, crushed garlic and mushrooms; saute 5 minutes over high heat.

3. Add flour; blend. Add tomato paste and beef stock; stir smooth while bringing to a boil.

4. Add sour cream and sherry; stir smooth. Combine meat and sauce; simmer 8 minutes. Remove from heat.

5. Serve with rice pilaf. Garnish with parsley.

*SEASONED FLOUR

Yield: 1-1/8 quarts

Ingredients

FLOUR, HARD WHEAT (bread)	1 quart
SALT	1/2 cup
BLACK PEPPER	2 teaspoons

Procedure

1. Place ingredients in flat pan; mix thoroughly.

BEEF STROGANOFF II

Yield: 2 gallons, 48 2/3 cup portions

Ingredients

ROUND STEAK, cut into 1-inch cubes	10 pounds
SHORTENING	1-1/2 ounces (3 tablespoons)
HOT WATER	1 gallon
ONION SOUP BASE	8 ounces (1 jar)
TOMATO PUREE	1 cup
WORCESTERSHIRE SAUCE	2 tablespoons
MUSHROOMS, FRESH, sliced	4-1/2 pounds (1-1/2 gallons)
SHORTENING	3-1/2 ounces (1/2 cup)
HEAVY CREAM	3 cups
SOUR CREAM	3 cups
FLOUR	4 ounces (1 cup)
WATER	1 cup

Procedure

1. Brown meat in first amount of shortening. Add hot water, soup base, tomato puree and Worcestershire. Cover, simmer 1-1/2 hours, or until meat is tender.

2. Cook mushrooms in the second amount of shortening until lightly browned. Add mushrooms, heavy cream, and sour cream to meat. Cover and cook over low heat about 15 minutes.

3. Make a paste of flour with remaining water. Stir gently into meat mixture. Cook until gravy is slightly thickened. Serve over rice or noodles.

PEPPER STEAK ⟶

Yield: 50 portions

Ingredients

FLOUR	2 cups
SALT	1/4 cup
PEPPER	2 teaspoons
BEEF SHORT LOIN STEAKS, 4-OUNCE, FROZEN	50
SHORTENING	2 cups
ONION, chopped	1 quart
GARLIC CLOVES, minced	4
WATER	1 gallon
BEEF EXTRACT	1/4 cup
WORCESTERSHIRE SAUCE	2 tablespoons
TOMATO PASTE	10 ounces
LEAF OREGANO	2 tablespoons
GREEN PEPPER, sliced	2 pounds

BOURBON FLANK STEAK

Yield: 24 portions

Ingredients

TOMATO SAUCE	2 quarts
CHIVES, chopped	1 cup
SEASONED SALT	1 tablespoon
SEASONED PEPPER	1 teaspoon
CELERY SALT	2 teaspoons
BOURBON	1 cup
FLANK STEAK	12 pounds
MUSHROOMS, sliced	1 pound

Procedure

1. Combine tomato sauce, chives, seasoning and bourbon in a large shallow pan; mix well. Add steak and mushrooms; chill 2 hours, turning meat occasionally.

2. Drain steak and mushrooms, reserving marinade.

3. Broil steaks 5 minutes. Turn; top with mushrooms, broil 5 minutes or until steak is the desired doneness.

4. Slice steak diagonally to serve.

5. Heat marinade. Serve with steak and mushrooms.

Procedure

1. Combine flour, salt and pepper; mix thoroughly.

2. Coat steaks in seasoned flour. Reserve remaining flour.

3. Brown steaks in shortening. Remove to steamtable pans.

4. Saute onion and garlic in fat remaining in skillet until onion is transparent.

5. Blend in remaining seasoned flour.

6. Stir in water, beef extract, Worcestershire sauce, tomato paste and oregano. Cook and stir until slightly thickened.

7. Pour sauce over steaks. Cover pans; bake in oven at 350°F. for 1-1/2 hours or until tender.

8. Add green pepper for the last 15 minutes baking time.

OVEN-BARBECUED STEAK

Yield: 50 portions

Ingredients

ROUND STEAK, 4-ounce	50
SALAD OIL	1/2 cup
ONION, thinly sliced	2 cups
CATSUP	1 quart
VINEGAR	2 cups
SUGAR, BROWN, packed	1/2 cup
WATER	1-1/2 quarts
MUSTARD, PREPARED	1/2 cup
WORCESTERSHIRE SAUCE	1/4 cup
SALT	1 tablespoon
PEPPER	1/2 teaspoon

Procedure

1. Brown steaks in oil turning to brown both sides. Transfer to roasting pans.

2. Saute onion in fat remaining after browning steaks. Add remaining ingredients. Simmer and stir 5 minutes.

3. Pour sauce over steaks. Cover; bake in oven at 350°F. for 2 to 2-1/2 hours or until meat is tender.

BOEUF BRAISE

Yield: 100 portions

Ingredients

BEEF, BONELESS, 10-POUND PIECES	4 (40 pounds)
SHORTENING, melted	1 pound
ONION, chopped	1 pound
GARLIC, chopped	2/3 ounce
BEEF STOCK or WATER	1 gallon
SALT	6 ounces
PEPPER	1/2 ounce
FAT, FROM DRIPPINGS	2 cups
FLOUR	3 cups
DRIPPINGS PLUS WATER to make	6 quarts

Procedure

1. Brown beef in hot fat. Add onion and garlic; saute 5 minutes.

2. Add stock and seasoning; simmer until meat is tender, 3 to 3-1/2 hours.

3. Pour drippings into a small pan; skim off fat; measure amount needed for gravy.

4. Blend flour into fat; add liquid. Cook and stir until gravy is thickened and smooth. Reduce heat; simmer 10 minutes. Season to taste.

5. Slice meat; serve with gravy.

BEEF WITH SOUR CREAM SAUCE

Yield: 50 3/4-cup portions

Ingredients

ROUND STEAK, cut in 1-inch cubes	15 pounds
FLOUR	1-1/2 cups
FAT	1 cup
ONION, thinly sliced	2-1/2 pounds
SOUR CREAM	2 quarts
MUSHROOMS, CANNED, drained	1-1/4 quarts
MARJORAM	1-1/2 teaspoons
THYME	1-1/2 teaspoons
SALT	1/4 cup
PAPRIKA	1/3 cup
GARLIC, finely chopped	1 clove

Procedure

1. Dredge meat in flour. Brown meat and onion in hot fat.

2. Combine all ingredients in 2 roasting pans, 12-inch by 15-inch by 5-inch. Cover tightly. (Aluminum foil may be used for covering.)

3. Bake in oven at 350°F. for 2-1/2 hours. Remove cover during last hour of baking. Stir occasionally. Serve with hot cooked rice or noodles.

BRAISED STEAK AND MUSHROOMS

Yield: 48 portions

Ingredients

BEEF ROUND, 1-inch thick	20 pounds
SALT	3 tablespoons
BLACK PEPPER, GROUND	2 teaspoons
FLOUR	3 cups
SHORTENING	2 cups
WATER	2 quarts
TOMATOES, CANNED, broken up	2 quarts
ONION, sliced	1 quart
GARLIC, finely minced	2 cloves
BAY LEAVES	2
MUSHROOMS, FRESH, sliced	4 quarts
or	
MUSHROOMS, CANNED, sliced	2 1-pound cans

Procedure

1. Cut steak into 6- to 7-ounce pieces.

2. Season with salt and pepper. Dredge in flour.

3. Brown steaks in shortening. Remove to baking pans. Add water, tomatoes, onion, garlic and bay leaves.

4. Cover pans with foil. Cook in oven at 325°F. for 1-1/2 to 2 hours or until meat is tender, adding mushrooms 10 to 15 minutes before meat is done.

5. Garnish with chopped fresh parsley or sprigs of parsley.

BURGUNDY BEEF

Yield: 20 portions

Ingredients

BEEF, CLOD OR CROSSRIB, BOTTOM OR TOP ROUND (larded with pork back fat and carrots)	7-1/2 pounds
RED WINE, DRY	3 cups
CARROTS, coarsely cut	5 ounces
ONION, coarsely cut	4 ounces
CELERY, coarsely cut	3 ounces
GARLIC, minced (optional)	1 clove
MIXED SPICE	1/3 ounce
FLOUR	6 ounces
BROWN BEEF SAUCE	1 quart

Procedure

1. Marinate beef two days with wine, vegetables and spices, turning occasionally.

2. Remove meat from marinade; drain well. Drain vegetables.

3. Season meat; brown on all sides in skillet. Remove meat; saute vegetables until golden brown. Add flour; cook until grainy.

4. Transfer vegetable mixture to a baking pan; add marinade, cook and stir until mixture boils. Add meat; cover, simmer in oven until about half done.

5. Add brown sauce; cook until tender.

6. Remove meat. Reduce sauce to 2/3 its original volume. Strain. Correct seasoning. Serve with sliced meat.

BAKED BEEF CUBES IN RED WINE

Yield: 24 portions

Ingredients

ROUND STEAK, cut in 2-inch cubes	8 pounds
SALT	3 tablespoons
PEPPER	1 teaspoon
RED WINE	1 quart
GARLIC CLOVES	4
BAY LEAF	4
BACON SLICES, chopped	1/2 pound
BEEF STOCK	1 quart
CLOVES, WHOLE	8
ONION, medium, cut in half	12 onions
CARROTS, sliced	1 quart
FLOUR	1/2 cup
PARSLEY, chopped (to garnish)	as needed

Procedure

1. Sprinkle meat with salt and pepper.

2. Add wine, garlic and bay leaves; marinate in refrigerator for several hours.

3. Fry bacon in a heavy pot or kettle. Remove bacon bits.

4. Drain beef; reserve marinade. Brown meat in bacon fat. Add stock, cloves and marinade; simmer for 2 hours.

5. Place onion and carrots in a baking pan. Pour meat mixture over vegetables; bake in oven at 350°F. until vegetables are tender. Remove meat and vegetables to serving pan.

6. Blend flour with a little cold water; add to liquid; cook for a few minutes, stirring constantly. Pour gravy over the meat.

7. Garnish with chopped parsley.

SAUERBRATEN SWISS STEAK

Yield: 50 portions

Ingredients

VINEGAR, cider	1 quart
WATER	2 quarts
SUGAR	1/4 cup
PEPPERCORNS	1 tablespoon
BAY LEAVES	12
CLOVES, WHOLE	1 teaspoon
ROUND STEAK, 4-ounce portions	50
LARD or SHORTENING	1 cup
SALT	1/4 cup
FLOUR	1 cup
WATER	1-1/2 quarts
GINGERSNAPS, crushed	4 ounces
ONION, sliced	2 pounds

Procedure

1. Combine vinegar, first amount of water and sugar.
2. Divide the peppercorns, bay leaves and whole cloves equally. Tie in cheese cloth squares to make two spice bags.
3. Add spice bags to vinegar mixture; heat to boiling.
4. Pour the warm liquid and spice bags into a crock or deep stainless container. Add steaks, turning to cover with marinade. Refrigerate; marinate overnight.
5. Remove steaks; drain, reserving marinade and spice bags. Brown steaks slowly in small amount of lard.
6. Place browned steaks into two steam table pans; sprinkle with salt. Place one of the spice bags in each pan.
7. Measure drippings; add enough lard to make 1 cup. Blend in flour. Add marinade and remaining water; cook and stir until thickened.
8. Stir in gingersnap crumbs. (This will make gravy thicker.)
9. Cover steaks with sliced onion; pour gravy over all.
10. Cover pans; bake in oven at 350°F. for 1-1/2 to 2 hours or until done.
11. Serve on hot cooked noodles, if desired.

Lively Accents for Special Meals

VEGETABLES

APPROACHED WITH imagination and with care, vegetables can add a bright and lively accent to the special meal. Their variety is infinite and their color unrivaled for catching the eye. What is more, they are remarkably versatile and responsive to change.

One way to gain attention is to feature some of the more exotic vegetables, varieties that are not seen on many occasions. On the other hand for special meals where patrons are not given a choice, you will be on much safer ground when you keep to the better known vegetables and look for intriguing new ways to change their appearance and enhance their taste.

Simply changing the style of cutting can make a vegetable seem quite different. For example, carrots, celery and zucchini take on new interest when sliced diagonally. Mushrooms change appearance as they are cut into slices or quarters or allowed to remain as small whole caps.

Combining two—possibly three—vegetables can create a new offering that has more charm than one of the vegetables used alone. Mixing cut green and wax beans is like finding a new vegetable. Putting half-slices of zucchini and strips of carrot together produces a similar result.

A little originality in presentation can go a long way toward setting a menu apart. A baked tomato makes an impressive appearance when stuffed with an inverted mushroom cap. Beets in a tasty orange sauce delight the eye when portions are presented in orange shells.

A vegetable with an imaginative seasoning can bring distinction to the meal. A seasoned butter, for example, can provide an impressive flavor boost. Try a lemon butter on asparagus or broccoli, mustard butter with green lima beans. Try other unexpected seasoning touches; a dash of sherry adds zest to creamed mushrooms and to mashed sweet potatoes or winter squash. A hint of nutmeg enhances spinach or crookneck squash. A combination of fresh dill and parsley adds a new dimension to small new potatoes. Chopped mint does the same for young carrots or peas.

ALMOND BUTTERED CELERY

Yield: 48 portions

Ingredients

CELERY, sliced diagonally	1-1/2 gallons
ALMONDS, BLANCHED, SLIVERED	2 cups
BUTTER or MARGARINE	1/2 pound
SALT	as needed
PEPPER, WHITE	as needed

Procedure

1. Cook celery until crisp-tender. Drain, if necessary.
2. Saute almonds in butter until golden brown.
3. Pour almonds and butter over celery; toss to mix. Season with salt and pepper.

GLAZED CARROTS

Yield: 25 portions

Ingredients

CARROTS, RAW, medium size	10 pounds
BUTTER	4 ounces
SUGAR, brown	1 pound
SALT	1 teaspoon
PEPPER	1/4 teaspoon
BITTERS	1 tablespoon

Procedure

1. Cook whole carrots in small amount of water until crisp-tender; drain.
2. Melt butter; add brown sugar, salt, pepper and bitters. Mix well until smooth and syrupy.
3. Add carrots; place over low heat. Turn carrots carefully until well glazed.

CINNAMON MASHED LOUISIANA YAMS

Yield: 25 portions

Ingredients

YAMS, cooked, mashed	3 quarts
BUTTER or MARGARINE, melted	1/2 pound
MILK	3 cups
SALT	2-1/2 teaspoons
CINNAMON	1-1/2 teaspoons

Procedure

1. Combine ingredients.
2. Heat over low heat, stirring as needed. Garnish with pecan halves which have been lightly browned in vegetable oil, if desired.

Note

Fresh or canned mashed yams may be used.

BAKED TOMATO STUFFED WITH MUSHROOM CAP

Yield: 48 portions

Ingredients

MUSHROOMS, FRESH, medium size	48
TOMATOES, large	48
OLIVE or SALAD OIL	as needed
SALT	3 tablespoons
INSTANT ONION POWDER	3 tablespoons
INSTANT GARLIC POWDER	2 teaspoons
BLACK PEPPER, GROUND	1 teaspoon
PARSLEY, chopped	as needed

Procedure

1. Rinse mushrooms; pat dry. Cut stem to base of mushroom cap.
2. Slice off stem end of tomato. Scoop out enough of centers for mushroom cap to fit into cavity in tomato.
3. Brush mushroom caps and outer skin of tomatoes with oil.
4. Mix salt, onion powder, garlic powder and pepper. Sprinkle tomatoes and mushroom caps with mixture. Set mushroom, rounded side down, into tomato.
5. Bake in oven at 400°F. for 25 to 30 minutes or until tomatoes are tender yet firm. Garnish with parsley.

LYONNAISE GREEN BEANS

Yield: 50 portions

Ingredients

GREEN BEANS, FROZEN	10 pounds
ONION, thinly sliced	1 pound
BUTTER	1/2 pound
SALT	1-1/2 tablespoons
PEPPER	3/4 teaspoon

Procedure

1. Cook green beans according to package directions; drain.

2. Saute onion in butter until tender and lightly browned. Add to beans. Season with salt and pepper. Heat thoroughly.

FRESH BROCCOLI SUPREME

Yield: 50 portions

Ingredients

BROCCOLI, FRESH (prepared for cooking)	10 pounds
BUTTER or SHORTENING	3/4 pound
FLOUR	2 cups
MILK	3-1/2 quarts
ONION	1 medium
CLOVES, WHOLE	3
SALT	2 tablespoons
BLACK PEPPER	1/2 teaspoon
MUSTARD, DRY	1/2 teaspoon
EGGS, hard-cooked, chopped	9
PARSLEY, chopped	1/2 cup

Procedure

1. Cook broccoli in boiling, salted water until just tender. Drain.

2. Melt butter; blend in flour. Cook slowly 5 minutes.

3. Heat milk with the onion stuck with the 3 whole cloves.

4. Add hot milk to flour mixture; stir until smooth. Add salt, pepper and mustard. Cook 15 to 20 minutes over low heat, stirring frequently.

5. Remove from heat; strain. Add chopped eggs.

6. Ladle over stems of hot broccoli. Dust with chopped parsley.

NEW POTATOES WITH FRESH DILL

Yield: 24 portions

Ingredients

NEW POTATOES, small	8 pounds
BUTTER or MARGARINE	1/2 pound
FLOUR	3/4 cup
SALT	1 tablespoon
PEPPER	1/2 teaspoon
WATER FROM POTATOES	2 quarts
LEMON JUICE	2 tablespoons
DILL, FRESH, chopped	as needed
PARSLEY, chopped	1/4 cup

Procedure

1. Scrub potatoes thoroughly. Cook in boiling salted water until tender, about 20 minutes. Drain, reserving water for sauce. Keep potatoes hot.

2. Melt butter; blend in flour, salt and pepper. Add potato water gradually. Cook and stir until thickened. Add lemon juice. Place potatoes in steam table pan. Pour sauce over them. Sprinkle generously with dill and parsley.

PEPPY SOUR CREAM POTATOES

Yield: approximately 90 3-ounce portions

Ingredients

WATER, boiling	1-1/4 gallons
SALT	3 tablespoons
MILK, cold	1-1/2 quarts
INSTANT POTATO FLAKES	2-1/2 pounds
SOUR CREAM	2-1/2 quarts
PARMESAN CHEESE, grated	1 cup
GREEN ONIONS, chopped (including tops)	1 cup
SEASONED SALT	6 tablespoons
BUTTER	6 tablespoons (3 ounces)

Procedure

1. Place boiling water and salt in mixer bowl; add cold milk.
2. Add potato flakes; stir slowly until wet.
3. Let stand 1/2 minute.
4. Mix at low speed to desired consistency (about 1/2 to 1 minute).
5. Add sour cream, cheese, onion and seasoned salt; blend well.
6. Turn into two 12-inch by 20-inch pans. Dot with butter.
7. Bake in oven at 350°F. for 20 to 30 minutes.

Give Strawberry Desserts a Special Touch

California Strawberry Advisory Board

In Strawberry Cookie Shell Sundae (recipe page 292) ice cream and berries are cupped in crisp filbert cookie; Strawberry Ice Cream Shortcake is presented in a layered triangle topped with whipped cream.

DESSERTS

DESSERTS, LIKE appetizers, have an important part to play. Appetizers give the first impression; desserts come in to win final approval. Appearing, as they do, toward the very end, they are given the part that is likely to be remembered and that will set the image for the meal. A dessert with exciting good looks and exceptional flavor can carry off honors and, in effect, extend a cordial invitation to return.

Desserts are the treats that top off a special meal with a festive touch. A rich, satisfying dessert rounds out a menu that is light in character. A light, refreshing dessert, on the other hand, provides a pleasing finale to a bounteous meal. In either case, comely desserts with an imaginative twist will win praise from dessert lovers who often are not apt to enjoy these delicacies at home.

Lofty chilled souffles, chiffon pies, decorative cakes and other showy creations go over well. A fine chocolate dessert never fails to please, while ice cream in fancy dress has a tremendous appeal.

Baked Alaska has become something of a "banquet special." But other ice cream-and-cake concoctions are worthy of *trial. Ice cream as a pie is another idea. Try presenting ice cream in a brandy snifter with an elegant sauce or put it inside a cream puff or crisp cookie shell. Serve it as a coconut snowball with a sparkly red sauce or as a glamorous parfait made with a complementary liqueur. Creme de Menthe, Tia Maria and Grand Marnier are among liqueurs that make delightful ice cream sauces ready to pour.*

Cakes

AMBER CREAM ANGEL FOOD

Yield: 1 10-inch cake

Ingredients

CREAM, whipping	2 cups
SUGAR, LIGHT BROWN	3/4 cup
VANILLA	1 teaspoon
ANGEL FOOD, 10-INCH ROUND	1 cake

Procedure

1. Combine cream, brown sugar and vanilla. Refrigerate 30 minutes.
2. Whip cream until stiff enough to spread.
3. Cut cake into three layers. Spread cream between layers, over the top, and around the sides. Chill for several hours.

ICE CREAM AND CANDY CAKE

Yield: 2 9-inch cakes

Ingredients

VANILLA ICE CREAM	2 quarts
CHOCOLATE ICE CREAM	2 quarts
CAKE LAYERS, WHITE OR YELLOW	2 9-inch
SEMI-SWEET CHOCOLATE PIECES	6 ounces (1 cup)
CREAM, HEAVY	1/2 cup
VANILLA	1/2 teaspoon
CREAM, HEAVY (for whipping)	2 cups
SUGAR	1 cup
PEPPERMINT STICK CANDY, crushed	1/3 cup

Procedure

1. Alternate scoops of vanilla and chocolate ice cream in each of two 9-inch cake pans. Pack firmly with back of spoon. Cover; freeze firm.

2. Wrap cake layers; freeze.

3. Heat chocolate and first amount of cream over low heat until chocolate melts. Stir in vanilla. Cool.

4. To assemble cakes: Dip pans with ice cream into cool water. Turn out onto chilled serving plates. Return to freezer to harden surface.

5. Spread tops of each layer of ice cream with 1/4 cup of the cool chocolate sauce; top with cake layers. Spread top of each cake layer with remaining chocolate sauce.

6. Whip remaining cream until soft peaks form. Add sugar; beat until stiff.

7. Spread whipped cream on sides of cakes. Using a pastry bag, pipe a border of whipped cream around edge of top layer. Sprinkle candy over edge.

8. Hold in freezer for serving.

SCOTCH CHOCOLATE CAKE WITH ICE CREAM SAUCE

Yield: 50 portions

Ingredients

CHOCOLATE, UNSWEETENED	8 ounces
FLOUR, ALL-PURPOSE	1-1/4 pounds
SODA	4 teaspoons
SALT	2-1/2 teaspoons
SHORTENING	7 ounces (1 cup)
SUGAR	1 pound, 10 ounces
EGGS, unbeaten	3
BUTTERMILK	3-3/4 cups
VANILLA	2 teaspoons

Procedure

1. Melt chocolate; cool.

2. Sift flour, soda and salt together.

3. Cream shortening; add sugar gradually; continue beating until well blended.

4. Add eggs; beat until light and fluffy. Add chocolate; beat until well blended.

5. Combine buttermilk and vanilla. Add flour to creamed mixture, alternately with the liquid. Stop mixer and scrape bowl and beater after last addition, then beat until smooth.

6. Turn into well-greased baking pans to a depth of 3/4-inch. Bake in oven at 350°F. for 25 to 30 minutes, or until done. Cut in squares; serve warm with Ice Cream Sauce. *(Recipe, facing page)*

ICE CREAM SAUCE

Yield: 2 quarts

Ingredients

CREAM, HEAVY	2-1/2 cups
EGGS	4
SUGAR	5 ounces (3/4 cup)
SALT	1/4 teaspoon
BUTTER, melted	1/2 pound
VANILLA	1 tablespoon

Procedure

1. Whip cream until stiff.

2. Beat eggs until light. Gradually add sugar and salt; continue beating until thick.

3. Add melted butter and vanilla to egg mixture beating constantly. Fold into whipped cream. Chill until ready to serve.

ALMOND PRALINE CAKE

Yield: 26-inch by 18-inch by 1-inch sheet cake

Ingredients

BUTTER or MARGARINE, melted	1 pound
SUGAR, LIGHT BROWN	1 pound, 5 ounces
CREAM, LIGHT or MILK	1-1/2 cups
ALMONDS, SLICED NATURAL	3 cups
COCONUT, FLAKED	7 ounces (about 3 cups)
VANILLA	1 tablespoon
SALT	1/2 teaspoon
WHITE or YELLOW CAKE, baked, hot	1 sheet (26-inch by 18-inch by 1-inch)

Procedure

1. Mix butter, brown sugar, cream, almonds, coconut, vanilla and salt. Spread over hot (just baked) cake.

2. Return to oven heated to 350°F.; bake 10 to 15 minutes or until topping is golden brown.

3. Cool; cut 8 by 6 for 48 3-inch portions.

CHOCOLATE CAROUSEL CAKE ———➤

Yield: 1 cake

Ingredients

FLOUR, ALL-PURPOSE, sifted	1/3 cup
COCOA	1/4 cup
BAKING POWDER	1/2 teaspoon
SALT	1/4 teaspoon
EGG YOLKS	4
VANILLA	1 teaspoon
EGG WHITES	4
SUGAR, GRANULATED	3/4 cup
COCOA	1 to 2 tablespoons
ALMONDS, BLANCHED, WHOLE	1 cup
BUTTER or MARGARINE, softened	1/3 cup
CONFECTIONERS' SUGAR, sifted	3 cups
CREAM or MILK	1/4 cup
ALMOND EXTRACT	1/2 teaspoon

Chocolate Carousel Cake

California Almond Growers Exchange

Procedure

1. Sift flour with first amount of cocoa, baking powder and salt.
2. Beat egg yolks and vanilla until thick and lemon colored.
3. Beat egg whites until foamy. Add granulated sugar gradually, continuing to beat until stiff but not dry.
4. Fold egg yolk mixture into meringue.
5. Fold in sifted flour mixture.
6. Spread evenly in waxed-paper-lined 15-inch by 10-inch by 1-inch jelly roll pan. Bake in oven at 375°F. for 15 minutes or until done.
7. Invert cake on towel sprinkled with remaining cocoa. Remove paper from cake. If necessary, trim crisp edges from cake. Cover cake with pan; let cool.
8. Grind almonds until fine in electric blender or on grinder.
9. Mix butter with one-third of the confectioners' sugar until light and fluffy.
10. Add remaining sugar alternately with cream, beating until very smooth and of spreading consistency. Fold in almonds and almond extract.
11. Spread filling evenly over cooled cake.
12. Cut cake lengthwise into 4 strips, each about 2-1/4 inch wide.
13. Roll up one strip as for a jelly roll. Place roll, flat side down, on serving plate. Wrap remaining strips around roll, starting each strip where last ended. Chill.
14. To serve, cut into wedges with sharp, thin-bladed knife.

SAINT-HONORE GATEAU ⟶

Yield: 5 cakes

Ingredients

FILLING	
VANILLA PUDDING AND PIE FILLING	1 pound,10 ounces
CRUSHED PINEAPPLE, undrained	1 No. 10 can
WATER	1 cup
CREAM, HEAVY (for whipping)	1 quart
PASTRY	
CREAM CHEESE, softened	15 ounces
PASTRY DOUGH	1 pound, 9 ounces
CAKE	
WHITE CAKE, baked 9-inch layers (warm)	5
LIGHT RUM	2/3 cup
PUFF SHELLS, MINIATURE, baked	90 to 100
TOPPING	
CREAM, HEAVY (for whipping)	1-1/4 quarts
SUGAR	2/3 cup
CANDIED CHERRIES	as needed
ANGELICA	as needed

Procedure

FOR FILLING

1. Combine pudding mix, pineapple and water. Cook and stir until mixture boils and is very thick. Cover; chill.

2. When ready to use, whip first amount of cream. Stir pineapple mixture; fold in cream.

FOR PASTRY LAYER

1. Blend cream cheese with pastry dough thoroughly. Shape into 5 8-ounce balls.

2. Roll each to a 9-1/2-inch circle.

3. Place on baking sheet; prick with fork.

4. Bake in oven at 400°F. for 12 to 14 minutes or until lightly browned. Slide onto rack to cool.

FOR CAKE LAYERS

1. Turn warm layers out onto rack; sprinkle with rum. Cool thoroughly. Split each horizontally into two layers.

TO ASSEMBLE GATEAU

1. Place each pastry layer on a flat serving plate; spread with thin layer of pineapple filling.

2. Cover each with a cake layer; spread with filling. Top with a second cake layer; spread with filling.

3. Split puff shells; fill with remaining filling.

4. Whip remaining cream with sugar until stiff.

5. Spread tops of gateau with thin layer of whipped cream.

6. Place filled puffs close together in circle around edge of tops.

7. Using pastry tube, pipe rosettes of remaining whipped cream between puffs.

8. Garnish with candied cherries and angelica.

CALIFORNIA DESERT BROWNIES

Yield: 36 portions

Ingredients

DATES, FRESH	3 cups
BUTTER or MARGARINE	8 ounces
CHOCOLATE, UNSWEETENED	6 ounces
EGGS	6
SUGAR	1 pound 5 ounces
FLOUR, ALL-PURPOSE	8 ounces
BAKING POWDER	1-1/2 teaspoons
SALT	3/4 teaspoon
WALNUTS, chopped	1-1/2 cups
VANILLA ICE CREAM	1 gallon
BRANDIED CHOCOLATE SAUCE	1 quart
(Recipe, facing page)	

Procedure

1. Chop dates coarsely.

2. Combine butter and chocolate; melt over hot water or very low heat.

3. Beat eggs until thick and lemon colored; beat in sugar.

4. Blend in chocolate.

5. Combine flour, baking powder and salt; sift. Add to chocolate mixture; mix until blended. Add walnuts and dates.

6. Turn batter into 3 well greased 9-inch by 13-inch baking pans. Bake in oven at 350°F. for 20 minutes or until done. Do not overbake.

7. Cut into squares. Serve topped with ice cream and brandied chocolate sauce.

BRANDIED CHOCOLATE SAUCE

Yield: 1 quart

Ingredients

CHOCOLATE, UNSWEETENED	6 ounces
CORN SYRUP, LIGHT	3/4 cup
SUGAR	1 pound
EVAPORATED MILK, undiluted	1-1/2 cups
SALT	1/4 teaspoon
BRANDY	1/2 cup

Procedure

1. Combine chocolate and corn syrup; cook and stir over very low heat until chocolate is melted.
2. Blend in sugar, milk and salt; cook and stir until well blended.
3. Remove from heat; stir in brandy.

Fresh Lemon Polar Pie (Recipe, page 272)

Sunkist Growers Inc.

Pies

FRESH LEMON POLAR PIE

Yield: 8 9-inch pies

Ingredients

BUTTER	1-1/2 pounds
SUGAR	3-1/2 pounds
SALT	1 teaspoon
LEMON RIND, grated	1/2 cup
LEMON JUICE, FRESH	2-2/3 cups
EGG YOLKS	24 (2 cups)
EGGS, WHOLE	8
VANILLA ICE CREAM	2 gallons
PASTRY SHELLS, 9-INCH, baked	8
EGG WHITES	24 (3 cups)
CREAM OF TARTAR	1-1/2 teaspoons
SUGAR	1 pound, 5 ounces

Procedure

1. Melt butter in top of double boiler. Blend in first amount of sugar, salt, grated lemon rind and lemon juice.

2. Combine egg yolks and whole eggs; beat thoroughly.

3. Combine beaten eggs with butter mixture.

4. Cook over simmering water, stirring frequently, until very thick and smooth. Cool.

5. Smooth one pint softened ice cream into each pastry shell; freeze. Top with one cup of lemon mixture; freeze. Repeat the two layers, freezing after each addition.

6. Beat egg whites until frothy. Add cream of tartar; continue beating until egg whites hold stiff peaks. Gradually add remaining sugar, beating until sugar is completely dissolved.

7. Spread pies with meringue, completely covering and sealing to edge of pastry.

8. Place in baking sheet filled with crushed ice. Brown in oven at 475°F. for about 3 minutes.

9. Serve at once or freeze.

PUMPKIN CHIFFON PIE

Yield: 9 9-inch pies

Ingredients

GELATINE, UNFLAVORED	3 ounces
SUGAR, DARK BROWN	1 pound
SALT	1 tablespoon
CINNAMON	4 teaspoons
NUTMEG	2 teaspoons
GINGER	2 teaspoons
MILK, hot	2-1/4 quarts
EGG YOLKS, well beaten	12 ounces (1-1/2 cups)
PUMPKIN, cooked, mashed	1-3/4 pounds
EGG WHITES	1-1/8 pounds (2-1/4 cups)
SUGAR, GRANULATED	1 pound
CREAM, HEAVY (for whipping)*	2 cups
PIE SHELLS, 9-INCH, baked	9

Procedure

1. Mix gelatine, brown sugar, salt and spices.

2. Combine milk and egg yolks; add gelatine mixture. Cook over boiling water, stirring occasionally, until gelatine is dissolved (8 to 10 minutes).

3. Remove from water. Blend in pumpkin. Chill until slightly thickened.

4. Beat egg whites until foamy throughout. Gradually beat in granulated sugar, beating to soft peaks. Fold in pumpkin mixture.

5. Whip cream. Fold into pumpkin mixture.

6. Fill pie shells, allowing 1 quart filling per pie. Chill until firm.

*Or 1 quart prepared whipped topping.

WARM APPLE 'N ICE CREAM PIE

Yield: 5 9-inch pies, approximately 5 quarts sauce

Ingredients

ICE CREAM, BUTTERED ALMOND or VANILLA	1-1/2 gallons
PIE SHELLS, 9-INCH, baked	5
APPLE SLICES	1 No. 10 can
BUTTER	1-1/2 pounds
SUGAR, DARK BROWN	2-1/4 pounds
SALT	1 tablespoon
CORNSTARCH	1/4 cup
WATER, cold	1-1/2 cups

Procedure

1. Soften ice cream slightly. Fill pie shells. Hold in freezer unit until ready to serve.

2. Drain apple slices thoroughly.

3. Combine butter, sugar and salt in large saucepan. Cook and stir over medium heat until caramelized.

4. Add apples; mix until well coated.

5. Combine cornstarch and cold water. Blend some of hot liquid into the cold cornstarch mixture. Add to apples; continue to cook one minute.

6. Spoon warm, caramelized apples over portions of the ice cream pie.

Note

For a sundae version, serve warm caramelized apples over scoops of ice cream.

Fresh Strawberry Cream Pie

California Strawberry Advisory Board

FRESH STRAWBERRY CREAM PIE

Yield: 6 9-inch pies

Ingredients	
WATER	2-1/2 cups
SUGAR	1-1/2 pounds
CORNSTARCH	4 ounces
WATER	1/2 cup
STRAWBERRIES, washed, hulled	6 quarts
PIE SHELLS, 9-INCH, baked	6
CREAM, WHIPPING	3 cups

Procedure

1. Combine water and sugar; bring to a boil.

2. Blend cornstarch with remaining water. Thicken hot liquid. Cool.

3. Pour over strawberries. Turn into baked pie shells. Chill 2 hours before serving.

4. Whip cream. Garnish pies.

SHERRY ALMOND PIE

Yield: 3 9-inch pies

Ingredients

GELATINE, UNFLAVORED	4 tablespoons
WATER, cold	1 cup
MILK	2-1/4 quarts
SALT	1/2 teaspoon
SUGAR	1-1/2 cups
EGG YOLKS, beaten	9 (3/4 cup)
ALMOND EXTRACT	2-1/2 tablespoons
SHERRY	1/2 cup
EGG WHITES	9 (1-1/8 cups)
PIE SHELLS, 9-INCH, baked	3
CREAM FOR WHIPPING	1-1/2 cups
ALMONDS, SLIVERED, lightly toasted	1 cup

Procedure

1. Soften gelatine in cold water.

2. Scald milk with salt and 1/2 cup of the sugar; add gelatine.

3. Add beaten egg yolks to the hot milk mixture gradually, stirring constantly. Cook and stir over hot water until mixture is slightly thickened.

4. Remove from heat; add almond extract and sherry. Cool until slightly thickened.

5. Beat egg whites; add the remaining sugar gradually, continuing to beat until meringue forms peaks. Fold into cooked mixture; pour into baked pie shells.

6. Chill until firm. Serve garnished with whipped cream and almonds. For special service, garnish each portion with orange sections, sliced banana or grapes.

BROWN DERBY PIE

Yield: 1-1/2 gallons filling, 6 9-inch pies

Ingredients

GELATINE, UNFLAVORED	1-1/3 ounces (1/4 cup)
SUGAR	2 pounds (4-1/2 cups)
SALT	3/4 teaspoon
EGG YOLKS, beaten	4 ounces (1/2 cup)
MILK	1-1/4 quarts
CHOCOLATE, UNSWEETENED	1 pound
VANILLA	2 tablespoons
WHIPPED TOPPING, prepared	4 quarts
PIE SHELLS, 9-INCH, baked	6
WHIPPED TOPPING, prepared	1-1/2 quarts
CHOCOLATE CURLS	as needed

Procedure

1. Combine gelatine, sugar and salt in top of double boiler. Combine egg yolks and milk; add to gelatine mixture. Add chocolate; cook and stir over boiling water until chocolate is melted.

2. Remove from heat. Add vanilla. Beat with a rotary beater 1 minute or until mixture is smooth and blended. Chill until thickened.

3. Place first amount of whipped topping into mixer bowl. Blend in chocolate mixture, using low mixer speed.

4. Ladle into pie shells, allowing 1 quart per pie. Chill.

5. Spread second amount of whipped topping over pies allowing 1 cup per pie. Garnish with chocolate curls, placing some of the widest curls upright.

Variation

For tarts, fill 3-inch tart shells with chocolate mixture, allowing a No. 16 scoop (1/4 cup) per shell. Chill. Spread with whipped topping and garnish with chocolate curls as above. Makes 8 dozen tarts.

Puddings, Souffles, Molds

FUDGE PUDDING

Yield: 40 4-ounce portions

Ingredients

CHOCOLATE, UNSWEETENED	9 ounces
SHORTENING	3-1/2 ounces (1/2 cup)
FLOUR	1 pound
BAKING POWDER	2-1/2 tablespoons
SALT	1-1/2 tablespoons
SUGAR	1 pound, 5 ounces
MILK	2 cups
VANILLA	1 tablespoon
NUTS, chopped	2 cups
WATER	1-3/4 quarts
SUGAR	2 pounds, 10 ounces
CHOCOLATE, UNSWEETENED	4 ounces

Procedure

1. Combine first amount of chocolate and shortening; melt over very low heat. Cool.

2. Combine flour, baking powder, salt and first amount of sugar in mixer bowl; mix, using paddle.

3. Add milk and vanilla; mix only until smooth. Mix in cooled chocolate mixture and nuts.

4. Spread in a greased 18-inch by 12-inch baking pan.

5. Combine water, remaining sugar and chocolate. Place over medium heat; stir until sugar is dissolved and chocolate melted. Then bring to a boil without stirring.

6. Pour hot syrup over batter. (This makes a sauce in bottom of pan after pudding is baked.)

7. Bake in oven at 350°F. for about 45 minutes or until cake tests done.

8. Cut warm cake in squares; serve with sauce from bottom of pan. Garnish with whipped topping, whipped cream or sour cream, if desired.

PINWHEEL TRIFLE

Yield: 12 portions

Ingredients

JELLY ROLL, 1/2-inch slices	12 slices
SHERRY	1/2 cup
CUSTARD SAUCE*	1-1/2 quarts
WHIPPED CREAM (garnish)	as needed

Procedure

1. Lay slices of jelly roll flat on pastry board. Sprinkle tops with half of the sherry.

2. With broad spatula, turn slices over on board. Sprinkle with remaining sherry.

3. Ladle 1/2 cup custard sauce into each serving dish. Top with cake slice. Refrigerate about one hour.

4. Garnish with whipped cream or topping as desired.

*CUSTARD SAUCE

Yield: 1-1/2 quarts

Ingredients

EGG YOLKS, slightly beaten	12
or WHOLE EGGS, slightly beaten	6
SUGAR	3/4 cup
SALT	1/2 teaspoon
MILK, scalded	1-1/4 quarts
VANILLA	2-1/4 teaspoons

Procedure

1. Combine egg yolks (or whole eggs), sugar and salt in top of double boiler. Add scalded milk slowly, stirring constantly.

2. Cook mixture *over* simmering water (bottom of double boiler should not touch the water) until mixture coats a metal spoon, stirring constantly.

3. Remove from heat. Pour at once into bowl or other container. Add vanilla. Chill.

CINNAMON CHOCOLATE SWIRL SOUFFLE ➤
(See picture, page 283)

Yield: 48 portions

Ingredients

VANILLA-MACE MIXTURE

GELATINE, UNFLAVORED	1/2 cup
WATER, cold	1 quart
SUGAR	2 cups
EGG YOLKS, beaten	2 cups (1 pound)
FLOUR	1/2 cup
MACE, GROUND	1 teaspoon
SALT	1 teaspoon
MILK	1 quart
VANILLA	2 tablespoons
EGG WHITES	3 cups (1-1/2 pounds)
SUGAR	2 cups
CREAM, HEAVY (for whipping)*	1 quart

CHOCOLATE MIXTURE

SUGAR, CONFECTIONERS'	3 cups
CINNAMON, GROUND	1 teaspoon
EGG YOLKS	1 quart (2 pounds)
CHOCOLATE, SEMI-SWEET, grated	1 pound
CREAM, HEAVY (for whipping)*	2 quarts

*Or, double the measure of prepared whipped topping.

Procedure

To make vanilla-mace mixture:

1. Soften gelatine in cold water

2. Combine first amount of sugar, egg yolks, flour, mace and salt; stir until smooth.

3. Blend in milk. Cook and stir over low heat until mixture coats a metal spoon.

4. Remove from heat. Add gelatine; stir until dissolved.

5. Add vanilla. Chill until mixture thickens slightly.

6. Beat egg whites until foamy throughout. Add next amount of sugar gradually, continuing to beat until meringue forms stiff glossy peaks.

7. Whip cream.

8. Gently fold meringue and whipped cream into gelatine mixture. Refrigerate but do not allow mixture to become firm.

To make chocolate mixture:

1. Combine confectioners' sugar, cinnamon and egg yolks in stainless steel bowl. Place over hot water. Beat with a whip until light and mixture ribbons from a spoon. Remove from water bath; whip until cool to prevent crusting.

2. Melt chocolate over hot water. Cool slightly; add to egg yolk mixture. Cool.

3. Whip cream. Fold into chocolate mixture. Refrigerate to keep cold.

To prepare souffles:

1. Place alternate spoonfuls of the two mixtures into individual souffle dishes prepared with foil collars. Cut through mixture with a knife to get marbleized effect.

2. Refrigerate until firm. Remove foil collars. Serve, without unmolding, in the souffle dishes.

CHERRY BELLS

Yield: 24 portions

Ingredients

MILK	2 cups
SUGAR, BROWN	1 pound
SUET, GROUND	5 ounces (1-1/3 cups)
BREAD CRUMBS, SOFT	1 pound
EGGS, WHOLE, beaten	2 cups
CINNAMON	4 teaspoons
NUTMEG	2 teaspoons
SALT	1 teaspoon
SODA	2 teaspoons
BAKING POWDER	2 tablespoons
ALMONDS, SLIVERED, toasted	1 cup
CHERRIES, FROZEN RED	1-1/2 pounds
CHERRIES, MARASCHINO, drained	48

Procedure

1. Combine milk, brown sugar, suet and soft bread crumbs with well-beaten eggs.

2. Mix spices, salt, soda and baking powder together; add to crumb mixture. Fold in almonds and frozen cherries.

3. Put a No. 8 scoop of pudding mixture into each of 24 greased, 6-ounce custard cups. Cover each cup with foil.

4. Place cups in wire or perforated steamer baskets. Steam 2-1/2 hours.

5. Cool 5 minutes before turning out puddings. Slice each pudding in half, vertically; place, cut sides down, on a serving plate.

6. Garnish with a Maraschino cherry at the bottom of each bell, a sprig of holly at the top. Serve with Fluffy Almond-Butter Sauce. *(Recipe, facing page)*

FLUFFY ALMOND-BUTTER SAUCE

Yield: 1-1/2 quarts, 48 2-tablespoon portions

Ingredients

BUTTER or MARGARINE	1/2 pound
CONFECTIONERS' SUGAR, sifted	1-1/4 pounds
EGGS, WHOLE	3/4 cup
NUTMEG	1 teaspoon
ALMOND EXTRACT	1 teaspoon

Procedure

1. Cream butter and sugar.
2. Blend in egg, nutmeg and almond extract, beating thoroughly. Chill.

Cinnamon Chocolate Swirl Souffle (Recipe, pages 280-281)

American Spice Trade Association

DEVONSHIRE MOLD ⟶

Yield: 32 portions

Ingredients

GELATINE, UNFLAVORED	3 tablespoons
WATER, cold	3/4 cup
COTTAGE CHEESE	3 pounds
CREAM CHEESE	2-1/4 pounds
SUGAR, CONFECTIONERS'	1/4 cup
CREAM, HEAVY	1 quart
STRAWBERRIES, FROZEN, SLICED, thawed	4 pounds

APPLE GELATIN JEWELS

Yield: 92 1/2-cup portions

Ingredients

GELATIN DESSERT, LEMON	2 pounds, 4 ounces
WATER, boiling	1 gallon
GELATIN DESSERT, LIME	2 pounds, 4 ounces
WATER, boiling	1 gallon
APPLE SAUCE, CANNED	1 gallon
WHIPPED TOPPING	as needed

Procedure

1. Dissolve lemon gelatin in first amount of boiling water. Dissolve lime gelatin in remaining boiling water.

2. Chill gelatins until slightly thickened.

3. Add half of the apple sauce to each of the two flavors, stirring well.

4. Pour each mixture into an 18-inch by 26-inch bun pan or four 9-inch by 13-inch pans. Chill until firm.

5. Cut into cubes. Arrange a layer of each flavor in dessert dishes or punch cups. Garnish with whipped topping.

Note

Dessert may be topped with toasted coconut, whipped cream or lemon sherbet, or serve with light cream, if desired.

Procedure
1. Combine gelatine and cold water; heat until dissolved.
2. Force cottage cheese through a fine sieve.
3. Soften cream cheese.
4. Combine cheeses; beat until thoroughly blended. Add sugar; add cream gradually, beating until mixed.
5. Add dissolved gelatine; blend well.
6. Turn into shallow pans. Chill until firm.
7. Cut into squares. Serve with strawberries.

SWEDISH CREAM

Yield: 24 portions

Ingredients

SOUR CREAM	1-1/2 quarts
SUGAR	3 cups
GELATINE, UNFLAVORED	3 tablespoons
CREAM, HEAVY	1-1/2 quarts
VANILLA	1 tablespoon

Procedure
1. Allow sour cream to warm to room temperature.
2. Mix sugar, gelatine and heavy cream in a saucepan. Heat and stir over low heat until gelatine has lost granular appearance and is completely dissolved.
3. Cool until just slightly thickened and approximately room temperature.
4. Carefully stir sour cream until smooth. Blend sour cream and vanilla into gelatine mixture until ingredients are well blended.
5. Turn into lightly oiled individual molds. Chill until firm.
6. To unmold, gently slip knife around edge of mold; turn into large sherbet dish. Serve with desired fruit sauce.

HAWAIIAN AMBROSIA

Yield: 16 portions

Ingredients

PINEAPPLES, FRESH	8 medium
MANDARIN ORANGES, drained	1 quart
BANANAS, sliced	6 medium
COCONUT	1 quart
CANDIED GINGER, diced	1 cup

Procedure

1. Cut pineapples in half, lengthwise through crown, keeping bright green leaves intact.

2. Using a grapefruit knife, cut around edge of fruit to loosen. Cut down either side of core, then make 4 or 5 crosswise cuts. Lift out fruit. Remove core. Reserve shells. Cut pineapple into chunks.

3. Combine pineapple chunks, oranges, bananas, coconut and ginger; toss lightly to mix. Return to pineapple shells.

FROZEN CREME

Yield: 2-1/2 quarts, 32 portions

Ingredients

COTTAGE CHEESE	2 pounds
LEMON JUICE	1/4 cup
SUGAR	2 cups
SOUR CREAM	1 quart

Procedure

1. Whip cottage cheese in mixer until smooth and creamy.

2. Add lemon juice and sugar; whip until smooth and blended. Continue whipping while gradually adding sour cream.

3. Place mixture in freezer. When frozen about 1/2 inch around edge, remove from freezer; whip until smooth.

4. Pour into deep containers or shallow pans to a depth of 1 inch. Return to freezer; freeze until firm but not hard.

5. To serve, dip with No. 16 scoop or cut into 2-inch by 3-inch squares. Serve with salty pretzel sticks or with just-thawed frozen, sliced strawberries or peaches.

Fruited Maple Pie (Recipe, page 297)

Cling Peach Advisory Board

NUT TORTE

Yield: 4 pies

Ingredients

BROWN SUGAR	12 ounces
SUGAR, GRANULATED	12 ounces
EGG WHITES	1-1/2 cups
CREAM OF TARTAR	1/2 teaspoon
VANILLA	1-1/2 tablespoons
GRAHAM CRACKER CRUMBS	10 ounces
NUTS, chopped	8 ounces
WHIPPED CREAM	1 quart

Procedure

1. Mix brown and granulated sugars.
2. Beat egg whites with cream of tartar. Add sugar gradually, continuing to beat for 30 minutes. Add vanilla; beat 2 minutes. Fold crumbs and nuts in by hand.
3. Spread in heavily greased pie pans, rounding slightly at the top.
4. Bake in oven at 350°F. for 30 minutes, then cool. Spread with whipped cream before serving.

SHERRY CHARLOTTE

Yield: 48 portions

Ingredients

GELATINE, UNFLAVORED	3 ounces
WATER, cold	1 quart
MILK, scalded	1 quart
SUGAR	3 cups
SALT	1 teaspoon
SHERRY	2 cups
CREAM, HEAVY, chilled	2 quarts

Procedure

1. Soften gelatine in cold water. Dissolve in hot, scalded milk.

2. Add sugar and salt; stir until dissolved. Cool.

3. Add sherry. Chill until slightly thickened.

4. Whip cream until thick and shiny. Fold into gelatin mixture. Turn into pudding pans. Chill until firm.

5. Spoon into dessert dishes. Garnish each portion with additional sweetened whipped cream. Top with a few pieces of broken walnuts, cut maraschino cherries and one or two shaved chocolate curls.

Ice Cream Desserts and Sauces

STRAWBERRY ICE CREAM MERINGUE

Yield: 50 (3-1/2-inch to 4-inch)

Ingredients

SUGAR	3-1/2 pounds
WATER	2 cups
EGG WHITES	1-1/4 pounds
SALT	1/2 teaspoon
VANILLA	1 tablespoon
CREAM OF TARTAR	1 teaspoon
STRAWBERRY ICE CREAM	2 gallons
FROZEN STRAWBERRIES, thawed	5 pounds

Procedure

1. Combine sugar and water; cook to 240°F. Cover for a few minutes after it begins to boil to dissolve all crystals.

2. Beat egg whites in a 30-quart mixer bowl until foamy. Add salt, vanilla, cream of tartar; beat until stiff.

3. Pour hot syrup slowly in a thin stream. Beat until cool and stiff.

4. Line baking sheets with brown paper. Using a pastry bag with No. 2 or No. 3 star tube, or a spoon, shape the meringue nests about 3-1/2 inches in diameter. Bake in oven at 225°F. for 40 to 50 minutes or until dry.

5. Loosen the meringues from the paper by brushing the back with a little warm water or placing the paper on a damp towel for a few seconds. Cool.

6. Just before serving, fill each meringue with a No. 12 scoop of ice cream. Serve with frozen strawberries.

STRAWBERRY ICE CREAM PUFFS

Yield: 50 portions

Ingredients

SHORTENING	1 pound
WATER, boiling	1 quart
FLOUR, ALL-PURPOSE, sifted	1 pound
SALT	1 teaspoon
EGGS (at room temperature)	16
STRAWBERRY ICE CREAM	1-1/2 gallons
FROZEN SLICED STRAWBERRIES, thawed	5 pounds
CREAM, HEAVY (for whipping)	1 quart

Procedure

1. Put shortening and water in a sauce pan over high heat.

2. When fat is melted and mixture is *actively* boiling, add flour all at once. Mixture should not stop boiling. Stir and cook until it comes from side of pan. Do not overcook.

3. Put into small mixer bowl with paddle attachment. Break eggs into quart measure; add, one at a time, to mixture with beater at high speed. Mix after each addition until egg is completely incorporated. After adding last egg, mix until smooth.

4. Drop on lightly greased and floured baking sheet using No. 20 scoop.

5. Bake in oven at 400°F. for 15 to 20 minutes until puffed and set. Reduce heat to 300°F.; bake 35 to 40 minutes longer, until dried out.

6. Split each puff. Fill with a No. 16 scoop of ice cream. Pour 1-1/2 ounces thawed strawberries over each puff. Top with whipped cream.

Variation

1. For Profiteroles, drop puff shell batter with a No. 60 scoop; bake in oven at 400°F. for 8 minutes or until set.

2. Reduce heat to 300°F. and bake 25 minutes longer or until puffs are golden and dry,

3. Split puffs; fill with ice cream or pastry cream.

4. For each portion, arrange 3 puffs in a serving dish. Top with chocolate or caramel sauce and garnish with sliced almonds, if desired.

*Cherry Eclairs Glace (See cream puff recipe,
Strawberry Ice Cream Puffs, page 290)*

National Cherry Growers & Industries Foundation

PRALINE SUNDAE SAUCE

Yield: 1 quart

Ingredients

SUGAR, LIGHT BROWN	2-1/2 cups
CREAM, LIGHT	2 cups
MARSHMALLOWS	1/2 pound
SALT	1/8 teaspoon
BUTTER or MARGARINE	1/2 pound
VANILLA	2 teaspoons
WALNUTS or PECANS, broken	2/3 cup

Procedure

1. Combine brown sugar, cream, marshmallows and salt in a sauce-pan. Heat, stirring constantly, until brown sugar dissolves and mixture comes to boil. Cook 8 to 10 minutes.

2. Remove from heat; add butter. Cool slightly, add vanilla and nuts.

3. Serve warm over ice cream.

PEAR FANTASY

Yield: 50 portions

Ingredients

PEARS, CANNED	50 halves
ICE CREAM, BUTTER PECAN or MAPLE WALNUT	1-1/4 gallons
BUTTERSCOTCH SAUCE	2 quarts

Procedure
1. Place a pear half, cut side up, in each dessert dish.
2. Place a No. 16 scoop of ice cream on top of pear.
3. Ladle 2 tablespoons sauce over each.

FILBERT LACE COOKIES

(See picture, page 260)

Yield: approximately 7 dozen

Ingredients

BUTTER or MARGARINE	1/2 pound
SUGAR, LIGHT BROWN	12 ounces
SALT	3/4 teaspoon
MILK	3 tablespoons
VANILLA or LEMON EXTRACT	3/4 teaspoon
BAKING POWDER	1-1/2 teaspoons
ROLLED OATS, QUICK COOKING (uncooked)	9 ounces
FILBERTS, CHOPPED or DICED, toasted	6 ounces

Procedure
1. Cream butter, sugar, salt, milk and vanilla until light and fluffy.
2. Mix in baking powder, oats and filberts.
3. Drop by teaspoons onto sheet pans, 2 inches apart.
4. Bake, one sheet at a time, in oven at 350°F. for 7 to 10 minutes.
5. Cool about 1 minute; carefully remove with wide spatula. If cookies harden before removal from pans, reheat in oven a few minutes.
6. For rolled cookies, remove, one at a time, from cookie sheet; quickly roll up around handle of wooden spoon; cool. For shells for ice cream, make cookies larger; shape, while warm, over bottom of custard cup or glass water tumbler.

ORIENTAL ICE CREAM SAUCE

Yield: 1 quart

Ingredients

SUGAR	1 quart
WATER	2 cups
ORANGE RIND, grated	3 tablespoons
ORANGE JUICE	1/2 cup
LEMON RIND, grated	3 tablespoons
LEMON JUICE	1/2 cup
GINGER, CANDIED, finely chopped	2/3 cup
ALMONDS, BLANCHED, SLIVERED	1 cup

Procedure

1. Combine sugar, water, orange rind and juice and lemon rind and juice. Heat, stirring constantly, until sugar is dissolved.

2. Add ginger; simmer, stirring occasionally, until of medium thick consistency.

3. Remove from heat; add almonds. Cool. Serve over vanilla ice cream.

PINEAPPLE JUBILEE SAUCE

Yield: 2-1/2 quarts

Ingredients

CORNSTARCH	3 ounces
SUGAR	1 pound, 2 ounces
SALT	1/2 teaspoon
PINEAPPLE TIDBITS	1 No. 10 can
ORANGE JUICE	2-1/2 cups
STRAWBERRIES, FRESH, sliced	1 pound, 4 ounces

Procedure

1. Combine cornstarch, sugar and salt; add to undrained pineapple. Cook and stir until sauce thickens and clears.

2. Add orange juice; remove from heat. Cool.

3. Add strawberries.

Serving suggestion

Slice a few pieces of banana over a scoop of vanilla or strawberry ice cream. Ladle sauce over top.

DATE-NUT SUNDAE SAUCE

Yield: approximately 1-1/4 quarts

Ingredients

HONEY	2 cups
WATER	1 cup
BUTTER or MARGARINE	1/3 cup
DATES, PITTED, sliced	2 cups
PORT, MUSCATEL or DESSERT WINE	1 cup
WALNUTS, coarsely chopped	1 cup

Procedure

1. Bring honey and water to boil. Boil rapidly 12 minutes, removing "foam" as mixture boils. Remove from heat.

2. Add butter and dates. Cool.

3. Add wine. Just before serving, add walnuts. Reheat and serve hot over ice cream.

SAUCE FOR COUPE SEVILLE

Yield: 4-1/3 cups (for 48 to 50 portions, 4 teaspoons each)

Ingredients

ORANGE MARMALADE	1 quart
COINTREAU	1/3 cup

Procedure

1. Combine marmalade and Cointreau; stir until blended.

TO MAKE COUPE

1. Place about 1 teaspoon of the sauce in the base of a coupe or sundae dish.

2. Fill dish with vanilla ice cream using spade or No. 12 ice cream scoop.

3. Spoon about 1 tablespoon sauce over top. Decorate with a skewer threaded with quarters of thick orange slices, red and green maraschino cherries.

Variation

Make with Raspberry Royal ice cream; use raspberry jam and Cassis for sauce.

COCONUT SNOWBALLS WITH
SPARKLING RED CHERRY SAUCE

Yield: 50 portions

Ingredients

ICE CREAM, VANILLA	1-1/2 gallons
COCONUT	2 pounds

Procedure

1. Shape ice cream balls, rounding a No. 16 scoop. Set in freezer to harden.

2. To coat balls with coconut: Have coconut, a tray and 2 serving spoons well chilled. Spread coconut out on tray. Place a firm ice cream ball in coconut; toss with serving spoons until coated.

3. Serve with Sparkling Cherry Sauce.*

*SPARKLING RED CHERRY SAUCE

Yield: 1 gallon

Ingredients

FROZEN RED SOUR PITTED CHERRIES AND JUICE (PACKED 5 PARTS CHERRIES TO 1 PART SUGAR)	4-1/2 pounds
SUGAR	2 cups
WATER	1-1/2 quarts
GELATIN, CHERRY	8 ounces

Procedure

1. Combine cherries, sugar and water; bring to a boil.

2. Add cherry gelatin to the hot mixture; stir until dissolved. Chill until slightly thickened.

Frozen Rainbow Tower Torte (Recipe, page 298)

California Strawberry Advisory Board

Miscellany

FRUITED MAPLE PIE
(See picture, page 287)

Yield: 4 9-inch pies

Ingredients

CANNED FRUIT COCKTAIL, drained	7-1/2 cups
FRUIT COCKTAIL SYRUP	4-1/2 cups
GELATINE, UNFLAVORED	1 ounce
SALT	1-1/2 teaspoons
MAPLE EXTRACT	1 tablespoon
LEMON JUICE	3 tablespoons
CREAM, WHIPPING	3 cups
SUGAR	1/3 cup
BAKED 9-INCH PIE SHELLS	4
FLAKED COCONUT, toasted	1/4 cup

Procedure

1. Drain fruit cocktail for required amount of fruit and syrup. (Approximately 1 No. 10 can.)

2. Soften gelatine in 1 cup syrup.

3. Add salt to remaining 3-1/2 cups syrup. Heat. Dissolve softened gelatine in hot syrup. Add maple extract and lemon juice. Chill until slightly thickened.

4. Whip cream with sugar until thick and glossy. Fold into gelatine mixture. Fold in drained fruit cocktail reserving 2 cups fruit for garnish.

5. Turn filling into cooled, baked shells allowing 3-1/3 cups filling per pie. Garnish each pie with 1/2 cup fruit. Sprinkle with 1 tablespoon coconut. Chill until firm.

FROZEN RAINBOW TOWER TORTE
(See picture, page 296)

Yield: 3 8-inch torten

Ingredients

EGG WHITES	2-1/4 cups
VANILLA	2 tablespoons
CREAM OF TARTAR	1-1/2 teaspoons
SALT	3/4 teaspoon
SUGAR	1 pound, 10 ounces
STRAWBERRY ICE CREAM	1 gallon
PISTACHIO ICE CREAM	1/2 gallon
CREAM, HEAVY or CONCENTRATED	
LIQUID NON-DAIRY CREAMER	1-1/2 quarts
RUBY SAUCE (Recipe, facing page)	as needed

Procedure

1. Beat egg whites, vanilla, cream of tartar and salt until foamy. Add sugar gradually, beating until very stiff.

2. Pipe or spread meringue onto paper-covered baking sheets to form 12 8-inch circles.

3. Bake in oven at 275°F. for 1 hour. Turn off heat; let stand in oven at least 1 hour. Cool. Lift meringues from paper. Chill.

4. Let ice cream stand at room temperature until slightly softened.

5. Spread about 1-1/4 pints strawberry ice cream on each of 6 meringue layers. Hold in freezer.

6. Spread pistachio ice cream over 3 layers of meringue. Stack ice cream covered layers to form 3 torten, with pistachio layer in middle. Top each torte with one of remaining layers of meringue. Hold in freezer while whipping topping.

7. Whip cream or concentrated liquid non-dairy creamer (for pink topping, see recipe below). Frost torten; freeze until very firm, at least 6 hours, preferably overnight.

8. Drizzle with small amount of Ruby Sauce just before serving. Serve with additional sauce.

Note

For pink topping, color heavy cream with red food coloring. Or, mix 1 quart *chilled* concentrated liquid non-dairy creamer with 2-1/2 to 3 cups syrup drained from thawed frozen strawberries. Whip 3 to 4 minutes. Do not overbeat.

RUBY SAUCE

Yield: 6-1/2 pounds

Ingredients

STRAWBERRIES, FROZEN WHOLE	6-1/2 pounds
ARROWROOT or CORNSTARCH	as needed
ORANGE RIND, grated	1/4 cup
ORANGE EXTRACT	as needed

Procedure

1. Thaw berries; drain. Measure juice.
2. Thicken juice with starch allowing 1 tablespoon arrowroot or cornstarch per cup of juice. Cool mixture; add to berries.
3. Blend in orange rind and orange extract, checking for flavor.

HOLIDAY ANGEL TOWER

Yield: 24 portions

Ingredients

CREAM CHEESE	1 pound
MINCEMEAT	3-1/2 cups
WALNUTS, chopped	1/2 cup
ANGEL FOOD CAKE, 10 inch	2
CREAM, WHIPPING	1 cup

Procedure

1. Beat cream cheese until softened. Add mincemeat gradually, continuing to blend. Add walnuts.
2. Slice each angel food cake horizontally into three uniform layers.
3. Re-assemble cakes, spreading mincemeat mixture over bottom and middle layers.
4. Cover; refrigerate overnight.
5. Whip cream; sweeten if desired. Spread top of cakes before serving.

CHOCOLATE FUNNY CAKE

Yield: 7 9-inch cakes

Ingredients

CHOCOLATE, UNSWEETENED	6 ounces
WATER	3 cups
SUGAR	1 quart
	(1-3/4 pounds)
BUTTER or MARGARINE	12 ounces
VANILLA	2 tablespoons
PASTRY DOUGH FOR PIE	3-1/2 pounds
YELLOW CAKE BATTER	7 pounds
NUTS, chopped	1-1/4 cups

Procedure

1. Combine chocolate and water. Place over low heat, stir until chocolate is melted.

2. Add sugar; stir constantly until mixture comes to a boil.

3. Remove from heat; stir in butter. Add vanilla; set syrup aside.

4. Roll pastry 1/8 inch thick. Line seven 9-inch pie pans, turning edge of pastry under to make a high fluted rim.

5. Prepare cake batter. Pour into unbaked pie shells allowing 1 pound per pie.

6. Carefully pour lukewarm sauce over batter, allowing 1 cup per pie. Sprinkle with nuts.

7. Bake in oven at 350°F. for 50 to 55 minutes or until done.

Note

Cake is best served warm. Top with whipped topping, or ice cream if desired.

PEACH PARTY MACAROON

Yield: 24 portions, 4 8-inch pans

Ingredients

CANNED CLING PEACH SLICES	1 quart
EGGS, LARGE	3
SUGAR, GRANULATED	2 cups
VANILLA	1 tablespoon
FLOUR, ALL-PURPOSE, sifted	6 ounces (1-1/2 cups)
BAKING POWDER	1-1/2 teaspoons
SALT	1/2 teaspoon
ALMONDS, CHOPPED	2/3 cup
WHIPPING CREAM	2 cups
SUGAR, CONFECTIONERS'	1/4 cup
CLING PEACH SLICES, drained (for garnish)	24

Procedure

1. Drain peach slices thoroughly.

2. Beat eggs; add granulated sugar, continuing to beat until thoroughly combined. Add vanilla.

3. Sift flour, baking powder and salt together. Stir into egg mixture. Fold in peach slices and chopped almonds as gently as possible. Divide evenly in 4 well-oiled 8-inch pie pans. Bake in oven at 350°F. for 45 minutes.

4. Whip cream; sweeten with confectioners' sugar.

5. Serve dessert warm with a spoonful of cream and a peach slice. Or, if desired, cool baked desserts; decorate with whipped cream and peach slices.

FROZEN FRUITCAKE

Yield: 40 1/2-cup portions

Ingredients

WHIPPED TOPPING MIX	12 ounces
WATER, ice-cold	1 quart
SOLUBLE COFFEE	1/4 cup
SUGAR	2 tablespoons
VANILLA	1 tablespoon
RUM EXTRACT	1 tablespoon
CINNAMON	1 teaspoon
NUTMEG	1 teaspoon
CLOVES, GROUND	1 teaspoon
MINCEMEAT, MOIST	1 quart
NUTS, chopped	2 cups
MARASCHINO CHERRIES, (red or green) sliced	2 cups
PECAN HALVES	as needed
MARASCHINO CHERRIES, WHOLE	as needed

Procedure

1. Combine topping mix, water, coffee powder, sugar, flavorings and spices. Blend thoroughly with whip by hand or at low speed.

2. Whip at high speed 5 to 8 minutes until mixture forms soft peaks.

3. Fold in mincemeat, nuts and cherries.

4. Pour into wax paper-lined loaf pans or into tube pans. Freeze overnight.

5. Unmold. Garnish with pecan halves and maraschino cherries.

6. Serve at once or return to freezer.

CREAM CHEESECAKE

Yield: 4 9-inch cakes

Ingredients

GRAHAM CRACKER CRUMBS	1 quart (14 ounces)
MARGARINE, melted	1/2 pound
SUGAR, BROWN	1 cup
RAISINS	6 ounces (1 cup)
CREAM CHEESE LOAF, softened	6 pounds
SUGAR, GRANULATED	1-1/2 pounds
VANILLA	2 tablespoons
LEMON RIND, grated	1 teaspoon
EGGS	12
SOUR CREAM	2 cups
SOUR CREAM	3 cups

Procedure

1. Combine crumbs and margarine. Press 1 cup mixture into bottom of each 9-inch spring-form pan.

2. Combine brown sugar and raisins; sprinkle 1/2 cup of the mixture over each crust.

3. Combine cream cheese, granulated sugar, vanilla and grated lemon rind in mixer bowl. Mix on low speed until well blended.

4. Gradually add eggs and first amount of sour cream; mix until blended. Scrape bowl occasionally to prevent lumping.

5. Portion 1-1/4 quarts batter into each pan. Bake in oven at 350°F. for 60 to 70 minutes.

6. Cool; spread with remaining sour cream, allowing 3/4 cup per cake. Garnish with mandarin orange sections and pineapple chunks as desired.

CREPES MACAROON

Yield: 12 portions (2 crepes each)

Ingredients

FLOUR, ALL-PURPOSE, sifted	2 cups (8 ounces)
SUGAR	2 tablespoons
SALT	1/4 teaspoon
EGGS	4
MILK	1 cup
CREAM	1/2 cup
BUTTER, melted	1/4 cup
ALMOND MACAROONS, crushed	1 cup
ALMONDS, SLIVERED, TOASTED	1 cup
BUTTER	2 ounces
ORANGE JUICE	1-1/2 cups
CORN SYRUP, LIGHT	1/2 cup
CURACAO	2 ounces

Procedure

1. Combine flour, sugar and salt.

2. Beat eggs with milk and cream. Gradually stir into flour mixture.

3. Add melted butter. Add macaroons. Let stand 1 hour at room temperature.

4. Preheat a 6-inch crepe pan; brush lightly with butter. Add about 1/4 cup batter. Swirl and tilt pan so bottom gets an even coat of batter.

5. Pour off any excess of batter. Cook on medium heat until underside is brown. Turn; brown lightly on other side.

6. Remove from pan. Keep warm or reheat in oven at 300°F. before serving.

7. Saute almonds in butter.

8. Combine orange juice, corn syrup and Curacao; bring to simmer.

9. Roll warm crepes; sprinkle with almonds. Spoon about 1-1/2 ounces sauce over each portion.

Crepes Flamed at Tableside

Cling Peach Advisory Board

Sweet Semillon Floating Islands (Recipe, page 307)

Wine Institute

CHOCOLATE HEAVENLY CROWN

Yield: 1 9-inch pan

Ingredients

LADY FINGERS, split lengthwise	18
ORANGE JUICE	1/2 cup
CHOCOLATE, SEMI-SWEET PIECES	6 ounces (1 cup)
CREAM CHEESE, softened	1/2 pound
SUGAR, BROWN (packed)	1/2 cup
SALT	1/8 teaspoon
EGG YOLKS	3
EGG WHITES	3
VANILLA	1-1/2 teaspoons
SUGAR, BROWN (packed)	1/2 cup
CREAM, WHIPPING	1-1/2 cups

Procedure

1. Place lady fingers, flat side down, in oven at 375°F. for 5 minutes. Cool about 10 minutes. Brush flat sides with orange juice.

2. Arrange about 22 pieces vertically around edge of lightly buttered 9-inch spring-form pan. Arrange remaining pieces of lady fingers on bottom of pan.

3. Melt semi-sweet chocolate over hot (not boiling) water. Remove from heat; cool about 10 minutes.

4. Blend softened cream cheese, first amount of brown sugar and salt. Beat in egg yolks, adding one at a time. Blend in chocolate.

5. Combine egg whites and vanilla; beat until stiff but not dry. Add remaining sugar gradually beating until stiff and glossy. Fold into chocolate mixture.

6. Whip cream; fold into chocolate mixture.

7. Pour into prepared spring-form pan. Chill at least 5 hours or overnight.

SWEET SEMILLON FLOATING ISLANDS
(See picture, page 305)

Yield: 16 portions

Ingredients

EGG WHITES	5
SUGAR	3/4 cup
MILK	2 cups
WATER	2 cups
VANILLA	1/2 teaspoon
POACHING LIQUID	3 cups
SWEET WHITE WINE	1 cup
EGG YOLKS, slightly beaten	5
SUGAR	3/4 cup
FLOUR	1/3 cup
NUTMEG (optional)	as needed

Procedure

1. Beat egg whites until foamy. Add first amount of sugar gradually, continuing to beat until whites reach a firm peak. With a star tube, pipe onto waxed paper. (See picture, page 305, for form)

2. Mix milk, water and vanilla; heat to simmering. *Do not boil.*

3. Drop islands into liquid; poach for about 2 minutes on each side. Lift out; drain on clean towel.

4. Strain poaching liquid; measure required amount. Bring liquid to a boil.

5. Mix wine, egg yolks, remaining sugar and flour; add to hot liquid. Cook and stir until thickened.

6. Cool sauce; serve topped with islands. Sprinkle with nutmeg, if desired.

INDEX